Table of Contents

FOUNDATION CENTER
Knowledge to build on.

NONPROFIT MANAGEMENT GUIDES

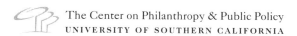
The Center on Philanthropy & Public Policy
UNIVERSITY OF SOUTHERN CALIFORNIA

The Center on Philanthropy & Public Policy

FOUNDATIONS AND PUBLIC POLICY

Leveraging Philanthropic Dollars, Knowledge, and Networks for Greater Impact

James M. Ferris, Editor

Library of Congress Cataloging-in-Publication Data
Foundations and public policy : leveraging philanthropic dollars, knowledge,
and networks for greater impact.
      p. cm.
  Includes bibliographical references and index.
  ISBN 978-1-59542-218-7 (pbk. : alk. paper)
  1. Charities—Political aspects—United States. 2. Endowments—United States.
3. Political planning—United States. I. Foundation Center.
  HV97.A3F65 2009
  361.7'632—dc22
                                     2008055565

Foreword

Public policy engagement is a natural extension of foundation efforts to address public problems. Foundations have a range of assets—dollars, knowledge, and networks—that can be leveraged to impact public policy. This book examines the choices foundations face when engaging in public policy work.

Foundation involvement in public policy is not new. Throughout the twentieth century, foundations have sought to influence public policy, and their work has often intersected or paralleled the work of government. In earlier days, the resources foundations had at their disposal were comparable to that of government, and the borders between government and philanthropy were not well-defined. Moreover, there were no limits circumscribing foundation involvement in the policy process, which raised concerns of corruption and self-dealing. By contrast, the size and scope of government today is overwhelming when compared to philanthropy and the boundaries are far less ambiguous. In addition, the role that foundations can play in public policy is perceived to be diminished, especially with the introduction of new rules contained in the Tax Reform Act of 1969, the last major federal action to regulate private foundations.

Over the last several decades, there has been a renewed interest in foundation engagement with public policy. This revival has been spurred by a variety of factors: the growing interest in philanthropy that has the potential to create greater value; the clarification of the legal possibilities for foundations engaged in public policy work; the increased attention that "conservative" foundations have garnered for their role in policy debates;

and the growing frustration with partisan stalemate in the policy process. The increasing numbers and scale of foundations, the focus on strategic philanthropy, and the devolution of public policy decisions to states and communities have further created a new landscape ripe with opportunities for greater philanthropic engagement with public policy. This is evidenced by the growing number of tools and guides for foundations, the increasing frequency of public policy staff within foundations, as well as the creation of the Paul Ylvisaker Award for Public Policy at the Council of Foundations in 2002.

This book is intended to answer three fundamental questions: What are the factors that are critical to a foundation's decision to engage in public policy work? What are the strategic and tactical options available to a foundation that becomes involved in public policymaking? And, what are the implications for a foundation that chooses to leverage its philanthropic assets to impact public policymaking? This is done cumulatively through four chapters that frame the analysis of recent foundation efforts in four policy arenas: school choice, wetlands preservation, child care, and health care insurance.

This volume reflects the combined efforts of an interdisciplinary team of experts—from a philanthropic consultant to academics to attorneys working with foundations—that participated in the development of commissioned papers for the Center on Philanthropy and Public Policy, and funded by a grant from the David and Lucile Packard Foundation. Authors include Lucy Bernholz, Jason Gerson, Jack Knott, Diane McCarthy, Michael Mintrom, Tom Oliver, Walter Rosenbaum, James Allen Smith, Thomas Troyer, Douglas Varley, and Sandra Vergari, a philanthropic consultant. This study benefited greatly from conversations with participants at two Center-sponsored meetings: a roundtable on foundations and public policy held in January 2002, hosted by the J. Paul Getty Trust; and a forum on leveraging philanthropic assets for public problem-solving held in May 2002. The publication of this volume was encouraged and supported by a grant from the California Endowment. In addition, Nick Williams, my graduate assistant at the Center on Philanthropy and Public Policy, was very helpful in the preparation of the manuscript as was Rick Schoff at the Foundation Center. We are appreciative to all who contributed to this effort, including those who reacted, commented, and shared their work with the authors.

The Center hopes that this analysis will enable foundations to consider the potential contributions that they can make to public problem-solving in an era of more devolved and fiscally constrained public decisionmaking. By engaging more foundations in public policy work, regardless of their points of view, philanthropy can strengthen policymaking in a pluralistic democracy. In so doing, foundation assets can be more effectively leveraged for public problem-solving.

James M. Ferris, Ph.D.
Director
The Center on Philanthropy and Public Policy

1

Introduction

James M. Ferris

Philanthropy can be more effective in its efforts to solve public problems by leveraging its assets—money, knowledge, and networks—to influence the public policymaking process. The actions of foundations, given their public benefit missions, intersect with the efforts of government. Since the earliest days of foundations in the United States, many have sought to impact public policy. Yet the relationship between foundations and public policy has continually been in flux, varying as a result of the dynamics of the size, role, and scope of government; the growth and evolution of the foundation sector; the changing interests and strategies that foundations have pursued in their work; and the reaction of foundations and government to each other.

This dynamic relationship has been a source of ongoing tension. At various points in time, this tension has been an impetus for changing the rules by which foundations can engage in public policy. As regulations have been adopted to constrain the activities of foundations, there has been a natural tendency to pull back from public policy engagement. This appears to have been the case in the immediate aftermath of the last major change in foundation regulations: the Tax Reform Act of 1969. Yet, in the ensuing four decades, the permissibility of foundation action in public policy has been clarified so as to establish the latitude for action, short of lobbying or electioneering.

At the same time, there appears to be a renewed interest in public policy on the part of some foundations as they work to leverage their philanthropic assets. This interest stems in part from a more concerted and conscious effort to create systemic change as a result of the challenges made by venture philanthropy to increase impact; the increasing emphasis on efficiency and performance for institutions in general; and the expanded opportunities for foundations in a world where public decisionmaking is being devolved and decentralized.

Given mounting interest and growing opportunities, there is a need to systematically analyze how foundations can leverage their assets to create public policies that further their public problem-solving missions, and to discern the implications of policy engagement for foundation practice. This volume examines foundation options for impacting public policy, both to inform foundations that are engaged in public policy as well as to introduce foundations that might be considering such an approach to the opportunities and challenges that such a move entails.

To develop a framework for understanding foundation options and assessing their relative effectiveness, there are three fundamental questions:

- What are the factors that are critical to a foundation's decision to engage public policy?

- What are the strategic choices and tactical options available to a foundation that decides to engage in public policymaking?

- What are the implications for a foundation that chooses to leverage its philanthropic assets to impact public policymaking?

To answer these questions, the chapters in this volume explore the strategies for foundation involvement in public policymaking and the associated benefits, costs, and risks through a set of framing chapters followed by four chapters that investigate foundation engagement with public policy in four specific policy arenas: school choice, wetlands preservation, child care, and health insurance.

Framing Foundation Choices for Public Policy Engagement

As a beginning point for the investigation of foundation engagement in public policy, in Chapter 2 James Ferris and Michael Mintrom develop a conceptual framework for understanding how foundations can leverage money, knowledge, and connections for solving public problems. They start with a discussion of the factors that shape a foundation's decision of whether or not to engage. Then, they examine the myriad points of impact, including the stages, venues, and jurisdictions in the policymaking process that foundations have to choose from, once they decide to engage in public policy work. In addition to determining where and when to engage in public policymaking, the authors maintain that foundations must make choices in terms of the form of engagement, from funding pilot projects to forging networks, and how those choices are reflected in a foundation's grantmaking.

In the following chapter, James Allen Smith explores nearly 150 years of American foundations' involvement in the policymaking process. In so doing, he analyzes how and by what means foundations have sought to influence public policy and government action, what specific outcomes they have successfully brought about, and he addresses important questions as to what the limits of foundation engagement ought to be in a democratic society. Beginning with Peabody's work in the South after the Civil War and ending with the Robert Wood Johnson Foundation's influence on health care reform in the 1990s, Smith further examines the commonalities and differences of particular foundations' strategies, tools, and tactics. Smith's narrative, grounded in a series of examples, underscores the fact that success in public policy is a result of patience, serendipity, and opportunities seized.

The current legal context for foundation engagement in public policy is provided by Thomas A. Troyer and Douglas Varley in Chapter 4. Their review of current law for foundations who seek to do public policy work establishes the wide latitude that foundations have to engage in public policy, despite the perceptions of some that it is quite limited. They present basic rules for private foundations to consider regarding what federal law defines as lobbying and what it does not. The authors further describe what activities are more favorable for foundation engagement in the policymaking process, including direct communications work, grantmaking to public charities that engage in lobbying, and nonpartisan voter education campaigns.

In the final framing chapter, Lucy Bernholz describes the burgeoning role of philanthropic associations in the public policy arena. She describes how these associations work, who does what, and how new associations relate to more established foundations and organizations. She outlines how foundations have organized to work together rather than always on their own to address and influence both policies that shape philanthropy (philanthropic policy) as well as policy issues that directly connect to programmatic areas of interest (public policy).

These chapters offer a framework to understand the decision to engage and the range of strategies and tactics for foundations who choose to do so; a historical context for understanding the importance of patience, coincidence, and concerted action; the wide latitude for foundation engagement under current law; and the need for foundations to align to enhance their leverage. To better understand this framework we investigate the conceptual models and issues in the context of specific policy arenas.

Investigating the Framework

In an effort to assess the usefulness of the framework, issues, and options identified in the framing chapters, four policy issue areas are examined in the subsequent chapters. The four cases were selected on the basis of factors that would help to discern general patterns and their implications beyond the more common single case method. This led us to define policy issues with a tighter focus, policy areas characterized by different levels of government and varying governmental roles, and foundation ecology.

In order to focus the cases, only one dimension of a broader policy domain is chosen. For example, school choice is but one dimension of a range of policy choices to improve education, and health insurance coverage is but one issue among many within the larger context of health access. Similarly, child care is only one of many policies that are aimed at strengthening children and families, and wetlands preservation is only one approach to enhancing environmental quality. Taking a slice of a larger domain allows a greater degree of specificity in analyzing foundation strategies and tactics, thereby providing greater insights into foundation choices for public policy engagement.

We selected policy issues that play out locally, regionally, and nationally. All too often public policy conversations, like textbooks on public policy, focus on Washington, D.C. This preoccupation with the nation's capital tends to place public policy engagement outside the reach of many foundations. By selecting cases that have a significant local, regional, or state focus, we are able to demonstrate the wide array of opportunities for policy work available to foundations. This is especially important as the number of leverage points for such efforts has increased due to the devolution of policy decisions from the federal government to the states, and from state capitals to local communities.

The public's acceptance of the role of government in a policy arena is another critical dimension. For example, there has long been a reliance on the market in health care that has implications for the nature of policy options that foundations can hope to influence, as well as for the benefits and costs of foundation efforts in public policy. This is in contrast to education, where the prevailing public view is of the centrality of government in ensuring the quality of schools.

Variation in foundation ecology is another important facet, as determined by the number of foundations working in the policy area, their scale and scope, and their focus and strategies. For example, among foundations—both large and small and both nationally and regionally focused—education is the primary area of interest. As a consequence, there are a large number of potential foundation actors, both locally and nationally, to engage education policy issues. In contrast, the number of foundations with an interest in environmental issues is relatively small, and they are quite diverse in terms of their geographic focus and scale. The ecology of foundations with health interests is uniquely characterized by a set of foundations with an exclusive focus on health. This sole focus and their relative size seem to increase their inclination to choose policy work.

Policy Issues

In the first case study, Thomas R. Oliver and Jason Gerson examine foundation efforts to expand access to health care. They begin with an important investigation of the similarities and trends, as well as the distinct interests, resources, and strategies of foundations involved in health policy. They then focus on the activities of twelve foundations aimed at expanding or protecting health insurance coverage. The authors categorize foundation activities into three broad strategies for shaping public policy: education, investment, and support. The chapter identifies some clear patterns in the allocation of resources and examines what those patterns suggest about foundation preferences and capabilities for improving health insurance coverage. Oliver and Gerson maintain that foundations are capable of becoming "policy entrepreneurs" that can create new products and courses of action, but may also choose the role of investor, providing financial support and technical assistance to one or more groups. Lessons are drawn from the successes and failures of policy activities and strategies of the foundations.

Walter A. Rosenbaum follows with an examination of foundation engagement in wetlands and habitat protection. He describes the substantial investment foundations have made in environmental conservation efforts and discusses their rationale for involvement. Rosenbaum further describes and explains the major strategic and tactical choices that foundations have made for this engagement, what jurisdictional level (national, state, local) they have preferred in their efforts, and which venues (executive, judicial, legislative, administrative) they have chosen. In addition, Rosenbaum argues that the perceived effectiveness of such efforts influences future engagement.

In their chapter, Jack H. Knott and Diane McCarthy focus on foundation involvement in child care programs and policies. They argue that foundation strategies toward child care began to emphasize early childhood development and after-school programs as a result of research indicating its significant effect on school performance and positive behaviors as adults. New opportunities for foundation engagement in policy arose with the development of major federal legislation. Knott and McCarthy survey and analyze how twelve large national foundations have chosen to engage the policy process and the strategies that those foundations have employed. They suggest that foundation strategy is selected based on the perceived risks and opportunities that each foundation confronts and describe the perspectives of various players, including program officers and members of foundation boards, to explain foundation strategy that mitigates risks and maximizes program and policy effectiveness.

In the last case examination, Michael Mintrom and Sandra Vergari look at foundation engagement in education policymaking. Mintrom and Vergari are particularly interested in examining philanthropic strategies used to gain influence in the debates concerning school choice. The chapter is built around answering five research questions: How and why have foundations supported the rise of school choice? What types of resources and strategies have foundations employed? What choices have they made with regard to the selection of where they engage in the policymaking process? What have been the outcomes of these choices? And, what are the lessons for theory and practice that emerge from these findings? The authors argue that foundations and individual philanthropists have provided support to school choice through significant sums of financial support to voucher and charter initiatives, by funding research and information dissemination, and by building networks and forging alliances. Mintrom and Vergari claim that foundations have made significant inroads in advancing school choice efforts onto the state and federal policymaking agenda.

The analysis of these four cases provides insights that deepen our understanding of how foundations are involved in policy work and the considerations for undertaking such work. These are summarized in the concluding chapter, which also considers the consequences and suggests the lessons learned about foundation practice in today's environment.

2

Foundations and Public Policymaking: A Conceptual Framework

James M. Ferris and Michael Mintrom

Introduction

A critical element in transforming philanthropy into more effective philanthropy is to leverage foundation assets—money, knowledge, and connections—for solving public problems. In this vein, foundations have an opportunity to maximize their impact on public problem-solving by deploying their full range of assets to shape public policy. In fact, there is an increasing opportunity for foundations to engage the policymaking process as governmental decisionmaking becomes increasingly devolved and decentralized.

Foundations can work to impact public policymaking at myriad points. There are many *stages* in the policymaking process, from problem definition to agenda-setting, and from policy formulation to policy implementation. There are also various *venues* for public decisionmaking, including the legislative process, ballot initiatives, administrative rules, and judicial review. Lastly, there are a variety of *jurisdictions* for action in a federal system of government: local, state, and national.

This multidimensional nature of the policy process makes mapping foundation action into public policy a complex undertaking. It requires an understanding of the various stages, venues, and jurisdictions where policymaking occurs. It also requires an understanding of the range of foundation strategies for shaping, influencing, and impacting public policy. This chapter provides a framework that helps to identify the range of possible foundation strategies; offers an assessment of the benefits, costs, and risks of these strategies; and explores the implications for the role of foundations in the policymaking process. Foundations may or may not make their choices in quite the same explicit fashion that our discussion suggests. However, by discussing foundation choices in a systematic fashion, we hope to shed light on the ways that foundations can engage the public policymaking process.

In what follows, we first present an overview of the policy process to provide a context for the role of foundations in public policy. We then discuss foundation approaches to policy engagement and the factors that shape their decision of whether or not to engage the policy process. This leads us to characterize foundations as influential outsiders. Being outside the policymaking process, but looking for ways to have influence, foundations encounter a range of strategic choices. We discuss how foundations might choose the jurisdictions where they seek influence, the venues they try to impact, and the stages of the policymaking process where they might choose to focus their resources. We also discuss the choices foundations face when determining the nature of the engagements they will have with policy partners, other foundations, nonprofits, and/or policy experts. We conclude the chapter by setting out research questions concerning the strategic choices foundations make. These questions are designed to help better understand the range of actions that foundations may take and their impacts.

The Public Policymaking Process

The public policymaking process is complex. Of course, if we were to limit ourselves to thinking of policymaking as what happens in legislatures, then developing an understanding of the process would be somewhat simplified. However, that simplification would come at considerable cost. It is true that foundations support the work of many policy institutes and that policy analysts from those institutes often give testimony at hearings of legislative committees (Weissert and Knott, 1995). This is an important means by which foundations engage with government in public policymaking. But there are many other means of engagement that deserve our attention. Given this, it is useful to characterize the policymaking process in a manner that gives due regard to its complexity and enables us to identify points of entry for foundation action, while keeping our characterization simple enough that it helps us understand foundation engagement in public policy.

Let us begin by thinking of the policymaking process as constituted from a variety of ongoing conversations about the role of government in society and how that role can be most effectively undertaken (Majone, 1989; Radin, 1997; Schön and Rein, 1994). These conversations are structured in significant ways by the formal institutions through which public policymaking becomes authoritative. However, the conversations take place in various forums, many of which appear reasonably removed from the rough and tumble of everyday politics. These conversations, like all conversations, involve a number of actors. The objective of the actors concerned is typically to make points that receive a fair hearing and that, through their merit, will come to shape policy decisions.

The federal system in the United States provides one of the structuring institutional forms that serve to channel and shape policy conversations. Policy of national importance is discussed and formulated at the federal government level. Conversations about such policies are centered in Washington, D.C., but, of course, they receive input from across the nation. Policies of significance to specific states are discussed and formulated within those states, while those of local significance are dealt with primarily within local jurisdictions. Often, policy conversations work in ways that break down these divisions of formal responsibility, just as a large number of public policies define and build upon intergovernmental relationships. But thinking in terms of divisions is a good way to begin making sense of policymaking in a federalist context, and the choices foundations face when they seek to have influence.

No matter whether policy formulation and adoption occurs at the jurisdictional level of the nation, state, or locality, the policymaking process follows fairly similar procedures in each. Thus, policy scholars have often characterized the process as involving a series of five stages. These stages are: problem definition, agenda-setting, policy adoption, implementation, and evaluation (Eyestone, 1978). This "stages" model of public policymaking has come under some criticism because it assumes an orderly, linear path that follows from stage to stage (Jenkins-Smith and Sabatier, 1993). Obviously, this is not always the case. It often happens that aspects of problem definition are not fully worked out until a policy is being implemented. In addition, evaluations of existing policies and programs can help to identify new problems and to set the agenda for future policy change. Furthermore, the stages approach is better suited to thinking about the making of public policy through legislative processes rather than through administrative and judicial action or initiative processes, all of which play highly significant roles in the shaping of public policy in the United States. Having said that, the stages approach does provide a convenient starting point for us to think about the evolution of policy conversations. It is especially helpful for allowing us to think about the ways that influential outsiders such as foundations might position themselves to shape public policy.

This conception of public policymaking, as constituted through ongoing conversations, structured by various formal institutional arrangements, and divided into a series of stages, serves as our starting point for considering the public policy efforts of foundations. Thinking of the policymaking process in this way allows for simplification that can guide more nuanced investigations of foundation strategies. But before showing how this perspective can guide our thinking about foundations and public policymaking, it is important that we first pay attention to foundation approaches to public policy and the factors that shape foundation decisions to engage in public policy work.

Foundation Approaches to Public Policy

Foundations have money, knowledge, and networks. These resources can be used to generate further knowledge, expand connections, and cultivate strong relationships with influential members of public policy communities. Through such efforts, foundations can leverage their assets to make a difference in public policymaking, thus advancing problem-solving in the policy areas of interest to them.

There are five general approaches that foundations adopt in engaging the policymaking process. Foundations may:

- Fund activities that can potentially have significant effects on public policy.

- Create stores of knowledge that can affect how others think about policy issues.

- Forge networks among individuals and organizations, bringing their knowledge, resources, and skills to bear on policy debates.

- Build good relations with influential policymakers.

- Develop reputations as credible, reliable policy players.

Funding Activities. Foundations can fund activities and programs that serve to promote ideas for policy change, to demonstrate viable alternatives to current policy settings, or to ensure policy implementation. While they have far fewer resources at their disposal than governments, foundations are better situated to support activities that facilitate change in government. For example, McKersie (1999) has documented the efforts of several foundations to contribute to changes in the governance of public schools in Chicago, ranging from funding the efforts of policy analysts and advocates to influence debate on the design of school governance, to funding efforts to ensure that the new governance arrangements were implemented in ways that conformed to their original visions for reform.

Creating Stores of Knowledge. Foundations can foster the development of creative thinkers and bodies of knowledge through fellowships and research institutes that can shape the thinking of others. This approach to influencing public policy places the emphasis on the role of ideas in society. For example, the Lynde and Harry Bradley Foundation and the John M. Olin Foundation have supported academic research and training programs conducted by scholars who are focused on the importance of markets and limited government. And the Robert Wood Johnson "Scholars in Health Policy" program has sought to develop a new generation of creative thinkers in health policy research.

Forging Policy Networks among Individuals and Organizations. Foundations can put ideas and new knowledge into play by creating an infrastructure for the communication and diffusion of policy ideas and innovations. Some foundations have been quite conscious in developing networks among individuals and organizations, with the purpose of creating an infrastructure of well-articulated arguments and empirically grounded policy analysis that can support strong and sustained efforts to shape public policy, both at the state and national levels. For example, the Heritage Foundation is noted for its adeptness at bringing politicians, policymakers, and policy analysts together to discuss topics on the policy agenda with a focus on markets and market-based policy solutions (Smith, 1991).

Building Good Relations with Policymakers. Foundations can establish close ties between their board members and program staff and policymakers. Regular distribution of policy briefing papers and sponsoring conferences and similar gatherings represent activities through which foundations can gain sway in policy communities, including influential policymakers. Those good relations can be supported through the funding of high-quality, timely contributions to policy debates. Foundations can also nurture such relations through what McKersie (1999) refers to as "gap-funding"—providing support for governmental actors as they seek to implement and evaluate new policies.

Developing a Reputation as a Credible Policy Player. Foundations can cultivate reputations for high-quality, timely contributions to public policymaking, thereby enhancing their influence in successive policy debates. For example, in the early 1960s, the Kennedy administration requested a group of private foundations with long-standing programs in race relations to fund the Voter Education Project (VEP). These efforts on the part of several foundations were designed to channel the actions of militant groups, and thus give the administration a freer hand to push for the passage of civil rights legislation, which eventually came in 1964 and 1965 (Jenkins, 1998). Without the efforts of these foundations, it is possible that the actions of militant groups might well have turned public opinion against civil rights. More importantly for our discussion, it is noteworthy that the foundations' earlier efforts to eliminate the Jim Crow system of electoral politics signaled their strong commitment to change. Having shown that commitment, the foundations opened the way for the Kennedy administration to make its overtures regarding further action. Thus, a good reputation can smooth the way for foundations to leverage the resources they have and achieve even more influence in public policymaking.

These five approaches are neither mutually exclusive nor collectively exhaustive. In fact, pursuing multiple approaches might increase impact. Nevertheless, we believe these five approaches capture the essence of foundation approaches to public policy engagement, when they choose to pursue it.

The Decision to Engage in Public Policymaking

Choices about public policy engagement are shaped by the context of individual foundations. Among the factors that are critical to such decisions are organizational characteristics, such as the foundation's mission and financial resources, as well as the environmental context in which the foundation operates, including legal restrictions, the philanthropic environment, and the policy domain.

ORGANIZATIONAL FACTORS

Internally, the two most significant factors are mission and funds. Foundations are constrained in what they might do by their missions and, perhaps more importantly, by the board's interpretations of those missions. Many foundations view their mission as improving society through public problem-solving. And public policy work can be viewed as consistent with such a mission. However, if a foundation has a mission that emphasizes the pursuit of goals that fall beyond the scope of current government activities, and if board members seek to avoid any engagement with government, then this can effectively block the foundation from engaging in any efforts—direct or indirect—to influence public policy. The foundation might also have a geographic focus that does not neatly map onto the jurisdictional bounds in which foundation-interested policy issues are played out.

The second factor that impacts the decision is the foundation's financial assets. While some foundations do have large endowments and they are able to make sizeable grants on an ongoing basis, there are limits to how far the money can go. Many foundations have limited resources relative to the problems that they are committed to addressing. Thus they are circumscribed in their effort. As a consequence, foundations develop approaches that are possible given their resources. They often focus on promoting innovative ideas in government, rather than funding long-term initiatives that parallel or surpass government activities as a realistic response. For example, in recent years the Kellogg Foundation has engaged in local efforts to provide health insurance to the working poor. But these efforts have never been viewed as anything more than temporary programs designed to draw attention to problems of health insurance coverage, and to showcase innovative funding models that government policymakers might emulate (Klein, 2001).

Sometimes foundations are constrained from engaging in public policy by their geographic scope and financial resources. That need not be the case. For example, many foundations are locally oriented and have moderate levels of assets. They choose to focus their efforts on "ground-level," practical initiatives that generate rapid, readily visible results. In terms of making visible use of their resources, this can be an appropriate strategy. However, even within such constraints, foundations face many options for engaging public policy. For example, coupling geographically limited demonstration projects with broader efforts to disseminate information about those projects and their effects can do much to promote the diffusion of policy innovations. Ideas and information concerning policy innovations tend to be carried through policy networks. Foundations also can work to keep specific networks buzzing with discussions of policy ideas and demonstration projects. In recent years, the Walton Family Foundation has contributed money to the development of many charter schools across the country. This foundation has been careful to support charter schools only in states where the laws that authorize these schools are deemed suitably permissive to allow large numbers of charter schools to develop. The Walton Family Foundation has then sought to leverage these local efforts by providing funds to national organizations like the Charter Friends National Network. This network is specifically designed as a forum and conduit for the sharing of information and political war stories among charter school advocates (Finn and Annis, 2001). Such networks facilitate the diffusion of innovations.

THE EXTERNAL ENVIRONMENT

The environment in which foundations operate also shapes their choices. The law is the most obvious factor. As tax-exempt organizations, foundations are subject to a set of restrictions on their activities. Among these are prohibitions on engaging in electoral politics and lobbying. At first glance, these prohibitions suggest that foundations are severely restricted in their ability to engage in activities associated with public policymaking. Actually, there is considerable latitude for foundations under existing laws and regulations (see Chapter 4; Williams, 2000).[1]

With respect to lobbying, foundations are prohibited from doing so directly, which means communicating directly with legislators where specific legislation is referred to and a view on the legislation is given. Further, foundations are not to engage in grassroots lobbying concerning specific legislation, and they are forbidden from enjoining citizens to contact their legislators over an issue. These prohibitions leave a considerable amount of room for foundations to maneuver. For example, they can assemble interested parties, including legislators, executive officials, and their staff, to discuss policy issues so long as they do not address the merits of specific legislation. Further, foundations are allowed to fund policy analyses and research findings as well as to provide these directly to legislators, executive officials, and their staff. These activities are viewed as efforts to educate the public about issues. In the resulting documents, the foundations are even allowed to take a position on specific legislation, so long as they present enough alternative points of view that a reader can come to an independent

---

[1]The legal restrictions discussed here apply to private foundations; community foundations are subject to the regulations that apply to public charities. *See* Edie (1991), p. 50.

opinion on the matter. Distribution of these documents must extend beyond supply to people on one side of an issue. If called upon to testify at legislative hearings, foundation representatives are allowed to support or oppose specific legislation.

Along with the activities mentioned above, foundations are also allowed to fund nonprofit organizations that do engage in lobbying. The funding is deemed legal so long as money provided in general operating grants is not earmarked for lobbying. It is also legal for foundations to fund projects that contain a lobbying component, so long as the funding of the lobbying component constitutes less than the total amount that the grantee will actually spend on lobbying.[2]

Foundation decisions can also be influenced by the broader philanthropic environment. Foundations are quite aware of what others in the foundation community are doing. And depending on the posture that a foundation takes, the actions of other foundations can be either limiting or encouraging. To the extent that foundations compete for reputation and influence over public policy, the philanthropic environment works to constrain foundation actions. For example, Knott and Weissert (1994) find that foundations that focus on health policy issues adjust their actions to those of others. Some foundations take lead roles, either as pioneers or trendsetters; but other foundations react to their lead by being niche funders or followers who provide some funding to complement the leaders rather than compete. On the other hand, it is possible that foundations with shared policy interests can join forces to have a greater impact in policy work. In fact, with appropriate structures, foundations may be more inclined to engage public policy than they would have been if left to undertake it alone.[3]

The Strategic Choices Foundations Make as Influential Outsiders

Next we turn to considering more closely the choices that foundations have in engaging the policy process. We divide these strategic choices into four groups. First, foundations face choices concerning the *jurisdictions* where they seek to influence public policy. These include national policymaking, as well as policymaking within states, regions, and localities. Second, foundations face choices concerning the *stages* in the policy process at which they act. These stages include problem definition, agenda-setting, policy adoption,

---

[2]Asher (1995) provides the following example. Suppose a foundation makes a grant of $10,000 in a year for a public charity's project. The grantee's project budget lists $20,000 for lobbying expenses out of total project expenses of $35,000. If the grant is not earmarked for lobbying, it is permissible, because the project's budget for non-lobbying expenses ($15,000) exceeds the grant's amount ($10,000).

[3]*See* Chapter 5 for Lucy Bernholz's discussion of how foundations form strategic alliances to engage in public policy.

policy implementation, and policy evaluation. Third, foundations can choose the *venues* in which they will participate. Since the vast majority of public policy is made through the legislative process, this serves as a critical venue in which to seek influence. However, the courts and the initiative process represent extremely important alternative venues. Fourth, foundations can choose the *instruments* that they will use to engage in policymaking.

For analytical purposes, we treat these strategic choices separately. In practice, of course, it is likely that foundations make these choices in combination, and in ways that differ from the neatness implied by our more linear presentation. It might also be the case that some foundations, because of their missions, do not consider the full menu of strategic choices that are available to them when it comes to leveraging their assets to influence public policymaking. But for the purposes of our analysis, it is important that we consider the full range of options. Having done so, we should be better able to understand the particular choices that any given foundation might make, and speculate on why it is that some strategies are rarely put on the table and others are the norm.

Choosing Jurisdictions

The federal system in the United States allocates governmental responsibilities among the national, state, and local governments. The justification for this system is the view that jurisdictions with the best information about particular issues or problems and the greatest motivation to address them should have the greatest say over the crafting of relevant public policy. However, because many issues and problems, such as poverty, education, the regulation of business, and environmental degradation raise concerns that do not fall neatly into any particular jurisdiction, policymaking often involves intergovernmental conversations and agreements as well. The intergovernmental aspects of public policymaking can involve both vertical interactions (such as state-federal, state-local, or federal-local) and horizontal interactions (state-state or local-local). Here, we refer to the distinctive layers of government as jurisdictions. Of course, foundations need not—and many do not—restrict themselves to working within one particular jurisdiction. Often, efforts are made to work simultaneously in multiple jurisdictions. Most complex policy issues are addressed through contributions made in multiple jurisdictions. Given this, where resources are available to do so, pursuing policy influence in several jurisdictions at once can be an effective strategy.

Foundations seeking to influence public policymaking face choices concerning the jurisdiction or jurisdictions within which to take action. Sometimes, this choice will be dictated by the scope and purpose of the foundation. For example, many relatively small family foundations have been established primarily as a means through which philanthropists can offer direct assistance to individuals and groups in need of support. The possibility of using foundation resources to influence public policy is not seriously entertained, partly because that would be a departure from the foundation's mission, and partly because of resource constraints. Often foundation trustees, particularly those associated with family foundations, desire to take actions that will have observable, local-level impacts. While policy change might be a broader objective, more energy is poured into providing direct services to people. Here, a trade-off is made between accomplishing immediate results that change a few people's lives and patiently working with policymakers to try to achieve breakthroughs that hold major implications for many people.

Instances can be found of nonprofits that deliberately mix their forms of engagement, and hence find themselves operating in a number of jurisdictions simultaneously. The San Francisco-based Bay Area Partnership is an example (Drabble and Abrenilla, 2000, p. 23).

When the federal and state governments instituted welfare reform in 1996, the Partnership worked with multiple local groups, including foundations, to ensure that children's basic needs would be met. The result was the establishment of new breakfast programs and after-school programs in many schools. But the Partnership did not focus exclusively on the local jurisdiction. To influence public policymaking, the Partnership targeted both the state and federal levels with the goal of shaping public policies that directly affect the children it serves. As a result, the Partnership was instrumental in expanding the nature of the program. This occurred when lawmakers raised the eligibility ages for children affected by the Federal Nutrition Act, during its 1998 reauthorization. In addition, the Partnership worked at the state level to affect the After-School Learning and Safe Neighborhoods Partnership Act so as to make the program more accessible to older children.

Foundations seeking to influence public policymaking can increase their likelihood of success if they carefully choose the jurisdictions within which they take action. Foundations with considerable resources at their disposal and with national reputations are likely to face the greatest opportunities for explicitly choosing the jurisdictions they will enter. Some might enter multiple jurisdictions simultaneously. For example, large national foundations such as the Ford Foundation or the Rockefeller Foundation can seek to influence national policy, state policies, or local policies, depending on the policy domain of concern (e.g., education, poverty alleviation, voting rights). In contrast, large state or regionally based foundations, while enjoying national profiles, are more likely to seek influence at the state or local level.[4] Meanwhile, as mentioned previously, smaller foundations, in particular smaller family foundations, are more likely to focus on local concerns, and might engage in public policymaking in a more limited fashion.

None of this is inevitable. Given the federal system and the multiple jurisdictions that come with it, all foundations seeking policy influence face important choices concerning the jurisdictions within which they might feasibly engage the policy process. Issues of focus, uncertainties, and risks associated with policy engagement suggest that foundations are likely to be confronted with trade-offs between the potential influence they will have and the likelihood of that influence leading to policy changes. Figure 1 characterizes the strategic choices foundations face when choosing jurisdictions.

Figure 1: Choosing Jurisdictions

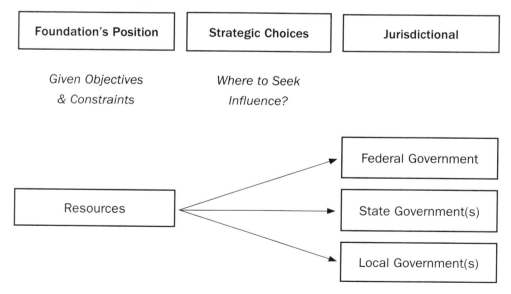

---

[4] It is possible that such an effort might reflect a mission that has a state focus.

Choosing Stages

Along with choosing the jurisdictions where they will seek to influence public policymaking, foundations also face choices regarding the stages of the policymaking process in which they will seek to engage. While jurisdictions concern the *place* of policy engagement, stages concern the *phase* of engagement. Here, we discuss issues of timing, and the points in the policymaking process where foundations might seek policy influence. Within the public policy literature, there is a bias toward viewing legislative politics as central to the policymaking process. In many respects, this bias is justifiable given that a majority of public policies are adopted by legislatures on behalf of the people they represent. However, the legislature is not the exclusive venue within which public policymaking occurs. For example, policy is also made during the implementation stage. It is here that many of the broader issues dealt with by legislative policymakers must be transformed into action by public organizations. More will be said about this shortly. Beyond the venues of policymaking mentioned here, two other critically important alternative venues require discussion. First, there are the courts. Second, there are citizen initiatives—a form of direct democracy—found most frequently in the western states. We will discuss public policymaking in those two alternative venues, and how foundations might seek influence there, in a separate section following.

Figure 2: Choosing Stages

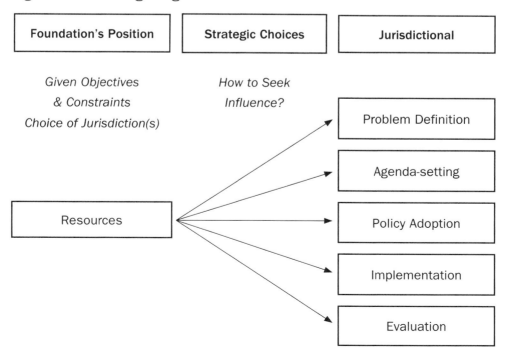

Problem Definition. Public policies are typically developed to address particular social problems that have been identified as significant. However, just because a problem is significant, it is not always clear that action on the part of government could contribute to its alleviation. For this reason, several scholars of the policymaking process have observed that policy problems cannot be separated from the solutions that are proposed to address them. According to Aaron Wildavsky (1979), it is only when people have an understanding of a potential solution that they come to define a phenomenon as a problem that calls for a policy response. Those who seek to represent a social phenomenon as a policy problem must present their ideas in ways that hold intuitive appeal to others, many of whom might not have noticed or previously thought about the "problem" (Mintrom, 2000).

Foundations seeking to influence public policymaking have the potential to significantly affect problem definition within particular areas of public policy. For example, funding basic research that involves developing information and statistics about particular social phenomena is one way to start the process of problem definition. In its annually updated "Kids Count" data book, the Annie E. Casey Foundation has sought to draw attention to the conditions faced by America's children. This project tracks the status of children in the U.S. It is designed to give policymakers and citizens benchmarks of child well-being, and hence promote local, state, and national discussions concerning ways to secure better futures for all children. Likewise, some of the early research on AIDS was funded by foundations for the purpose of drawing attention to a social problem, which could be construed as calling for a public policy response. It is also the case that foundations can draw attention to problems and their potential solutions by funding projects that help individuals or communities in need. The very action taken by foundations can be construed as defining a problem and providing a "model" program or policy showing how it might be solved.

Foundations can also work more explicitly in the realm of ideas. Foundations with strong beliefs in conservative principles have gained much attention for their work in recent decades to shape ideas about public policy. These efforts include the funding of university professorships and programs with the expectation that recipients of the funds will formulate and promote conservative ideas about government, markets, and society. But these efforts do not simply target the lecture hall. Research undertaken by university faculty with conservative sympathies is also widely disseminated. For example, the work by Murray (1984) on welfare delivery was funded by the Manhattan Institute. There, Murray argued that government welfare programs were themselves the source of problems, since they bred dependency behavior on the part of recipients. Murray's ideas helped set the agenda for the welfare reform efforts undertaken by the federal and state governments in the mid-1990s. Similarly, the work of Paul Peterson on education vouchers and their effects has been underwritten by a variety of foundations, such as the Thomas B. Fordham Foundation. Among his many activities in this area, Peterson has recently established a glossy journal for public consumption, *Education Next*. It is designed for a popular audience, appearing in large bookstores such as Barnes and Noble. Clearly, the journal is designed to change public discourse concerning public education and the nature of the policy reforms that would be most effective for addressing problems of student achievement.

Many foundation efforts to fund basic research can be seen as holding the potential to contribute to problem definition and, hence, to public policymaking. However, targeting the problem definition stage is likely to hold few rewards for foundations that want to see quick and demonstrable results from their grantmaking. Problem definition emerges primarily by the accretion of evidence and by careful efforts to sift through that evidence and present the findings in coherent and convincing ways; this is how advocates of policy change come to develop what Stone (1997) refers to as "causal stories" about problems and how they might be solved.

Agenda-setting. Once a problem has been defined and feasible policy solutions identified, it is possible for agenda-setting to begin. Agenda-setting can be thought of as taking two distinct forms. First, there is agenda-setting in the broader policy community. Second, there is agenda-setting within government (driven primarily by key members of the legislature and the leader of the executive branch, such as the president or a governor). Typically, items must be on the broader policy agenda if they are to gain the attention from political influentials necessary to get them placed on the government agenda. The process of agenda-setting in the broader policy community is typically quite open. Given this, political outsiders engaged in savvy efforts to promote their ideas for policy change can have considerable influence (Mintrom, 2000). According to Kingdon (1995), items get elevated onto government agendas when links are made between three distinctive "streams" of activity: political, policy, and problem. The political stream is punctuated primarily by elections and changes of administration. The policy stream is where ideas formulated in the broader policy community emerge. The problem stream is comprised of emerging crises or focusing events that attract popular attention. Actors in the policymaking process who seek to have particular issues placed on the government agenda must be able to connect problems with policies in ways that are sufficiently compelling to attract interest from politicians, who can then go on to promote ideas for government action.

Foundations face many opportunities to contribute to broad agenda-setting in policy communities. Using their grantmaking abilities combined with their relationships and knowledge networks, foundations can work to forge coalitions and build a critical mass of advocates pressing for policy change. This can be particularly helpful for agenda-setting activities when the coalitions create linkages among research organizations, analysis shops, and advocates. Greenberg and Laracy (2000) highlight the importance of foundations "... creating an 'echo chamber,' through which public policymakers repeatedly hear, understand, and retain messages educating them about policies..." (p.18). These authors argue that the release of one or two reports, even when they represent very good work, is not sufficient to create an echo chamber. Rather, foundations need to engage in "effective social marketing," just as businesses do through advertising campaigns. Foundations can leverage their knowledge and ideas through effective message development and communication strategies. Beyond coalition-building efforts and the development of an echo chamber, Greenberg and Laracy list the following strategies that foundations can use for agenda-setting:

• Disseminating findings from evaluations and assessments

• Synthesizing previous research

• Using web sites to disseminate research knowledge

• Briefing congressional staff

• Striving for a bipartisan convergence

• Organizing the grassroots

• Creating a public will for policy change

• Focusing on single issues, but linking them to broader issues

Most of these strategies for agenda-setting involve the packaging of information. Thus, efforts to develop bipartisan convergence might include the running of regular lunchtime seminars where the featured speakers are experts who approach the issue of interest from different ideological perspectives. These efforts might also include the holding of a conference on a broad issue, such as welfare reform, and providing opportunities for presenters and attendees to engage in discussions that have the potential to lead to greater consensus about the key policy concerns that need to be resolved, and how such resolution might be achieved.

Policy Adoption. The policy adoption stage of the policymaking process can be thought of as starting with legislative committee consideration of a bill and ending with government adoption of a new policy. Although the policy adoption stage is heavily influenced by political insiders such as elected officials and their staff, outsider influence can still be critical for guiding the actions of decisionmakers. For example, advocates will often organize key constituents and ensure that members of that group are in the public gallery of the legislature when representatives are debating or set to vote on a particular legislative change. In addition, advocates can take steps to "educate" representatives and their staff about issues on the government agenda. This can be done in a variety of ways, including the circulation of policy briefs, legislative analyses, and the giving of testimony during committee hearings. Foundations can contribute to efforts of this sort. However, it is at this stage in the policymaking process that foundations and other nonprofit organizations must take care to keep within the laws regarding lobbying.

Implementation. Once a new policy has been adopted by legislators and the political executive, it must be implemented. Policy implementation involves transforming ideas into actions. This process of taking legislative intent and making it happen inevitably opens spaces for additional, derivative policymaking. This micro-level policymaking frequently gets devolved to people on the ground. As Lipsky (1980) has documented, implementation of human services like police work and teaching require that service providers continually make judgments that bear upon their relations with their clients, and the quality of the service that is provided. Thus, in many ways, police officers and teachers can be seen as exerting ongoing influence on public policy through the choices they make on a daily basis. Certainly, the choices made by people in these positions can greatly affect citizens' impressions of government.

Foundations can influence policymaking at the implementation stage. McKersie's (1999) documentation of the role foundations played in the implementation of Chicago's school reforms demonstrates how such influence can be achieved. In that instance, ongoing foundation funding allowed analysis shops to provide technical assistance to schools and district personnel. The efforts of the Woods Foundation are useful to consider in this regard. The foundation has had a long-standing interest in community empowerment. The school reforms in Chicago were designed to increase community involvement in the schools. The Woods Foundation paid special attention to this matter during the implementation phase. The approach taken was twofold. First, the foundation took care to ensure that one of the agencies being funded to provide technical support for the reforms was indeed following an agenda that reflected what a diverse group of Chicagoans wanted. Second, the foundation led several collaborations among Chicago foundations to fund community- and school-level reform activity and convened several citywide meetings of school reform stakeholders.

In general, foundations have the potential to weigh in at the implementation stage with both funding and advice. Foundations may build partnerships among stakeholders to smooth the implementation of policy reforms. During implementation, foundations can follow a strategy of working in collaboration with government agencies. Thus, we commonly find examples of foundations providing funds to new school programs or to community health initiatives. But in addition to such efforts, foundations can also choose to work with nonprofit organizations, providing funds to temporarily address gaps not appropriately anticipated during policy design and adoption.

Evaluation. Once a new item of public policy has been adopted and implemented, it is important to know how well it actually works. Yet politicians are often somewhat reluctant to fund studies evaluating the effectiveness of new public policies or programs. The main reason for this is that politicians like to be able to claim credit for having put a new program in place. Solid evidence that the new program is working could well provide further grounds for credit-claiming. However, it is also the case that evaluation studies might point to problems of policy design and implementation or shed light on unintended consequences of the policy change.

The information generated by program evaluations is potentially of great value to policy analysts and program designers. However, for politicians, this new information can be a source of danger. Opponents of a new policy might seize upon the results to prove that they were right to resist it. Supporters of the policy might seize upon the results to show that more needs to be done to address the issues that concerned them in the first place. For the politicians who lent their support to the policy, funding evaluation work can be seen as inviting trouble. Given the risks, the question of "Does the policy work?"

often goes unanswered within government. This is a stage where foundations can have a great deal of scope for policy influence. It is also true that a lot of evaluation work can feed into new efforts concerning problem definition and agenda-setting for additional policy change.

Alternative Venues

Our discussion of the stages of the policymaking process indicates that there are many potential "pressure" points for foundations to have policy influence within the legislative process. However, other entry points also exist in venues that are deliberately separate from the legislative and executive branches of government. Here, we discuss the opportunities that the courts and the initiative process provide for foundations to influence policymaking.[5]

The Courts. The courts are important venues for policymaking in the United States because frequently individuals and groups will question the constitutionality of new policies that have been adopted through the legislative process. For example, charter school laws in several states, including Michigan, have been challenged in state courts. Likewise, public voucher programs in Wisconsin and Ohio have been challenged in state and federal courts. These challenges can lead to rulings against the laws in question. They can also force legislatures to make new or amended laws regarding the policy issue in question, with the purpose of addressing problems raised in the court challenges. These changes can sometimes be made before the legal challenges are fully dealt with in the court system.

Aside from adjudicating on the constitutionality of new laws, courts are also important venues in which individuals can file suits against other individuals, organizations, or governments for actions that they believe violate their rights. Judgments in disputes of this sort can have important implications for the interpretation of laws and, thus, for policymaking and policy implementation.

Since taking legal action is time-consuming and expensive, foundations can be important resources for individuals and groups seeking to use the courts to protect or promote their interests. Covington (1997, p. 23) has reported how conservative foundations have funded "… a core group of

---

[5]Most conceptual work concerning stages of policymaking has been developed on the assumption that the legislature is the focal point for policymaking. But, on reflection, thinking in terms of policymaking stages can also be helpful for analyzing what happens in alternative venues for policymaking—such as the court and the initiative process. The mapping of appropriate stages for these alternative venues, and the drawing of comparisons between those stages and stages in legislative policymaking, is yet to be done.

pro-market law firms and other law-related institutions actively seeking to overturn affirmative action, environmental regulations, rent control laws, and other government programs or statutes deemed inconsistent with the principles of economic liberty, freedom of contract or association, and private property." Meanwhile, Drabble and Abrenilla (2000, p. 14) have reported on the ways that progressive foundations in California have assisted individuals and groups in the venue of the courts. According to these authors, ". . . in recent years, California legal advocacy groups ... defended affirmative action and immigrant rights in the face of hostile ballot initiatives, protected teen abortion rights, worked on redistricting to increase Latino political representation, and fought court battles to defend the rights of people with disabilities to health care, education, and employment, and physical access." They also have noted that legal advocacy organizations are often involved as leaders or collaborators in litigation to advance or defend the rights of groups.

The Initiative Process. As an alternative way of making public policy, many states and localities in the United States allow for citizen initiatives to be placed on the ballot. These citizen initiatives—sometimes referred to as direct democracy—have been important in recent years as venues for making public policy regarding a range of measures including the rights of immigrants, education policy, tax policy, environmental regulation, and the regulation of insurance companies. Initiatives can only be included on the ballot after petitions have been circulated and a sufficient number of signatures have been collected in support of the initiative. Thus, to place an initiative on the ballot requires a high degree of political coordination and, hence, financial resources.

Initiatives are viewed, in the context of legal limits on foundations, as legislation where the public in the jurisdiction acts as the legislative body (Colvin, 1995). Foundations are prohibited from engaging in lobbying directly, or funding the lobbying of their grantees. Nevertheless, foundations can fund activities that support ballot measure work but which do not meet the definition of lobbying, or that qualify under exceptions, such as nonpartisan research and analysis or when the amount of the grant is less than a charity's non-lobbying budget.

Of course, there are stages in the initiative process just as in the case of legislation. There are three critical periods: the period prior to the circulation of signature petitions; the period when signatures are being collected to place it on the ballot; and the campaign after it is placed on the ballot. There is considerable latitude for foundation activity in the pre-circulation phase, but it is diminished in the later two phases (Fei, 2001). But, it is still possible for foundations to act to impact the campaign. For example, in 1994 the California Wellness Foundation undertook an effort to provide information to the public on Proposition 188—a statewide initiative in California that was viewed as undoing the stringency of antismoking laws that had been passed locally in many communities across the state (Colvin, 1995). The foundation chose to make a grant to the Public Media Center, a nonprofit media agency serving the nonprofit sector, which mounted a media-based public education campaign. The campaign did not rely on nonpartisan analysis, but rather offered information on the positions of those on both sides of the issue, and identified the major contributors.

Forms of Engagement: Instruments and Mechanisms

In our discussion to this point, we have frequently mentioned various forms of engagement that foundations can choose when seeking to influence public policymaking. However, it is important that we lay out the instruments and mechanisms of engagement in a somewhat more systematic fashion. Here, we do just that. We discuss forms of engagement under four broad categories: funding policy analysis and technical support; building knowledge communities; supporting advocacy; and public education. As the following figure indicates, we view the foundation's strategic choices concerning forms of engagement as deriving from its other choices concerning the jurisdiction to focus on, the stage of the policymaking process to target, and the venue to work within. Of course, the foundation mission, philosophy, and context will also frame the choices. A well-resourced foundation with a national reputation that is interested in shaping welfare policy is likely to make very different strategic choices than a family foundation interested in improving the educational performance of students in local schools. We expect that foundations will make more or less use of each of these instruments and mechanisms depending upon the stage of the policymaking process in which they choose to seek influence. But we do not have strong theoretical reasons for ruling out, at any given stage in the policymaking process, any given instrument or mechanism.

Figure 3: Choosing Instruments and Mechanisms

Foundation's Position	Strategic Choices	Instruments and Mechanisms

Given Objectives & Constraints
Choice of Jurisdiction(s)
Stage(s), & Venue(s),
& Forms of Engagement

What Forms of Engagement?

Resources

Funding Analysis & Technical Support

Building Knowledge Communities

Supporting Advocacy

Public Education

Evaluation

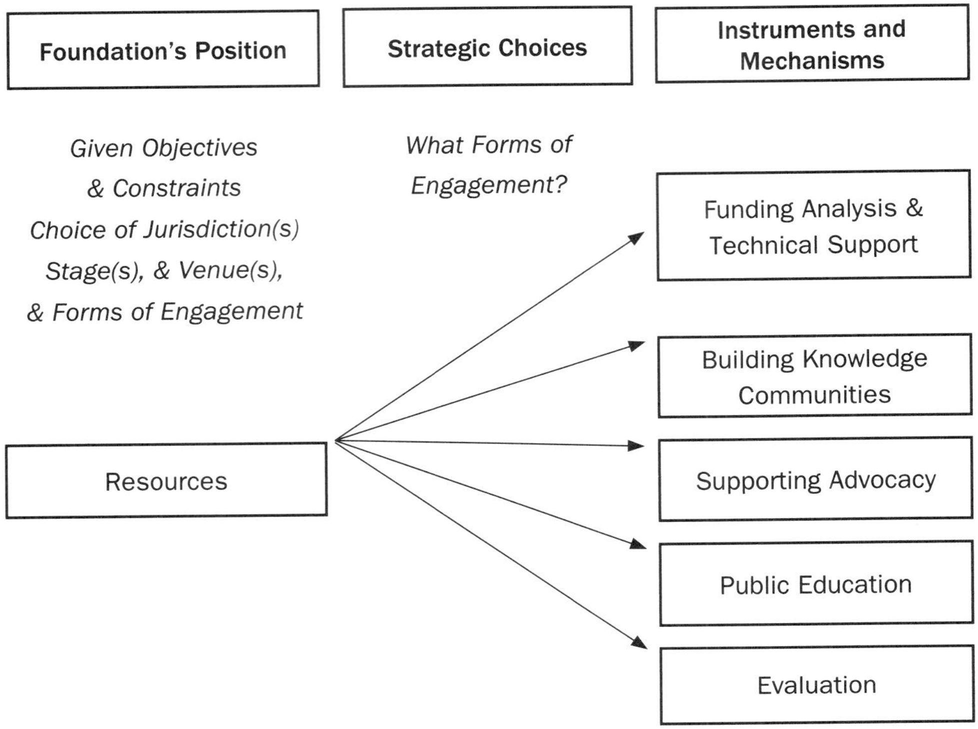

Funding Policy Analysis and Technical Support. A common and obvious way that foundations can contribute to public policymaking is through the funding of the intellectual work and research that can guide policymakers and practitioners. Funding these kinds of activities can create opportunities for foundations to have influence at every stage of the policymaking process. Policy analysis and research is most important at the early stages of the process, such as problem identification and agenda-setting. Funding technical support is most critical for foundations that seek to have influence during the implementation stage of the process. Often, funding technical support makes it possible for policy shops to collaborate with bureaucrats and others who have been charged with policy implementation. And since many micro-level policy decisions must be made as policy ideas are transformed into actions, there is a wide scope for foundations to have influence through supporting this kind of policy work. Funding program evaluations is important for filling knowledge gaps about the workability of policies. Since program evaluations will often identify weaknesses in current policies, they can be especially important as starting points for new rounds of agenda-setting for policy change.

Foundations also have opportunities to develop new policy knowledge through the funding, development, and monitoring of pilot programs. Such initiatives can have a variety of benefits for those who seek to influence public policymaking (see Mintrom, 2000). First, they can demonstrate that policy ideas are, in fact, able to be transformed into working programs. This is important for demonstrating to risk-averse politicians that policy change is possible and that the resulting program will not create unintended consequences. Second, pilot programs can help with coalition-building efforts. By providing services to a group of individuals who were previously unknown to one another, pilot programs can solve an important collective action problem, and allow people to come together and recognize their shared interests. Involvement in the programs can be a starting point for advocacy for broader, government-inspired policy change. Finally, pilot programs can generate important information about policy design and potential implementation problems. This information can be of value to policymakers and practitioners when government programs that take the pilot programs to scale are introduced.

Building Knowledge Communities. Through their grantmaking activities, foundations develop contacts and generate information flows. In the language of network analysis, foundations come to represent nodal points, creating weak ties across a range of individuals and organizations, past and present grantees. But a network of weak ties does not, in itself, constitute a knowledge community. Foundations can achieve increased influence by being proactive in creating and maintaining such communities, and orienting them in ways that comport with the public policymaking interests of the group. One way to do this involves hosting ongoing policy workshops that bring foundation grantees and other interested members of the policymaking community together for focused discussions. Hosting conferences is another way that foundations can influence the structure and help to promote the cohesion and growth of knowledge communities. Another mechanism that can help to build knowledge communities involves finding ways to have researchers, policy analysts, and practitioners work together on common problems. Making collaborative efforts a criterion for grantmaking is one way that foundations can create incentives for diverse groups of individuals and organizations to find common ground and begin working together. With the development of Internet tools, the opportunities for foundations to contribute to the development and maintenance of knowledge communities have now expanded significantly.

Two examples are the Welfare Information Network (WIN) and the Research Forum for Children, Families, and the New Federalism. According to Greenberg and Laracy (2000, p. 22),

> WIN is an information clearing house that serves as an intermediary and facilitator between organizations and individuals generating data, knowledge, and lessons about welfare, welfare reform, and poverty; and policy-makers, administrators, the media, and advocates using such information. The primary means through which it facilitates the dissemination of knowledge is its award-winning Web site.

The web-based Research Forum fulfills a similar function.

> The Research Forum promotes rigorous and policy-relevant research to monitor and evaluate the new welfare law. Working closely with WIN, the Research Forum supports collaboration among and between researchers and policymakers, with a particular emphasis on the need for researchers to address questions relevant to the interests of policymakers and practitioners.

Supporting Advocacy. Foundation support for advocacy is typically achieved through grantmaking to other nonprofit groups, such as policy analysis and advocacy shops. But support for advocacy can also be provided through support for legal defense funds and funding of other legal initiatives designed to protect and promote the rights of individuals and groups. Support for advocacy can be provided through grants to grassroots citizen groups for their activities.

There is considerable room for creativity on the part of foundations seeking to promote policy advocacy while still ensuring that their grantmaking provides financial support to those in need. Drabble and Abrenilla (2000, p. 27) quote Christina Regalado of the Los Angeles Women's Foundation on this matter:

> One of our biggest barriers to overcome in policy-related grantmaking is the notion of when you do "policy work" it requires a certain expertise. That is a barrier, even among our grantees, that often feel, "Policy work? Oh, that's work done by specialists, by people that have been working in Sacramento." Demystifying what policy work means is critical for community organizations. . . [O]rganizations can overcome the myths attached to policy and believe ". . . this is do-able, I actually have access, and I have a lot to say because I work out there in the community."

Public Education. Foundations can support public education on policy issues in at least two important ways. First, they can fund media campaigns concerning particular issues of the moment. Just as efforts can be made to create "echo chambers" that direct targeted messages at legislators and other policymakers, so too efforts can be made to embed important ideas in the minds of citizens. Public education media campaigns are most likely to be effective during the agenda-setting stage of policymaking and in the time leading up to legislative votes, elections, or ballot initiatives.

Public education can also be supported through grants to university-based teaching and research programs. For example, a group of foundations have provided resources for the development of conservatively oriented campus societies for law students. In addition, they have endowed professorships and new programs in the areas of public policy, law, economics, and political science (Covington, 1997). Do these university-based initiatives promote policy change? Writing of the changes made in regulation policy, Wilson (1980, p. 393) observed, "we must be struck at every turn by the importance of ideas." In saying this, Wilson noted the ways that ideas and arguments presented in lecture halls during the 1960s had come to gain dominance in the policy discourse in the late 1970s. Of course, what happens in the lecture halls is not all that counts. But, clearly, academics with particular points of view regarding public policy can make important contributions to the "echo chamber" of public ideas, especially when a long-term perspective of policy change is adopted.

Deploying Assets and Grantmaking

We have argued that foundations have assets in the form of money, knowledge, and connections. Given an aspiration to influence public policymaking, how might a foundation deploy these assets to get the most leverage? Foundations face choices concerning what activities to fund and how to fund them. Of course, issues of uncertainty and risk come into play here, and are likely to seriously shape the choices that foundations make. In general terms, foundations can be thought of as having control over the scope and duration of funding. Funds can be provided to other nonprofits in the form of general operating grants. Such funds place few constraints on the expenditure choices made by the recipients. For example, conservative foundations have now been providing general operating grants to the American Enterprise Institute (AEI) for several decades. With this funding, the Institute's leaders are free to make their own choices about the research projects and policy analysis work that they will fund. However, in 1986 the Olin and Smith Richardson foundations withdrew their support from AEI citing disagreements with some of its policies. Since that time, the Institute has assumed a more aggressive and conservative policy role. This change has been seen as a direct response to the wishes of foundation funders (Covington 1997, p. 15). The change suggests the influence that foundations can have when it comes to shaping policy analysis, building knowledge communities, and supporting advocacy and public education.

Foundations seeking greater control over the activities of those they fund can do so by designating how grants will be spent. This is why foundations often make program grants or the even more limited project grants. Such grants can be short-term or long-term in nature. Inevitably, foundations with larger endowments are better placed to make large, long-term commitments to their grantees. From the perspective of grant recipients, the nature of the grants being made can significantly affect their operations and the choices they make with respect to engaging in activities that could influence public policymaking. Drabble and Abrenilla (2000, 24) suggest that foundations are often ineffective in promoting policy change because they lack familiarity with policy activities and the role of policy in helping individuals and specific communities. In addition, foundation efforts are sometimes constrained because of "the appeal of short-term success and measurable outcomes of service grantmaking."

Advocates and researchers who are familiar with public policymaking often express frustration at the preference that foundations exhibit for funding short-term projects. Drabble and Abrenilla (2000, p. 25) report the following comments from a grantee: "[F]oundations move on to new programs after one to three years... Supporting member agencies is not sexy or new... To obtain new funding [for ongoing programs] you have to dress it up so that it looks like a new project and eventually it does become a new project." When looking to influence public policymaking, foundations need to think strategically about what they really want to achieve and how they can organize their grantmaking to maximize the likelihood that they will realize their policy objectives.

In Figure 4, we present an approach to categorizing foundations' choices when it comes to deploying their assets. The figure is designed to link foundations' choices with features of the broader public policy environment. Actions taken in the policy environment are expected to yield benefits, such as the shaping of public policy in accordance with the foundations' objectives. However, uncertainty characterizes the policy environment. For this reason, foundations deploying assets in pursuit of policy goals are forced by the nature of the situation to embrace some amount of risk. Inevitably, on some occasions grants are made or conferences are held, and the outputs yield little or nothing in terms of movement toward desired policy changes. Foundations engaged in the policy work must be willing to accept that risk.

Figure 4: Asset Deployment and Grantmaking Strategies

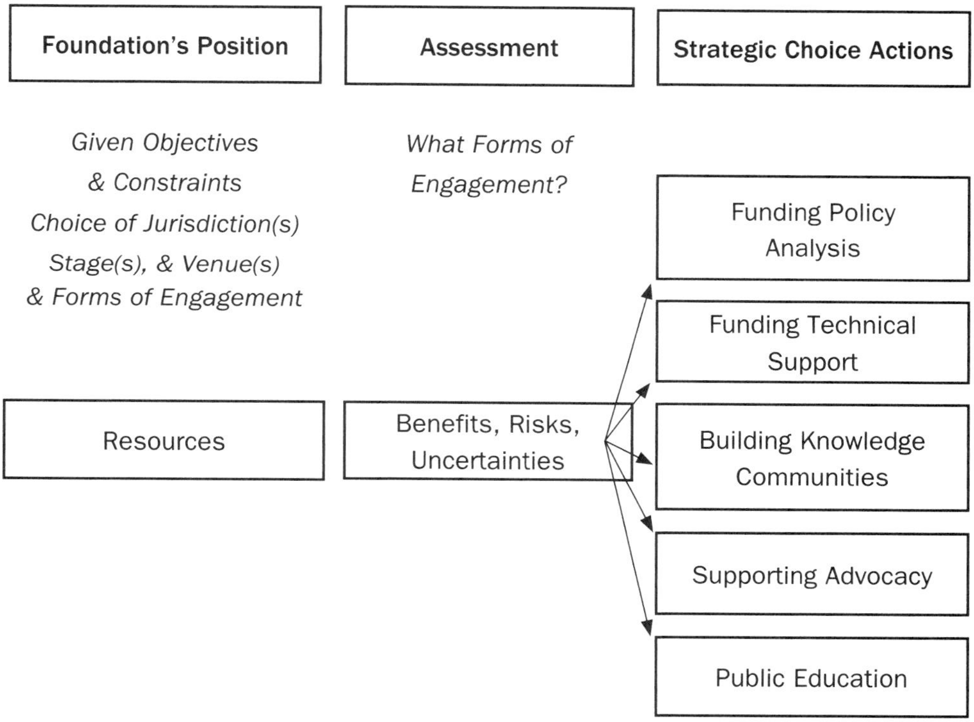

Foundation's Position	Assessment	Strategic Choice Actions

Given Objectives & Constraints
Choice of Jurisdiction(s)
Stage(s), & Venue(s)
& Forms of Engagement

What Forms of Engagement?

Funding Policy Analysis

Funding Technical Support

| Resources | Benefits, Risks, Uncertainties | Building Knowledge Communities |

Supporting Advocacy

Public Education

Conclusions

Our goal in this chapter has been to develop a conceptual framework useful for understanding foundation roles in public policy and the options foundations have when they choose to seek to influence public policy.

The policymaking process is made up of complex social interactions. When seeking influence in that process, foundations need to find productive ways to work with others to define and achieve common goals. Like other policy players, foundations are forced to act within well-defined formal institutional structures and more informal, but nonetheless important, social conventions that serve to delimit what actions are possible and feasible. Nevertheless, foundations have considerable assets that they can potentially leverage to impact public policy: money, knowledge, and connections.

To be effective players in public policymaking, foundations must be strategic. They need to make critical decisions as to where to engage the policy process, how to engage it, and how to deploy their assets.

Foundations face choices concerning where to engage public policy: what *stage(s)* of the policymaking process—problem definition, agenda-setting, policy formulation, policy adoption, and/or policy implementation; what *venue(s)*—the legislative process, the initiative, administrative rulemaking, and/or the courts; and, what *jurisdiction(s)*—local, state, and/or national. Those choices emerge from a set of feasible options given the organizational imperatives and the environmental context of the individual foundations and the institutional structure of the policy domain (e.g., schools, health, and smart growth).

Foundations face choices concerning how to engage public policy. Foundations may choose to fund work of policy relevance: policy analyses, pilot programs, and technical support; to build stores of knowledge and create networks; and to engage in the policy process through support of those directly involved in policymaking. They have the options of becoming involved in the policy process at different levels of intensity, duration, and commitment.

Foundations, then, can choose how to deploy their grantmaking assets, given their decisions concerning what activities they want to support. Foundations that select the funding of policy-relevant work are likely to do programmatic grantmaking of limited duration. Foundations that decide to go beyond such policy-relevant work, and to put that work into play to shape the policy environment are likely to commit resources that are more general (i.e., operating support) and of longer duration. And, some foundations may become more directly involved by choosing to support advocacy organizations and/or to engage with policymakers directly by devoting resources to their own activities such as convening policymakers and policy experts and distributing reports.

There is risk and uncertainty in public policy engagement. Foundations work from the outside, often through nonprofit partners. And there is a considerable amount of chance in getting the various policy forces to align. But there is not likely to be a big payoff unless foundations are willing to take such calculated risks. Yet, it is not always clear what foundations choose to pursue and why they do so. This raises a series of research questions about foundations and the policymaking process:

- What are the factors that encourage or inhibit foundations from becoming involved in the policy process—mission, resources, legal restrictions?

- For foundations that do engage in the process, what are the strategic choices they make regarding leverage points in the policy process, form of engagement, and asset deployment? And why?

- How might foundations work together to increase their joint effectiveness—in terms of greater leverage, policy innovation and diffusion, and risk-pooling?

These are questions that are critical to understanding the role of foundations in public policymaking and to developing strategies that expand foundation capacity to advance public problem-solving.

REFERENCES

Asher, Thomas R. 1995. *Myth v. Fact: Foundation Support of Advocacy.* Washington, DC: Alliance for Justice.

Berry, Jeffrey. 1984. *The Interest Group Society.* Boston, MA: Little, Brown.

Colvin, Gregory L. 1995. "A Case Study in Using Private Foundation Funds to Educate Voters." *Journal of Taxation of Exempt Organizations,* Vol. 6, No. 6, May/June 1995.

Covington, Sally. 1997. *Moving a Public Agenda: The Strategic Philanthropy of Conservative Foundations.* Washington, DC: National Committee for Responsive Philanthropy.

Covington, Sally. 2001. "In the Midst of Plenty: Foundation Funding of Child Advocacy Organizations in the 1990s." In *Who Speaks for America's Children*, Carol DeVita and Rachel Mosher-Williams, eds. Washington, DC: The Urban Institute Press.

Drabble, Laurie, and Michelle Abrenilla. 2000. *A Democratic Landscape: Funding Social Change in California.* Washington, DC: National Committee for Responsive Philanthropy.

Edie, John. 1991. *Foundations and Lobbying: Safe Ways to Affect Public Policy.* Washington, DC: Council on Foundations.

Eyestone, Robert. 1978. *From Social Issues to Public Policy.* New York, NY: John Wiley and Sons.

Fei, Rosemary. 2001. Unpublished memo on Charitable Funding of Ballot Measures Activities.

Finn, Chester E., and Kelly Annis. 2001. *Making It Count: A Guide to High-Impact Education Philanthropy.* Washington, DC: The Thomas B. Fordham Foundation.

Greenberg, Mark, and Michael C. Laracy. 2000. *Welfare Reform: Next Steps Offer New Opportunities.* Public Policy Paper No. 4. Washington, DC: Neighborhood Funders Group.

Heclo, Hugh. 1978. "Issue Networks and the Executive Establishment." In *The New American Political System*, Anthony King, ed. Washington, DC: The American Enterprise Institute.

Jenkins, Craig J. 1998. "Channeling Social Protest: Foundation Patronage of Contemporary Social Movements. In *Private Action and the Public Good*, Walter W. Powell and Elisabeth S. Clemens, eds. New Haven, CT: Yale University Press.

Jenkins-Smith, Hank C., and Paul A. Sabatier, eds. 1993. *Policy Change and Learning: An Advocacy Coalition Approach.* Boulder, CO: Westview Press.

Kingdon, John W. 1995. *Agendas, Alternatives, and Public Policies.* Second ed. Boston, MA: Little, Brown & Company.

Klein, Gregory. 2001. Change Agents and Policy Entrepreneurs at the Local Level. Unpublished doctoral dissertation. East Lansing, MI: Department of Political Science, Michigan State University.

Knott, Jack H., and Carol S. Weissert. 1994. "Foundations and Health Policy: A First Cut." Paper presented at the Annual Meeting of the Association of Public Policy and Management. Chicago, IL, October 28.

Lipsky, Michael. 1980. *Street-Level Bureaucracy: Dilemmas of the Individual in Public Services.* New York, NY: Russell Sage Foundation.

Macdonald, Dwight. 1956. *The Ford Foundation: The Men and the Millions.* New York, NY: Reynal.

Majone, Giandomenico. 1989. *Evidence, Argument, and Persuasion in the Policy Process.* New Haven, CT: Yale University Press.

McKersie, William S. 1999. "Local Philanthropy Matters: Pressing Issues for Research and Practice." In *Philanthropic Foundations: New Scholarship, New Possibilities*, Ellen Condliffe Lagemann ed. Bloomington, IN: Indiana University Press.

Mintrom, Michael. 2000. *Policy Entrepreneurs and School Choice.* Washington, DC: Georgetown University Press.

Murray, Charles A. 1984. *Losing Ground: American Social Policy, 1950–1980.* New York, NY: Basic Books.

Nagai, Althea K., Robert Lerner, and Stanley Rothman. 1994. *Giving for Social Change: Foundations, Public Policy, and the American Political Agenda.* Westport, CT: Praeger.

Radin, Beryl A. 1997. "The Evolution of the Policy Analysis Field: From Conversation to Conversations." *Journal of Policy Analysis and Management* 15: 438–43.

Schön, Donald A., and Martin Rein. 1994. Frame Reflection: *Toward the Resolution of Intractable Policy Controversies.* New York, NY: Basic Books.

Smith, James A. 1991. *The Idea Brokers.* New York, NY: The Free Press.

Stone, Deborah. 1997. *Policy Paradox: The Art of Political Decision Making.* New York, NY: W.W. Norton.

Weissert, Carol S., and Jack H. Knott. 1995. "Foundations' Impact On Policymaking: Results From A Pilot Study." *Health Affairs* 14: 275–286.

Wildavsky, Aaron B. 1979. *Speaking Truth to Power: The Art and Craft of Policy Analysis*. Boston, MA: Little, Brown.

Williams, Malcolm V. 2000. *Strategies for Shaping Public Policy: A Guide for Health Funders*. Washington, DC: Grantmakers In Health.

Wilson, James Q., ed. 1980. *The Politics of Regulation*. New York, NY: Basic Books.

3

Private Foundations and Public Policymaking: A Historical Perspective

James Allen Smith

George Peabody (1795–1869) has been strangely neglected in the history of American philanthropy. His name remains attached to Baltimore's famous conservatory, to museums in New England, and to housing projects in London. Yet it is the names of industrial magnates and financiers, Rockefeller, Carnegie, Sage, Rosenwald, and Harkness, all born a generation or two later, that resonate far more prominently when the beginnings of modern American foundations are discussed. Widely celebrated in his day for pioneering philanthropic initiatives, Peabody died in London in 1869 and was mourned in a memorial service that flowed into the streets surrounding Westminster Abbey. "The gaunt, famished London poor were gathered in thousands to testify their respect for the foreigner who had done more than any Englishman for their class," wrote the *New York Times* correspondent (Parker, 1971, p.183; also see Dillingham, 1989).

The Peabody Donation Fund, established in 1862, had already begun to build model dwellings for London's impoverished workers. Peabody flats would house nearly 15,000 Londoners by the 1880s. Recognizing Peabody's contributions to London's working classes and to his nurturing of Anglo-American relations, which had been so severely strained during the Civil War, Queen Victoria, the Dean of Westminster, and many others wanted to honor him with permanent burial in Westminster Abbey. But Peabody's last will and testament was clear. He insisted on interment in Salem, Massachusetts, near a walnut grove where he had played as a boy. His casket was transported across the Atlantic by Britain's largest and newest warship, H.M.S. *Monarch*, joined en route by an American naval vessel, U.S.S. *Plymouth*, dispatched hastily from the Mediterranean by order of President Ulysses S. Grant. From the beginning of the voyage to his final burial in Salem, the financier and philanthropist received solemn honors and dignities befitting a head of state.

Peabody's lifetime giving and final bequests totaled only about $10 million, an insignificant sum when measured by the standards of later donors. Many of the institutions he created in the 1850s and 1860s, including a Lyceum in his native Danvers, Massachusetts, a half dozen libraries, an institute for promoting the mechanical arts in Baltimore, a museum of ethnology and archaeology at Harvard, and a museum of natural science at Yale, seem quaintly traditional today. Nevertheless, Peabody's philanthropy is a useful point of departure for understanding how foundations have devoted their resources to public policy matters. His $2 million donation to endow the Peabody Education Fund in 1867 created the first foundation in the United States fully engaged in addressing major national policy issues.

When announcing his gift establishing the Fund just three years before his death, Peabody claimed that this was the endowment "nearest my heart, and the one for which I shall do the most, now and hereafter" (Parker, 1971, p. 157). The foundation reflected both his hope for national reconciliation after the Civil War and his lifelong ardor for education, a passion no doubt reinforced by the fact that his own schooling had been abruptly truncated at the age of eleven when he was apprenticed to a general store. Peabody, optimistic enough to think that the foundation's work could be completed in about thirty years, never intended his foundation to live in perpetuity. Ultimately, the foundation endured for forty-seven years, closing its doors in 1914 and transferring a part of its resources to the Slater Fund and using most of its remaining assets to establish the teachers college in Nashville that bears the Peabody name.

How did the Fund define its policy role? From the beginning, the Fund was able to attract prominent Americans to its board. The Fund's trustees included Presidents Ulysses S. Grant, Rutherford B. Hayes, Theodore Roosevelt, and Grover Cleveland; Justices of the Supreme Court; a handful of governors, including New York's Governor Hamilton Fish as vice-chairman and two southern governors; some of the nation's wealthiest businessmen and financiers, including J. Pierpont Morgan; and prominent educators and clergymen. The chairman for more than a quarter century was Robert Winthrop, scion of the famous Massachusetts family and one-time leader of the "Cotton Whigs" in Congress.

Peabody and Winthrop sought to assemble a national board, a politically well-connected board, and many of its northern members, like Peabody himself, had enjoyed cordial relations with southerners in the years before the Civil War. Indeed, Peabody had kept a considerable distance from the Abolitionist cause, leading some Americans to mutter that his behavior in London during the war was treasonous. Although ultimately declaring his whole-hearted commitment to preserving the Union, he felt that the war was fomented needlessly by extremists on both sides. In creating the Fund, Peabody was making a grand gesture toward binding up the wounds of war. He and his trustees, northerners and southerners alike, were committed to improving education in the South and to remedying, through education, what they saw as a dangerous level of economic underdevelopment in the defeated Confederate states. And they were wary, some overtly hostile, to the more far-reaching Reconstruction policies of the federal government.

Within the context of Reconstruction, the Fund's principal policy aim was to launch a movement for public education in the South. Although in its first years the movement envisioned by Peabody's associates was concerned almost exclusively with expanding public education for whites, its successes inspired other new foundations, including the John F. Slater Fund for the Education of Freedmen (established in 1882) and the Anna T. Jeanes Fund (founded in 1907) which worked to establish programs of industrial education and training for blacks. In time, the Peabody Fund also began to work with black schools, although funding them at only a fraction of the level allocated to white schools. These three funds pursued strategies that pointed the way for even more substantial work in the South in the early twentieth century, most notably the Rockefeller and Commonwealth philanthropies' work in public health and education and the Rosenwald Fund's expansive initiatives in support of black education and libraries.

How did the Peabody Education Fund pursue its goals? Some historians have seen the politically powerful boards of trustees of these early foundations as their principal source of policy influence. According to one scholar, "The foundation subsector concerned most with Southern work was informally integrated into the central state by the active participation of prominent public officials on foundation governing boards, and by way of occasional foundation financing of governmental programs and offices" (Stanfield, 1987, p. 122). Tactically, the Fund pursued astute publicity campaigns by reaching out to religious and educational leaders, journalists, and state legislators, always seeking to popularize a single animating idea: universal education for whites.

It also sought to influence policy through its funding decisions, using financial leverage to alter local educational practices and policies. It directed its grants, approximately $100,000 per year, toward public schools, always with a view toward selecting schools in towns and cities "where large numbers can be gathered, and where a model system can be organized," as Barnas Sears, the Fund's first "general agent," put it. His aim was "the widest possible influence upon the surrounding country" so that local school district successes would ultimately transform state educational systems, inspire the establishment of state normal schools, and improve teacher training (Bremner, 1980, p. 188). Matching grants were also a familiar tool. Each district was required to commit twice as much money as the Fund contributed and to agree to adopt certain educational standards, among them recruiting one teacher for every fifty pupils and assigning students to specific grade levels. Direct lobbying was also a tactic. At the national level, trustees and staff pushed hard but ultimately unsuccessfully for the passage of a bill that would provide federal financial support for state education systems, arguing especially for a land grant program to aid the education of the black population. Reviewing the role of the Peabody Education Fund in the 1880s, Jabez L. M. Curry, Sears' successor as general agent, concluded that by

> . . . showing the people what a good graded school was, [the Fund] did more to enlighten the people, disarm opposition, and create a sound public educational sentiment, than all the verbal argument that could have been used. The chief benefit did not arise from what the fund gave, but from what it induced others to give and to do. (Bremner, 1980, p. 189)

The Peabody Education Fund was the first among a handful of prototypically modern American foundations. These foundations made their tentative appearance in the decades after the Civil War, the very moment when a newly united nation was emerging from the crucible of war. Political reconciliation and reconstruction posed one immediate set of challenges for the government in Washington. At the same time, governmental responsibilities at all levels were being transformed by more fundamental forces: technological, demographic, and economic. Small isolated communities were being woven together by rail and telegraph, national markets for goods and services were being created, large-scale business enterprises and trusts were being established, new industries were transforming the old agricultural economy, cities were burgeoning with migrants from the countryside and immigrants from abroad. And as the burdens and responsibilities of government at all levels were beginning to change, private charitable organizations were also compelled to change, seeking ways to be more efficient, more professional, and, in the end, more scientific in their approaches to social and economic problems. This is the environment in which American foundations were born and within which they began their work. The large foundations established in the first two decades of the twentieth century—Russell Sage (1907), Carnegie (1911), Rockefeller (1913), Rosenwald (1917), and Commonwealth (1918)—shared a vision of making philanthropy more efficient and scientific. All of them understood that they had to engage government. Indeed, the emergence and evolution of private foundations is closely linked to the history of the public sector in the United States. In large measure the story of foundations and their policymaking role is about the changing expectations Americans have of government at various levels. And those expectations have been shaped by the reciprocal interaction of government and foundations as well as external crises and long-term trends.

Framing the Questions

This historical prologue suggests that there is nothing especially novel in the subject of foundations and public policymaking, especially when we ask what tactics foundations have had at their disposal in the pursuit of new or changed public policies. They have worked to shape policies by using the influence of their boards, by molding elite public opinion, by pursuing campaigns of public information and education, by creating demonstration projects, by using their financial resources strategically to leverage public funds, and by pursuing direct legislative lobbying, judicial strategies, and executive branch persuasion. They have worked at every level of government. Clearly, though, many external circumstances have changed since the late nineteenth century: technologies for communicating with and engaging the public are different; the relative roles and responsibilities of the different levels of government in our federal system have shifted; the scale and diversity of institutions operating in the nonprofit sector have expanded; laws and regulations restricting nonprofit and foundation lobbying have come into force, among many other changes.

Yet, the fundamental question that foundations must ask themselves about their policy role remains much the same as the problem framed by Barnas Sears: how do foundations induce others, at all levels of government and in the private sector, to give and to do? That deceptively simple question requires refinement and unpacking. Four questions are embedded in any discussion of foundations and public policymaking:

- How and by what means do foundations influence public policymaking?

- What specific policy outcomes have they brought about?

- How do foundations effect broader social, economic, and political change?

- What are and what ought to be the limits of their role in a democratic society?

Each of these questions allows us to construct a distinctive intellectual frame around the subject, permitting us to view the problem from a slightly different angle.

If the focus is merely on the "how," the question has primarily instrumental answers. It concerns the tools, tactics, and strategies that foundations have at their disposal to influence public policy decisions. It is easy enough to compile a historical inventory of those tools and to explore which have been the most effective, and, finally, to determine which tactics hold out the most promise today. It is easy enough to map out a schematic policymaking "process," as many political scientists have done, and to point to the most likely moments and best venues for foundations to intervene.

But the question also invites us to ask to what end: to induce others to do precisely what? The focus then must turn toward policy outcomes and results and to a consideration of what is possible at various historical moments. The answers require a careful look at the changing policy context, at the policy actors and interests that come into play whenever particular legislative and executive decisions are made. The answers demand that we consider the historical context and the opportunities presented by the particular political moment. Foundations are merely one player in the policy game, funding and collaborating with other nonprofit organizations and interacting with many other entities in and out of government who are often more powerful and consequential when policy decisions are finally made. In sorting out the lines of influence, it is also useful to recall the sage, cautionary comments of Kermit Gordon, president of the Brookings Institution in the late 1960s and early 1970s, when he tried to trace the relationships between policy research and policy decisions. "In the end," Gordon observed, "the [research] initiative may be decisive in inspiring an important policy decision, but it will have been strained through so many filters and combined with so many other ingredients that the causal chain may be untraceable" (Gordon, 1970, pp. 1–2).

But there are also ways of framing the question so that it becomes more significant, more relevant to the role that foundations have played over the long term as they seek to bring about social and political change. We must look beyond foundation involvement in formal policymaking processes where legislation or executive decisions result. The terrain should be wider, moving our exploration beyond legislative arenas, executive decisionmaking, and judicial processes. We must look not at discrete policy decisions but rather at a broader "politics of knowledge." In her study of the Carnegie Corporation, Ellen Lagemann has described how this politics of knowledge emerged in conjunction with the large-scale national state at the end of the nineteenth century. This politics "crystallized as knowledge of various kinds became more and more essential to economic activity and to the formulation, implementation, and evaluation of public policy" (Lagemann, 1989, p. 4). Foundations have been the key participants in this politics, building institutions and shaping the fields of knowledge that have a bearing on policy decisions, giving prominence to individual experts and to groups working in particular policy domains, structuring the lines of communication between experts and the public and, through training and education, fostering access to those knowledge-producing elites.

More broadly still, we should also ask about the political role of foundations in a democratic society. The answers, if indeed there are any final answers, force us to confront more enduring problems of political theory. These issues concern wealth and inequality, political power and influence, and, indeed, the political legitimacy of foundation involvement in democratic policymaking. Whose voices should be heard in a democracy? What role should trusts and endowments play?

Foundations have been regarded with suspicion, from the first warnings sounded by the Founding Fathers about privately endowed associations to the various congressional investigations in the twentieth century that have examined foundation power and influence. A web of myth and misunderstanding has surrounded foundations, starting in the 1910s with the investigations of Rockefeller philanthropy by the Walsh Commission on Industrial Relations, and continuing with congressional inquiries of Cox and Reece in the 1950s and Patman in the1960s. Gradually a regulatory regime for foundations has taken shape, culminating in the Tax Reform Act of 1969. That act defined the playing field and the rules for foundations engaged in the game of policymaking. While it is not the aim of this chapter to recount the history of congressional inquiry and regulatory reform, we should not forget how and why certain boundaries and rules were established.

All of this is to underscore the fact that we must formulate our questions about foundations and policymaking with precision, frame particular policy problems and policy outcomes with care, and understand that answers will inevitably reside in the details. This chapter, beginning with Peabody's work in the late nineteenth century, recounts the work of a half dozen foundations. The tools and tactics are often similar; the differences most often reside in the external environment, the opportunities presented by differing political circumstances, and the changing expectations Americans have had of the state. Edwin Embree, long-time president of the Rosenwald Fund, spoke of the "enlightened opportunism" pursued by the Fund during its thirty years of operation. It is a sage and useful phrase. Policymaking is a consequence of patience, serendipity, and opportunities shrewdly seized, all of which make theoretical generalizations about the foundation role in policymaking difficult.

POLICYMAKING AS ENLIGHTENED OPPORTUNISM

Certainly the first generation of foundations marked a break with older conceptions of charity, which is to say that the new general purpose foundations did not see their role as providing assistance merely to ameliorate the plight of needy individuals. In looking for the root causes of social and economic distress and in conceiving of their philanthropy as "scientific," they adopted new methods, especially in their interactions with government. How some foundations operated in the first three decades of the twentieth century, when the locus of public policymaking was at the level of town, county, and state government, can be seen in the story of the Julius Rosenwald Fund.

In 1917, three years after the Peabody Education Fund made its final grants, Julius Rosenwald incorporated his Fund, which over the course of its thirty-year life would transform education for blacks residing in the south. Rosenwald, whose organizational skills had turned Sears Roebuck into a national retailing enterprise, built a personal fortune that approached $80 million. He gave roughly one-third of it to the cause of black education, beginning in 1913 with a simple small gift. That year he donated $300 for the construction of a one-room school near Tuskegee, Alabama, whose total cost of precisely $942.50 was met by private funds from the local community, white and black, and the labor of the children's parents and friends. Not a dollar of public money went into that first project. Continuing to work with the Tuskegee Institute and Booker T. Washington, Rosenwald provided funds for another eighty schools and developed some of the fundamental principles that would shape the Fund's school-building program. When Washington died in 1915, Rosenwald pledged to build another 300 schools and he soon understood that his task was not merely to construct more buildings but to change the course of public policy in local school districts and southern states.

The appalling educational conditions that persisted when Rosenwald began its work more than a half century after the end of slavery were described by Embree:

> In all of the South there was not a Negro public high school approved for even two years of high-school work. The schools, such as they were, were open for an average of four months a year, often presided over by teachers whose average training was that of an eighth grade student and whose annual salary in many states was less than $150. (Embree and Waxman, 1949, p.12)

In 1917, the Rosenwald Fund began to formalize the school-building program that had begun with Rosenwald's personal donations four years earlier. It turned construction projects into community initiatives seeking to engage blacks and whites in a cooperative local enterprise. There was obviously something of the efficient mail-order businessman's spirit pervading the work as well. Simple, cost-efficient architectural plans were developed in Chicago for all sorts of school buildings, ranging from simple one-teacher elementary schools at a cost of $200 and six-teacher schools costing $2,600, all the way to twelve-teacher high schools priced at $6,000. Plans for teacher housing and classroom additions were also drawn up and priced accordingly.

Rosenwald and the foundation staff clearly understood the limits of private funding. They insisted that certain conditions be met before putting money into school building projects: the state and county had to contribute half the cost of construction and to agree that the building would be maintained as part of the local public school system; white citizens had to contribute some of the money since Rosenwald and his advisers knew that white leadership was essential to maintaining the local commitment to educating blacks; blacks also had to show their commitment by contributing money or labor; the school term had to be at least five months long and, as an incentive to extend the term to eight months, additional funds were offered to build housing for teachers.

By the time the school-building program ended in 1932, the Fund had supported the construction of 4,977 public schools and several hundred other buildings, principally teacher homes, in 883 counties in fifteen southern states. While the Rosenwald contributions of over $4.4 million were substantial, members of local black communities managed to raise $4.7 million and white supporters gave another $1.2 million. Even more significant was the transformation in public policy. Over the course of fifteen years, more than $18 million in tax revenues had gone to the construction projects; maintenance and other costs would continue to be met long into the future from public funds. And there were unintended policy consequences as well. *See*ing the well-conceived architectural plans for black schools, state education departments in several southern states turned their attention to improving the school facilities for white students and, on occasion, borrowed the Rosenwald school blueprints.

If rural schools and housing for teachers in black communities are the Rosenwald Fund's most noteworthy legacy, the Fund also showed a remarkable capacity to evolve. The Fund staff members saw that many southern communities lacked libraries (most had not been wealthy enough to benefit from the Carnegie program) and they devised demonstration projects in selected southern counties, propelling them over a five-year period toward county-funded, professionally staffed, and racially integrated library systems. The Fund's early health programs supported salaries in health departments so that counties and towns would be willing to hire black public health officers and nurses. Realizing that statistical data could be persuasive to policymakers and the public, the Fund soon began to support studies of the health conditions of blacks and, in the final years of the Fund's existence, began a program in medical economics.

Whether in higher education or health, the Fund staff knew that its resources were far smaller than those of local and state governments. Its method was to point the way with successful demonstration projects, with concerted efforts to build community interest, and with funds that they often described as "pump priming." Money was pledged for a fixed period and governments were expected to take over payments for the schools, libraries, or public health programs within a few years. As Embree put it:

> In the main the Fund followed the policy of stimulus rather than subsidy because of the strong belief of its officers that enterprises which were self-supporting through payment by beneficiaries or through absorption into the permanent social structure of government were preferable to those which would require continual charitable support. (Embree and Waxman, 1949, p. 126)

Progress had been substantial since 1917 and the Fund prepared scores of books and reports to measure and account for its work. In 1917 only about half of the South's two million black children of school age were in school and those who were spent scarcely four months in the classroom each year. Only 3,000 black Americans were in institutions of higher learning anywhere in the United States. Some thirty years later, 80 percent of the children between five and seventeen years of age were in school. And in a single year, 1947, over 6,000 degrees (500 of them Master's and higher) were awarded to students in black colleges and universities in the South alone. The Rosenwald Fund had helped to bring about an institutional transformation in both education and public health. Measurable progress had been made in terms of schools built, students enrolled, fellowships offered, teachers trained, library books circulated, health conditions improved, and public and private dollars committed to new programs.

However, as the Fund approached the end of its fixed life span, it became increasingly apparent to staff and board that the overriding problem in the United States was segregation. Educational opportunities, health care, and economic livelihoods could be improved, but the chasm between blacks and whites would never be closed as long as segregation, whether by law in the South or by habit and circumstance in the North, continued to exist. With the Fund wrapping up its programs, Embree concluded that America had to face a new reality. The nation had to move toward the "recognition that the integration and full participation of Negroes and all others in our society is not only possible but that it is imperative if we are to realize our democratic ideals" (Embree and Waxman, 1949, p. 162).

Changing deeply ingrained habits of thought about race—the predicate for more profound policy change—was a far less certain matter. Yet the Fund risked some $3 million in programs designed to overcome prejudice and to begin to build understanding between blacks and whites. In the North, the Fund supported the American Council on Race Relations and the Bureau of Intercultural Education, whose agendas reflected the growing racial tensions outside the South. And in this field, the Fund produced dozens of books and many more articles and pamphlets. Many were written by Fund staff members: Edwin Embree wrote popular books such as *Brown Americans* and *13 Against the Odds*; Charles S. Johnson produced volume after volume: *The Negro in American Civilization*, *Shadow of the Plantation*, and *Statistical Atlas of Southern Counties* and, at the request of President Roosevelt in 1943, began *A Monthly Summary of Events and Trends in Race Relations*. Howard W. Odum of the University of North Carolina received Fund support for his work on racial tensions and Joseph Lohman, a Fund staff member, examined police and their relationships with minority groups, drafting a training manual for police departments.

In appraising the Fund's work as it brought its activities to a conclusion, Embree was proud of the foundation's accomplishments, chastened by mistakes and failures, and concerned about the road ahead.

> Probably in no other area [race relations] was there so much thinking and careful planning nor such lack of full satisfaction with the given steps of the total results. While the Fund did play a part in the progress that has come, America is still so far from the democratic ideal that none of the agencies at work in the field has cause for self-congratulation. There is a long struggle ahead toward the goal of a society in which all of the diverse peoples who make up this nation will share equally in a common democracy. (Embree and Waxman, 1949, p. 195)

During its three decades, the Rosenwald Fund worked intensely with local communities and state governments. It set educational standards and provided incentives for school systems to meet them. It created model programs and demonstration projects. It invested in physical capital, building schools and libraries with the expectation that public expenditures would in time sustain their operations. It built human capital through teacher and library training programs and a vast national fellowship program. And it deployed some of that human capital in local and state government agencies, paying salaries for a fixed period until governments were ready to pick up the costs. It sought to measure its accomplishments, publish and disseminate the results, and convene and organize groups to advocate on behalf of its causes. Inevitably, its work was constrained by contemporary attitudes toward race.

While Rosenwald's accomplishments were exemplary, all its methods were familiar to other foundations. The famous Rockefeller public health campaigns pursued similar strategies at the county and state level in attempting to eradicate hookworm and other diseases prevalent in the South (see Ettling, 1981). In the 1920s, the Commonwealth Fund's mental health programs, which early on emphasized the prevention of juvenile delinquency, and their rural health demonstration projects, which led to a program for building rural hospitals, also invented creative strategies for working at the local level (see Commonwealth Fund, 1963; Sealander, 1997).

While many foundations have continued to employ similar tactics of direct engagement with local and state governments, other foundations have chosen to work at a somewhat greater remove from formal policymaking processes. They have grounded their approach in research, analysis, and expertise.

While the Rosenwald Fund, especially under Embree's guidance, came to understand the value of research and publication, others employed those means for influencing policy from the moment of their origin. The Russell Sage Foundation, for one, exemplifies this approach.

INSTITUTION BUILDERS: FROM A SCIENCE OF PREVENTION TO THE POLICY SCIENCES

When Russell Sage died in 1906 he left his widow, Margaret Olivia Slocum Sage, then approaching seventy-eight years of age, well over $60 million. Besieged in the half year after his death with some 20,000 letters requesting money, she turned for advice to lawyers experienced in charitable work, most notably Robert W. de Forest, longtime president of New York's Charity Organization Society and a national leader among social reformers. He conferred, in turn, with others who were knowledgeable about the conditions of the poor and the charitable agencies that served them. He asked his informants explicitly how $10 or $15 million might usefully be expended by a new foundation. The consensus was striking. De Forest's correspondents wrote about the need "for encouraging inquiry and publication," for "investigation," for "education, chiefly by publication," and "for paying, amply, persons of marked experience and ability for making studies (with time for real study, here and abroad) in the field of curative and preventive philanthropy, with the aim of adding to that body of knowledge which shall help to lessen human wants and ills" (Glenn et al., 1947a, p. 5).

Established in 1907 and thus older than the Rosenwald Fund by a decade, the Russell Sage Foundation represents yet another foundation approach to influencing public policy. The Sage Foundation was profoundly of its era in its conviction that research would reveal the root causes of social distress and lead to preventive measures and cures. It echoed the perennial message of John D. Rockefeller and Frederick T. Gates that philanthropy was a search for root causes, an effort to eradicate evils at their source. But in many other respects the Russell Sage Foundation signaled something new. It was the prototype for the American policy think tank, for institutions engaged in applied social and economic research, for institutions with an increasingly national perspective on public policies.

The Russell Sage Foundation's avowed mission was "the improvement of social and living conditions in the United States of America." Sometimes de Forest and others even spoke optimistically about the "permanent" improvement of those conditions. Its methods were to be "research, study, teaching, publication, initiation of concerted effort, establishment of necessary agencies and institutions, aiding such effort already existing and such agencies or institutions already established" (Glenn et al., 1947a, p. 8). The foundation's broad charge and its close ties to charity organizations initially propelled its research program in familiar directions: local fact-finding and institutional studies aimed at improving the efficiency of social services.

The staff was clearly building upon the data-collecting and analytic methods of late nineteenth century charity organization societies and the emerging profession of social work, whose case work method provided the rudiments of a social science. The foundation's early departmental structure with their quaint sounding names—Child-Helping, Charity Organization, and Child Hygiene (later divided into separate departments of Recreation and Education), Remedial Loans, Women's Work (later Industrial Studies), and Southern Highlands—reflect the agenda of problems addressed by the foundation in the 1910s and 1920s. Each of these departments and divisions has its own history of studies conducted, alarms sounded, education and training initiatives pursued, national organizations formed, government officials consulted and advised, model legislation drafted, and legal briefs researched. However, the Department of Surveys and Exhibits cut across many policy domains and its work is worth more detailed examination. It typifies some of the policy-oriented foundation activities not only of Sage, but also of Commonwealth, Carnegie, and others in the first three decades of the twentieth century.

One of the earliest Sage Foundation grants went to a project that would lead to the massive Pittsburgh Survey, a five-year investigation that produced six volumes on the city's housing, health, and working conditions. The survey's aim was to describe and to measure precisely the social and economic conditions of a complete urban environment. This survey method would become the most important research tool for the Sage Foundation's national work; many others would emulate its approach.

Between roughly 1900 and 1928, some 2,700 surveys were undertaken in American cities and regions, according to the survey movement's survey of itself (see Eaton and Harrison,1930; Dusenbury, 1969). While the surveys in Pittsburgh and a handful of other cities were of a general nature, other surveys began to focus more narrowly on specific problems such as education, juvenile crime, public health, and sanitation. The Sage Foundation, its resources not nearly large enough to fund all the hundreds of survey requests it received, provided technical assistance to projects in cities across the United States. It sought to improve the rigor of the data-collecting and to help with the public education campaigns and exhibits that were so crucial to shaping popular opinion. Survey organizers saw their efforts as a collaboration between expert investigators who would furnish accurate measures of social conditions and leading members of the community who would then mobilize public opinion to change the conditions exposed by the survey. In principle, public opinion, enlightened by the facts, would bring about the appropriate reforms.

This American obsession with data collection and measurement went well beyond foundations and charitable organizations. Indeed, it seems fundamental to American approaches to both public and private decisionmaking and to our continuing use of expert commissions, councils, and task forces. The language of surveys and measurement—and the conviction that a policy consensus will follow from the fact-collecting—owes much to the influence of engineers and efficiency experts in late nineteenth century business and government. As the scale and complexity of enterprises involved in transportation, mining, banking, and insurance grew, so did the need for data. Better data was also important to the network of federal regulatory agencies that sought to monitor business practices in the new economic environment. The survey, thus, became an instrument of central administration, allowing large organizations to keep abreast of routine operations or to track sudden changes in far-flung locales. It was a technique for improving efficiency, enforcing uniform standards, and assessing institutional change, whether organizations were public or private, business or philanthropic.

Surveys were widely used not only by Sage but also by Rockefeller's General Education Board in its famous report on medical education and by the Commonwealth Fund in its health and hospital work. Government commissions, usually with private foundation financial support, also pursued their work through fact-finding investigations and surveys. They were a hallmark of what some historians have described as the "associative state." In that conception of the state, governance involves a high degree of engagement between the private sector and government. The exchange of information between private organizations and government agencies is essential and policy is grounded in voluntary decisionmaking, informed by the facts, rather than coercive governmental fiat. Herbert Hoover's Committee on Recent Economic Changes (1929) and his far larger Research Committee on Social Trends (1932), sanctioned by government but privately funded and organized, were characteristic policy instruments of the associative state. These projects assumed that shared knowledge would lead to voluntary action by the appropriate private sector entities and that government's role would remain limited.

Whether or not they saw a sharply limited role for government, many American foundations at work in the years between the two World Wars were equally committed to building knowledge as a means of advancing public policy. Unlike Sage with its roots in social work and the charity organization movement, Rockefeller, Carnegie, Commonwealth, and the Twentieth Century Fund drew more often on the academically based social sciences, especially economics, sociology, and social psychology. These disciplines had played an important role during World War I. Indeed, many economists and businessmen realized that the federal government, having relied heavily during the war on statistical and economic analysis in such agencies as the War Industries Board, had dismantled these wartime analytic units much too hastily at war's end. Foundations began to build new independent research institutions and university social science programs. Work within those institutions would begin to change the conception of what government at the federal level could and should do.

In 1920, the Carnegie Corporation provided funding to enable Wesley Mitchell to establish the National Bureau of Economic Research (NBER) and to begin its work on business cycles and national income accounting. NBER's research led to the development of important analytic tools for policymakers, keeping the spirit of government's wartime analytic work alive and pointing the way for its resumption in Herbert Hoover's Commerce Department and in Franklin D. Roosevelt's New Deal agencies. The Carnegie Corporation made a ten-year financial commitment to develop applied economic work when it established another organization, the Institute for Economics (1921), which merged in 1927 with the Rockefeller-funded Institute for Government Research (1916) and the Robert Brookings Graduate School of Economics and Government (1924), to become the now familiar Brookings Institution. For decades Brookings stood virtually alone in Washington as a center of applied policy research and analysis. A magnet for foundation funds in the 1920s, it produced painstaking studies of federal administrative agencies, the budget process, tariff reform, Germany's war debts, and agricultural policy.

During the 1920s, the Rockefeller Foundation and especially the Laura Spelman Rockefeller Memorial, which was folded into the larger foundation in 1928, also played major roles in advancing university-based social science and, on occasion, building links between the research community and the practical realms inhabited by policymakers. Founded in 1918, the Memorial was originally intended to serve as a conduit for channeling money to the women's and children's causes that interested the late Mrs. Rockefeller, Sr. However, under the imaginative leadership of a young Chicago-trained social psychologist, Beardsley Ruml, the Memorial expended some $41 million on the social sciences between 1922 and 1929. For the most part, it pursued the Holy Grail of improved scientific method and objectivity rather than grittier realities of direct engagement with the policy process. In fact, the Memorial operated under strictures laid down by a distinguished committee of Rockefeller advisers, all of them still worried about the controversy sparked a decade earlier when the Rockefeller Foundation had begun to study industrial and labor relations, thereby provoking the wrath of congressional investigators. The Memorial was expressly prohibited from contributing to organizations whose purposes were "the procurement of legislation" or "to secure any social, economic, or political reform" (Fosdick, 1952, p. 201).

Despite these self-imposed limitations, the Memorial and the Rockefeller Foundation social science program that succeeded it had a huge impact on academic institutions in the United States and Europe and in diverse policy areas. Grants allowed researchers at the University of Chicago to study that urban community, while scholars at Harvard and Radcliffe pursued legal and economic research on international relations, researchers at Wisconsin explored rural tenancy and land ownership, and social scientists at the University of North Carolina examined state and local government in the South. Research organizations such as Yale's Institute for Human Relations were established and dozens of other universities in the United States and Europe saw their social science departments strengthened. The Memorial also founded the Social Science Research Council (SSRC) in 1923. While SSRC's primary aims were to foster interdisciplinary research, to explore methodological questions, and to serve as a conduit for fellowship funds, it also organized advisory bodies to address public problems and, with foundation funding, played a key organizational role in President Hoover's Research Committee on Social Trends.

As the academic training and research infrastructure grew, as statistical techniques and analytic methods improved, as broad claims to objectivity (or merely to basic technical competence) were strengthened, the long-term prospects for social scientists in both policymaking and administrative roles were substantially improved. Growing numbers of experts and technocrats possessing increasingly specialized knowledge would find their way into government in the New Deal and after. As the role of the federal government expanded between the Great Depression and the Cold War, new knowledge and new competencies were demanded of it. Foundations were also compelled to consider how their relationship to an expanding public sector and to the policymaking process in Washington would have to change.

POLICY TECHNICIANS, POLICY ENGINEERS

Foundations often think of their activities in metaphorical terms. In the early 1900s they often likened their endeavors to those of resolute medical researchers seeking out the root causes of diseases or bold doctors and public health workers taking preventive measures to avoid infectious disease. They saw themselves engaged in curing the social ills of the day while simultaneously laboring to build a solid research infrastructure and to establish training programs in the social sciences, much as medical research laboratories had been founded and the education of doctors reformed at the turn of the century. However, when economic, social, and political systems began to fail in the 1930s, a language of "balance" and "adjustment" began to permeate foundation conversations. Physics and psychology were the principal disciplines from which foundations began to draw their metaphors of social and political engagement. Retreating from large-scale institution building as their assets dwindled during the Depression, foundations looked for places where they might intervene to correct imbalances and maladjustments in social and economic processes.

Edmund E. Day, stalwart head of the Rockefeller Foundation's social science division through most of the 1930s, contended that swings in the business cycle were "the underlying forces in which much of our physical suffering, illness, mental disorder, family disintegration, crime, political upheaval, and social instability have their origins" (Day, 1933). Consequently, foundations had to be flexible and adaptable in their approaches. Raymond Fosdick, the president of Rockefeller, went so far as to argue that the advance of knowledge was too limiting a mission; instead the foundation had to be opportunistic, asking where human needs were greatest. Even though foundations were pressured to consider old-fashioned ways of alleviating human suffering in the 1930s and 1940s, they were also asking themselves how the rapidly changing role of government would alter their modes of operation. Sometimes staff members were seconded to new federal agencies, yet kept on the foundation payroll. Foundations and the experts they had funded were often called upon to advise in the design of new administrative structures for government programs or to pursue data-gathering efforts during the economic emergency. And some foundations began to turn their attention to international relations as the historically isolationist United States confronted turmoil in Europe and Asia.

With the Depression persisting through the 1930s, the Rockefeller Foundation and others continued to spend millions of dollars on projects that sought a better understanding of economic cycles and of the policy tools that might ameliorate the effects of economic instability. NBER, Brookings, and SSRC were recipients of Rockefeller funding, so were the Economic Intelligence Section of the League of Nations, the Dutch Economic Institute, the Austrian Institute for Trade Cycle Research, and the London School of Economics. Brookings (having failed to meet a Rockefeller matching grant and then seeing its Carnegie funding come to an end in 1931) received substantial funds from Pittsburgh's Maurice and Laura Falk Foundation to explore the causes of the Depression. Economists at Brookings examined national income levels, patterns of consumption and investment, and the productive capacities of the American economy, ultimately producing four data-rich volumes, the last of which had a distribution of over 100,000 copies. The Twentieth Century Fund devoted its attention in the early 1930s to studies in two key areas, the internal debt structure of the United States and the conditions of its financial markets. According to Adolf A. Berle, prominent member of the Roosevelt "brains trust" and longtime Fund chairman, the data it gathered on the stock market was essential when the Securities Exchange Act of 1934 was drafted (Berle, 1969).

The Russell Sage Foundation, after considering whether it should divert its resources into a program for the direct relief of New York's unemployed, decided instead to use the talents of its staff to advise government agencies on new programs. The various foundation departments prepared studies and reports for the President's Emergency Committee for Employment, the Works Progress Administration, the New York Emergency Relief Bureau, and other federal and state agencies. The staff also vetted plans for cash and work relief programs and developed statistical refinements for better measuring unemployment, costs of relief expenditures, and the cost of living (Glenn et al., 1947b, p. 490). When the staff was not advising on administrative matters or analytic methods, it served as a goad toward new programs and a critic of inadequate ones. A member of the Department of Charity Organization captured the anxious spirit of the time:

> The Department's program became a breathless rush to keep abreast of the changes and their implications. Constant field work, and much public speaking, all with promotional as well as research emphasis, became necessary. The output

of periodical articles by members of the staff doubled and trebled; there was no
time for the preparation of books and pamphlets which would have been out of
date before they saw print. (Glenn et al., 1947b, pp. 515–16)

Edmund Day and his Rockefeller colleagues administered the largest social
science program of any foundation in the 1930s. Like others, they assumed
that one of their most urgent tasks was to help government administer its
new and expanding programs. Characteristically, Rockefeller looked to the
university as the primary locus for strengthening public administration. A
grant to Harvard created a graduate level public service training program,
the forerunner of the Graduate School of Public Administration that
would later be funded by Lucius Littauer. University programs at Chicago,
Minnesota, Virginia, and Cincinnati also benefited from Rockefeller
funding. In Washington a special program was set up—a collaboration
between American University and the Civil Service Commission—to provide
for the recruitment and training of federal workers. The SSRC's Public
Administration Committee was given funds to compile and reflect on some
of the lessons learned as the federal government assumed its new burdens.

The Spelman Fund, endowed with $10 million when the Laura Spelman
Rockefeller Memorial was dissolved, received another $3 million to support
its work with state and municipal governments during the Depression. Its
work led to one of the most enduring foundation contributions to the field
of public administration. The Public Administration Clearing House, located
at 1313 East Sixtieth Street in Chicago and thus known simply as "1313,"
worked with nearly two dozen organizations to improve the competence
of public officials. From the American Public Works Association and the
Municipal Finance Officers Association to the Civil Service Assembly and
the International City Managers' Association, "1313" aimed to improve
standards of administration, develop uniform accounting and budgetary
concepts, and create professional and ethical codes of conduct.

While some foundations had worked in international health and education
before the 1930s, relatively few were concerned with broader issues of
policy. The Carnegie Endowment for International Peace, founded with a
$10 million gift from Andrew Carnegie in 1910, had pursued its quixotic
mission "to hasten the renunciation of war as an instrument of national
policy." It expended over $18 million prior to 1940. Much of its funding
went to support research institutions and publications concerned with
international law. The Endowment also produced a massive economic
and social history of World War I and devoted considerable resources to
international scholarly exchanges, foreign visits of teachers and journalists,

and international conferences, congresses, and symposia. Beginning in the early 1930s, the Rockefeller Foundation also saw the need to develop a set of institutions concerned both with research and discussion about international issues. Its roster of grantees included the Council on Foreign Relations, the Foreign Policy Association, the Institute of Pacific Relations, the Royal Institute of International Affairs, Geneva's Institute of International Studies, Paris's Centre d'Études Politique Étrangères, Berlin's Notgemeinschaft der Deutschen Wissenschaft, and the Fiscal Committee of the League of Nations.

One of Rockefeller's most far-reaching projects was to support the Council on Foreign Relations' work on "war and peace studies." As early as 1939 the Council had volunteered to gather experts to advise the government on the problems that it might face during and after the war. The State Department agreed to accept their help but had no financial assistance of its own to offer. With Rockefeller funding, the Council mobilized experts, prepared studies, and found that not only State but also the War, Navy, and Treasury Departments relied on their analyses. Anticipating the intellectual needs of the Cold War world, Rockefeller established the Russian Institute at Columbia in 1946 whose purpose according to Raymond Fosdick was to train students "as broadly based specialists who understand Russia and the Russians and who thus prepare themselves for careers of authority and influence" (Fosdick, 1952, p. 219).

It often seemed that the demand for competent personnel whatever the field was impossible to meet. In 1950, Joseph Willits, who had taken over as head of the foundation's social sciences program in 1939, wrote:

> The Social Science Research Council and the officers of the Social Sciences Division of the Foundation are deluged with calls from government, the United Nations and other agencies which need men trained in the social sciences. The demand far outstrips the supply. The danger is that the large sums being spent on surveys and other investigations will be partly wasted because competent and objective workers are far too few. (Fosdick, 1952, p. 225)

Training in policy-relevant disciplines remained central to the work of Rockefeller in the postwar period. And as the foundation took stock of the individuals who had received fellowships for training or grants for research projects over the years, it singled out people who had moved from the academic world into prominent public posts during the war and after.

More widely influential, however, were the various analytic tools that had been developed over more than thirty years, a credit not to any single foundation but rather to the sum total foundation grantmaking in the social sciences. That sustained commitment produced many useful insights: NBER's work on the size and distribution of national income had informed war production planning as well as budget and tax policy decisions and its work was replicated in other countries as the Marshall Plan took shape; NBER's work on business cycles also supplied methods of data collecting and analysis that undergirded postwar fiscal policymaking; demographic analysis undertaken by several academic research centers helped the Census Bureau and government planning agencies; advances in opinion research and sampling techniques were used by the Agriculture Department, Treasury Department, and Federal Reserve System as they assessed the public's economic attitudes; and diverse social science disciplines were employed during World War II by the Office of War Information, and the War and State Departments.

As World War II came to an end, the major foundations began to reassess their programs. Some, most prominently the Twentieth Century Fund, were concerned with the state of the economy as the nation stood down from its war footing. The Fund devoted its resources to schemes for economic planning and to questions of tax and fiscal policy. Others concerned themselves with the devastation of war and the challenges of reconstruction, often adopting the familiar wartime language of strategy and tactics. The Rockefeller program review of 1945–46 reflected a somber tone at war's end:

> The really significant destruction has been in the social and intellectual organization and in the faiths and codes of men. The countless points of self-adjusting equilibrium which existed in all fields prior to the war are now largely blocked off; and the formal and informal codes which regulated the relations of men over wide areas have lost their power as sanctions for conduct. (Rockefeller Archive Center, 1945–46)

The foundation's public policy work focused in the postwar years on questions of human behavior, the nature of democratic institutions, and international understanding.

A major new player entered upon the national philanthropic scene in the late 1940s. The Ford Foundation, which had operated as a regional philanthropy since the mid-1930s, embarked on a serious planning process under the guidance of Rowan Gaither, who had spent the war years directing MIT's Radiation Laboratory. Ford's financial resources would soon dwarf those of the older foundations. By 1954 its grant budget of $68 million would be four times Rockefeller's and ten times Carnegie's and, after selling 20 percent of its Ford Motor Company holdings in 1956, the foundation announced that it intended to give away $500 million over the course of eighteen months. Its ambitions and international reach would be unsurpassed in the postwar world. The program areas set out in Gaither's report were vast—establishing peace, strengthening democracy, strengthening the economy, educating democratic citizens, studying individual behavior and human relations—but the plans for action remained vague.

Wealthy as it was, the Ford Foundation acknowledged that it would have to operate selectively and with tactical agility: "The success of any program will not depend solely on the urgency of the problem it seeks to solve, or on the wisdom of the program's general approach, but upon finding the right projects headed by the right men at the times that offer the most strategic opportunities." It would be a job of "strategic selection and tactical execution" (The Ford Foundation, 1949, p. 100). The Ford planning team maintained that it should build on the lessons learned from other foundations, mixing tried and true strategies of research with practical experiences in applying and disseminating knowledge. But Ford's planning group also seemed to believe that the scope for private philanthropic activity was narrowing.

Dwight Macdonald looked at Ford and others in the mid-1950s and concluded, "In this silver age, therefore, most [foundations] have developed a policy of either going in for retail trade—small grants for marginal projects—or, when they do spend large amounts, giving money to established institutions. Their millions, in short, merely lubricate the gears of the status quo" (Macdonald, 1989, p. 48). Putting it more sympathetically at one point, Macdonald said, "In recent years, although the great foundations have not decreased their rate of spending, they have found it increasingly difficult to make the same splash with their money. The philanthropic frontier has been steadily closing as the government has taken over more and more of the fields that were pioneered by private enterprise" (Macdonald, 1989, p. 47). Even a foundation insider like Edwin Embree complained that foundations in the postwar world were handling their resources as "timid billions." The primary policy challenge for foundations in the 1950s and 1960s was to pursue meaningful work when the federal government had come to see few limits to its social, economic, and international role. With the greatest financial and staff resources and the shortest record of accomplishment, Ford tackled the challenge head on.

EXPERIMENT AND ACTIVISM

The Ford Foundation's urban program in the late 1950s and 1960s is a useful lens for seeing how a major foundation conceived of its relationship to government in a time of expansive federal policy innovation. Its urban program in those early years seemed to be yet another attempt by a foundation to study a problem, experiment with solutions, and ultimately persuade government to intervene. But Ford's work differed from earlier foundation programs in several key respects. Most notable was the external governmental reality: the liberal welfare state had evolved. By the mid-1960s the federal government needed little in the way of persuasion and prodding or of convincing research and analysis to embark on new programs. Thus, Ford's urban initiatives often seemed more oriented toward social activism than toward advancing social science research. Ford used research, not to gather data and build consensus, but rather to seek out the most promising points of intervention to foster social change. In the final analysis, Ford and other foundations were beginning to think more systemically about social problems, about the nature of communities, and about the diverse levers for bringing about social change.

The Ford Foundation's approach to urban issues in the 1960s evolved out of an earlier concern with juvenile delinquency, and particularly from ideas about delinquency advanced by Columbia University researchers Richard Cloward and Lloyd Ohlin. They focused not on the individual pathology of troublesome youth but on the communities where they lived, arguing that delinquent behavior occurred when other opportunities to succeed were foreclosed. In *Delinquency and Opportunity* they contended that gangs and gang behavior were a rational response whenever more legitimate avenues to success were blocked. Structural problems, largely economic and racial barriers, were the cause of juvenile delinquency, not psychological problems. Their argument overturned many of the behavioral assumptions—and the resulting programmatic responses—that focused on individual children. Community-based interventions, systemic thought about reforming schools, welfare agencies, and political structures together promised to hold the key to new opportunities for young people to succeed.

Paul Ylvisaker, the Minnesotan who headed Ford's Public Affairs Department, pushed the boundaries at Ford, where the trustees had generally tended to shy away from controversy, especially in social matters. After working with Philadelphia mayor Joe Clark in the 1940s and early 1950s, honing his skills as a coalition builder and pragmatic reformer, Ylvisaker moved to Ford in 1955 and began to reshape its lethargic urban program, focusing on urban redevelopment, metropolitan governance, and an abortive effort to create "urban extension" services at state universities. Ylvisaker's "Gray Areas" program allowed him to confront issues of race, albeit obliquely at first. He explained that in urban areas, slum neighborhoods were not functioning as the "staging grounds" for assimilation and upward mobility as they had for earlier generations of Americans. He focused on those he termed the "new immigrants," rural southerners, both black and white, and Puerto Ricans. Under Ylvisaker, Ford found a new focus for its urban strategy. But in seeking to change the culture of poverty, Ford would have to confront the fragmentation of education and welfare services in the inner city, the complicated relationships with diverse federal agencies and their funding arrangements, and ultimately a severe backlash against foundation activism.

Ylvisaker looked across Ford's programmatic divisions to the Education Department and, after fighting and winning internal battles with that department, crafted a joint Great Cities School Improvement Program in 1960. It would try to make schools the point of entry for services such as housing, employment, and health—for "culturally disadvantaged" families. Admitting that his search was akin to a quest for the Holy Grail, he soon aimed for "broader-than-school approaches to human problems of our urban Gray Areas" (O'Connor, 1999, p.175).

His quest was for both catalytic ideas, which he found in Cloward and Ohlin's opportunity theory, and for new institutional structures. These new organizations took the form of a cluster of quasi-public agencies— Community Progress, Incorporated in New Haven; Action for Boston; the United Planning Organization in Washington; and the Philadelphia Council for Community Advancement—whose boards included both elected officials and community members. They served as planning and coordinating mechanisms and, above all, as fundraising entities, aiming to tap into federal grant programs. They became intermediaries between the federal and local levels and Ylvisaker saw them as models adaptable to other cities. The Ford Foundation staff also took on an important intermediary role, helping to raise government grant money for the various demonstration sites while making the broader case for community action and reform.

By late 1962, some $30 million in federal and foundation funding had been allocated for the Gray Areas demonstration projects. But problems were also glaringly obvious. Planning was a contentious political process, rife with interagency rivalries. Community participation could also lead to sharply politicized processes with ethnic and class divisions intensifying in different locales. Aggressive organizing tactics, whether boycotts, rent strikes, or rallies, often made it difficult to sustain collaborative efforts among government agencies, nonprofit organizations, and foundations. New York's Mobilization for Youth group adopted some of the most radical organizing tactics and alienated many of its initial supporters. Racial politics also tore through New Haven's CPI and Philadelphia's PCCA. Charles Silberman's critique (a Ford-funded study) accused the Gray Areas program of being a "grandiose fusion of paternalism and bureaucracy" and of avoiding the fundamental racial and class realities that underlay urban problems (O'Connor, 1999, p. 180).

If the politics of major policy innovation proved overwhelmingly difficult to master, so too did the social science and research questions. Testing new theories and measuring results would have been hard in any case but there was also resistance from program administrators whenever social scientists tried to examine programs and to insist on consistency in practice. The testing of theory was hardly compatible with the needs for flexibility and adaptation as programs evolved. As Alice O'Connor concludes in her study of the program:

> Visions of cooperative, rational planning ran up against the realities of political infighting and bureaucratic resistance. Resident participation was racially charged, difficult to achieve within the limited framework of orderly bureaucratic reform, and highly unpredictable. (O'Connor, 1999, p. 192)

Ford's engagement with the central policy problems of the day reminds us in what ways foundations are subsidiary agents in the policy process, more often buffeted by external political and economic events than shaping and controlling them. In the 1960s, the budding national focus on poverty was spurred by Michael Harrington's *Other America*, a searing series of *New York Times* articles on Appalachia, and the extensive academic work by Robert Lampman, Gunnar Myrdal, and others, all of which intersected with Ford's experiments in community action. In June 1963, John F. Kennedy created an interagency task force under Walter Heller, the chairman of the Council of Economic Advisers, to begin to explore policy responses to poverty. At the Ford Foundation, Ylvisaker also announced that "poverty" would be the generic label under which the Public Affairs Department could address a host of linked issues.

The window of policy opportunity was suddenly thrust wide open when Lyndon Johnson summoned Walter Heller to a meeting in the Oval Office only a few days after President Kennedy's assassination. Concluding his general briefing on the economy, Heller told the president that he had been thinking about new ways of combating poverty. Johnson was intrigued and ordered him to move ahead full-tilt with ideas for a new program. Heller clutched at some of the themes being tested in Ford's program, lifting the concept of community action wholesale from the Ford experiments. The community action idea had appeal in Washington for a number of reasons, not the least of which was that it promised to cut through the rigid bureaucratic structures of existing federal agencies and in doing so to move the focal point of activism from federal departments to local organizations. What also emerged was a strong conviction that minority and impoverished communities should have a way of expressing their views in the making of policy. The phrase "maximum feasible participation" entered the vocabulary as the programs sought to engage local communities in policymaking and planning activities.

On the basis of only a small Ford Foundation experiment in a half-dozen cities (research and evaluation on them still incomplete), the federal government moved to implement programs in 600 cities. Ford's local experiments, though few in number, suddenly had to bear the weight of a nationwide model program. Whatever the ultimate failings of the legislation (and the debate has raged for more than thirty years), many at Ford immediately saw the passage of the Economic Opportunity Act of 1964 as one of the foundation's greatest successes. And the lure of working even more closely with government was difficult to resist. Henry Heald, Ford's exceedingly cautious president and someone who had always been wary of Ylvisaker's moves toward greater social and political activism, nevertheless sought to solidify the foundation's relationship with government officials. He created a foundation Office of Policy and Planning, one of whose functions was to maintain liaison with government officials and to coordinate staff contacts with government agencies.

Ford was not alone in moving closer to government in the 1960s. Other foundations also enjoyed close ties to the Johnson administration and had important roles to play as Great Society legislation churned out of Congress in the mid-1960s. John Gardner, the Carnegie Corporation president who was chosen by Johnson to serve as Secretary of Health, Education, and Welfare, had encouraged considerable research on early childhood education during his years at the foundation. He had also worked closely with the Rockefeller Brothers Fund as it prepared a series of reports on education. Focusing on educational "disadvantages," researchers provided a rationale for expanding the federal role in education. The Head Start program owes much to Carnegie-funded research as well as to Ford-funded educational experiments. While still at Carnegie, Gardner had also headed a presidential task force on education, which was one of the mechanisms ultimately responsible for triggering passage of the Elementary and Secondary Education Act of 1964. Other educational ideas—Basic Educational Opportunity Grants, the National Assessment of Educational Progress, and the Fund for the Improvement of Postsecondary Education—emerged from Carnegie commission and council reports. Carnegie, at the explicit request of the Johnson Administration, also organized a Commission on Educational Television in 1965. Not surprisingly, its recommendations were quickly endorsed by the president and embodied in the Public Broadcasting Act of 1967 (see Lagemann, 1989).

Yet as Ford and Carnegie enjoyed their policy successes in Washington, legitimate questions were being asked about foundations. Beginning in 1961, Congressman Wright Patman of Texas had compiled volume after volume of research on possible financial abuses. In 1968 and 1969, congressional hearings on tax reform raised further questions about the political role of foundations. While the most shocking financial abuses were clearly limited to a handful of renegade foundations, the political activities and the accusations of partisanship led directly to Ford's doorstep. The foundation had trod on dangerous and overtly political terrain with a grant in 1967 to Cleveland's Congress on Racial Equality for a voter registration drive. Democrats and Republicans both agreed that the drive had given Carl Stokes, the city's first black mayor, the margin of victory. Under McGeorge Bundy, the foundation had also used its resources for the Southern Regional Council's voter registration drives in the South, provoking white political leaders to complain about a tax-exempt foundation intruding upon the electoral process. And if that were not enough, John Rooney, a Democratic congressman from Brooklyn, accused his opponent, Henry Richmond, of using the Richmond Foundation to gain political advantages in his campaign to unseat Rooney.

Other, far more disturbing inequities came to light in the spring of 1969. A foundation established by Louis Wolfson, notorious for stock manipulations and high-handed corporate raids and consequently under indictment by federal authorities, had been making payments to Supreme Court Justice Abe Fortas since shortly after his appointment to the court. The $20,000 annual fee provided yet more evidence that foundations were being used to manipulate the American political system, to corrupt the nation's highest court. Not long after, another alarming story came to light. Justice William O. Douglas was receiving fees from the Parvin Foundation, whose founder, Albert Parvin, had been named as one of Wolfson's coconspirators. And, to complete the circle, Fortas's wife was retained by the Parvin Foundation as legal counsel. Fortas, who had returned the money after Wolfson's indictment in 1966, promptly resigned from the bench when *Life Magazine* revealed the story in May 1969. Thus, just as the Ways and Means Committee hearings on tax reform were drawing to a close, another grave and well-publicized charge against foundations was added to the indictment.

It is not the purpose of this chapter to describe the Tax Reform Act of 1969 and the regulatory changes that have followed from it. Nor is it particularly important for the purposes of this chapter to try to assess the overall impact of the legislation. Others have explained the current rules of the policy game and the boundaries within which it is played. But it is safe to say that it has had a chastening effect on foundations as they consider their policy-oriented activities. As early as 1972, Waldemar Nielsen ventured a warning about the politically chilling impact of the legislation: "The paralyzing effect of the new provision on innovativeness by even the most courageous of the large foundations has already been considerable. Their typically conservative boards have developed a new preoccupation with the possible reaction of Congress and the Internal Revenue Service to their grant decisions. This in turn has led to two common results: a greatly increased reliance on lawyers and legal advice in all program matters; and a tendency to restrict the latitude of discretion of typically more liberal staff members in dealing with grant proposals" (Nielsen, 1972, pp. 19–20). While Nielsen is certainly correct in his contention that lawyers are consulted more routinely, the legislation did not necessarily temper the policy battles in which foundations were engaged in the 1970s and 1980s. Indeed, policy battles in those years took on a far more ideological tone.

IDEOLOGICAL WARS

Countless new right-wing organizations emerged in the decade or so after Barry Goldwater's shattering 1964 presidential defeat. They represented American conservatism in all its many guises: Old Right, New Right, Paleo-conservative, Neo-con, Southern Agrarian, Libertarian, Old World Right, Catholic Conservative, Protestant Fundamentalist, and all their hybrid forms. Conservatives were seeking to regroup, having attributed their devastating electoral defeat in 1964 to the workings of a powerful liberal establishment, one that was certainly bolstered by the major foundations. In the early 1970s, many conservatives felt an even greater sense of loss in the face of what they considered the many policy betrayals of Richard Nixon, especially his embrace of wage-price controls, Keynesian economics, environmental and occupational safety and health regulation, and plans for welfare expansion, among his other apostasies. They redoubled their organizational energies.

Indeed it seemed to a core group of conservatives that their major failure had always been one of organization. Energies that had been diffuse, fragmented, and counterproductive needed to be consolidated. New institutions needed to be built. A handful of conservative foundations turned to that task in the late 1960s and early 1970s. They put their money into existing conservative think tanks such as the American Enterprise Institute, the Hoover Institution, and the Center for Strategic and International Studies, and they began to build new organizations such as the Heritage Foundation, the Institute for Educational Affairs, the Manhattan Institute, and the Cato Institute. In the 1970s, Richard Larry of Pittsburgh's Sarah Scaife Foundation began to talk about a conservative "resource bank," an organizational task that fell to the leaders of the Heritage Foundation in 1977–78. It is one measure of how far and how quickly the conservative movement emerged as an institutional force. From a meeting of some twenty academics and a few think tank organizers, which was an adjunct session to the Philadelphia Society annual meeting, in 1978, the resource bank has grown and flourished. In 1997, at its twentieth meeting, 170 conservative organizations were represented by about 270 people; the full roster of members now includes 400 free-standing policy groups and about 1,900 individuals, most of them academics and policy researchers.

This proliferation of organizations is a testimony to the concerted philanthropic effort on the part of conservative foundations. As a group, these foundations are large neither in numbers nor assets. A cluster of six stands out: the Lynde and Harry Bradley Foundation, the Koch family foundations, the John M. Olin Foundation, the Scaife family foundations, the Smith Richardson Foundation, and the Adolph Coors Foundation. Among these, only Bradley, with some $700 million, ranks among the top 100 American foundations in assets. Yet working together, they have constructed what one critic has termed a conservative "counter-establishment" (Blumenthal, 1986). Their efforts represent yet another way in which foundations have been able to assume a prominent policy role. These foundations have worked purposefully, from funding national think tanks and advocacy organizations to building regional and state-based counterparts, from funding those who can generate new ideas in universities and research organizations to supporting the journals and media outlets that can propagate them. Above all, they have provided general operating support over the long term to these institutions and their policy experts.

The John M. Olin Foundation, to take one example, concentrates its resources in a handful of leading think tanks and universities, often endowing chairs and fellowships there. Its commitment to the field of law and economics has endured for some thirty years, starting with an endowed chair at the University of Chicago. Other prestigious universities have also accepted money to establish chairs and various centers bearing Olin's name and committed to the research interests of conservative scholars and writers, prominent among them Robert Bork, William Bennett, Irving Kristol, and the late Allan Bloom. Olin has also supported a roster of conservative publications such as *The New Criterion*, *The Public Interest*, and *The American Spectator*. And it has backed a group of institutions whose goals are to investigate and criticize liberal organizations.

While the overarching strategy has been to build solid institutions and to advance the careers of conservative scholars and writers, the foundations have also proceeded on the basis of several assumptions about the nature of the policy process. The first is that large ideas and values matter. The second is that politics is a relentless intellectual contest, to be waged as an aggressive war of ideas. The third is that ideas can be propagated, marketed, and sold. All of these assumptions are reinforced by the changing framework of contemporary policy discourse, which is no longer mediated by political parties, interest groups, and elite opinion-makers but is instead contested on cable news channels, op-ed pages, talk radio, web sites, e-mail lists, direct mail campaigns, faxed broadsides, and push polling techniques. These new realities of the policy process have posed continuing, bewildering challenges to mainstream foundations whose work has been grounded in problem-oriented, field-specific, and, above all, pragmatic work.

When a National Committee for Responsive Philanthropy study of the conservative foundations' funding practices appeared in 1997, the response from mainstream and liberal foundations reflected the perplexity. A Ford Foundation spokesman simply had no comment on the report. A Rockefeller official maintained that while conservative foundations "have deliberately gone out and created institutions and trained scholars and worked with editorial boards to push an ideological agenda... that's not what we're really about." We focus, she said, on infectious disease, school reform, global food shortages, and interracial understanding. Another foundation leader conceded that he would continue to adhere to old-fashioned foundation values, saying:

> It would be a disservice to a real debate in the country if it's just ideological mudslinging. From the broad range of philanthropy in the middle, which is where most of us are, there ought to be much more of a push for serious, honest research on social issues that takes a longer range view than today's pocketbook and bank account. (Covington, 1997, pp. 15–17; also see *City Limits*, 1997)

It is as if two distinct philanthropic cultures had emerged, each operating in a separate universe. They were separated not so much by political ideology, but by differing ways of valuing research, by distinct styles of persuasion, and by fundamentally different convictions about how the political process ought to operate. Nevertheless, some large foundations have tried to learn from the conservative foundations' willingness to use the media.

The Robert Wood Johnson Foundation is one foundation that has tried to engage the public in ways that are novel for an organization that is also deeply committed to basic medical research. Ever since receiving some $1.2 billion in Johnson & Johnson stock from the founder's estate in 1972, the foundation has been the largest American foundation exclusively confronting issues of health. By the 1990s its program had evolved into a concentration on three fundamental problems: expanding access to health care, organizing health services for the chronically ill, and reducing the many and diverse harms of substance abuse. Occasionally it had added its public voice to medical and health policy questions over the years, but never more visibly than in 1994 when it contracted with NBC to produce and broadcast a two-hour program on national health care reform. The Foundation spent $2.5 million on air time for a program based on a simple town meeting format, while agreeing to leave editorial control securely in the hands of the NBC news division; it spent another $1 million to promote and advertise the program.

With the Clinton administration laboring to promote its legislative proposals and the health insurance industry and other interest groups weighing in with tens of millions of dollars on television and print advertising campaigns, the Johnson Foundation knew that most Americans were deeply confused about the issues. Indeed, the advertising campaigns were analyzed by the Annenberg School of Communications, which received a grant from the Johnson Foundation for that purpose. By mid-1994, the Annenberg researchers estimated that 49 different groups had spent some $50 million on advertising. The study found that more than half of the broadcast advertisements and a quarter of the print advertisements contained false, misleading, or unfair statements (*New York Times*, 1994a).

The Johnson-initiated NBC documentary "To Your Health" aired in June. Television critics generally awarded the foundation an "A" for effort, though they deemed it to be typical of television journalism: long on anecdote, short on deeper analysis. *New York Times* critic Walter Goodman characterized it as "a jumpy series of debates that touched many issues but explored few" (*New York Times*, 1994b). But partisans in the fray howled in protest, no doubt because Hillary Clinton was so prominent a part of the program and so persuasive. Haley Barbour, national chairman of the Republican Party, accused the networks of favoring the Democrats, giving and selling air time for a program featuring the First Lady and other proponents of reform, while refusing to sell blocks of time to the Republicans or to Ross Perot who opposed the Democratic plan.

These criticisms of the Johnson Foundation's efforts to inform and engage the public—and the critics were not limited to ideological opponents of health care reform—reveal the most significant challenge that foundations face as they attempt to participate in contemporary policy processes. How do they now define their role? Do they jump into the fray as ideological combatants? Do they insist upon maintaining their neutrality and claim that their role is purely to educate and to inform? Do they try to amplify as diverse an array of voices as possible? Do they work for fundamental reform of the public policy arena so that voices can be heard that are a counterweight to corporate economic interests? These are the unresolved questions that foundation trustees and staff must contemplate. They point the way toward even more profound questions about the legitimate role of foundations in policymaking processes.

THE USES OF MONEY, THE CLAIMS OF LEGITIMACY

This chapter, describing how a handful of major foundations have sought to influence public policy, has not been ambitious in its theoretical aims. The narrative has been grounded in a series of stories out of the simple conviction that an understanding of particular policy strategies and ultimate foundation influence resides in the narrative detail and, especially, in an appreciation of the given historical moment. If any overarching generalization can be offered it is this: a foundation's policy opportunities are largely shaped by external circumstances and sometimes battered by unforeseen contingencies. There are no formulas to assure success. Indeed, Edwin Embree's observation about the need for foundations to pursue a policy of "enlightened opportunism" still rings true.

It is also worth underscoring the fact that the particular issue area matters when we examine what foundations can and cannot expect to accomplish and what strategies they can successfully employ. Some domains, such as education, are primarily local and state responsibilities with only a limited role for the federal government. In contrast, some policy areas have cohered around long-established federal programs such as Social Security and Medicare. Other policy domains, such as arts and cultural policy, are more inchoate and involve small federal agencies, scattered programs, and complex relationships among federal, state, and local bureaucracies. Some issue areas, communications policy for one, are contested primarily in federal regulatory agencies; other policy problems are more susceptible to judicial remedies. We must always be mindful of how foundations are constrained by the particular policy domains in which they operate.

The ways in which policy problems are defined—and our criteria for judging policy success or failure—also determine how we view the policy role of foundations. For example, in the 1970s and early 1980s, the movement to deregulate air travel, interstate trucking, telephone service, and banking brought greater market competition to industries that had been subject to regulatory regimes that had been set in place, in some cases, since the 1930s. From one perspective this dramatic policy transformation can be viewed as the ideological triumph of conservative foundations and the various think tanks into which they poured their resources. These proponents of free market ideas had used diverse tactics to win over popular and elite opinion. From another perspective, however, this policy transformation was the consequence of long-term efforts, beginning in the mid-1950s at the Ford Foundation and continuing as a handful of other foundations committed themselves to funding basic microeconomic research. They had long sought to bolster the field of microeconomics by encouraging graduate students and young faculty. Their studies of particular industries, their applied research, their career paths from university economics departments to think tanks to government agencies created a policy community around which the ideas of deregulation could coalesce into concrete legislative and executive branch decisions. Our view of the role of foundations in this significant policy transformation will inevitably be shaped by our view of the success of deregulation. Moreover, this example compels us to ask how long-term policy strategies grounded in building intellectual and human capital are to be assessed against more direct activist and advocacy strategies.

However, there is a final lingering question about the role of foundations in democratic political processes. How do we justify or, more bluntly, why do we tolerate the involvement of private foundations in our public decisionmaking? Whose interests do foundations represent? What value do they add to public policymaking?

The historical justification for the existence of trusts, endowments, and foundations is strong: they have sought to provide some sort of public benefit despite being organized privately. The public benefits are perhaps easiest to see and accept when foundations provide a direct service rather than aim to influence public policies. But the historical rationale has been bolstered by economic theory which contends that foundations and other nonprofit organizations are a response to "market failures." When markets fail to provide sufficient public goods, nonprofit organizations step in to do what the market cannot. Foundations play a clear and beneficial role, even if it is not the largest financial role, in sustaining the nonprofit sector as that sector provides public goods.

But arguments grounded in theories of market failure still do not seem fully persuasive or to provide an adequate justification for the direct engagement of foundations in the policy process. Certainly, they can prod government to provide public goods when markets fail. But it is a concept of "government failure" that pushes us closer to a rationale for the role of foundations. When government policies fail to meet public needs or prove to be inefficient, rigid, wrong-headed, or outmoded, foundations and other civil society organizations are the institutional means by which we seek to remedy those failures of the public sector. James Douglas and Aaron Wildavsky offered one of the fullest explanations of this view in the mid-1970s. They asked specifically how foundation roles had changed as government's role had expanded over the course of the twentieth century. During the course of the twentieth century the role of foundations, they suggested, had evolved from direct social action to building a policy research infrastructure and, finally, to assisting with public administration and managerial matters. From their vantage point in the last quarter of the twentieth century, they argued that the primary role of foundations had evolved into one of evaluating the effectiveness of government activities and, thus, of serving as a kind of intellectual check and balance on government (Douglas and Wildavsky, 1978).

Their argument points toward an even deeper analysis, expanding on classical ideas of mixed government and pluralism and suggesting how we might best understand the relationship between foundations and government. We must ask what values private foundations embody as they pursue their policy role and how those values serve to counterbalance the weaknesses inherent in the values of the public sector and the marketplace. How can foundations enhance innovation in the face of government's programmatic rigidity? How can foundations move issues onto the policy agenda when political processes refuse to engage fundamental problems? How can foundations give voice to groups that are little heard or marginalized? How can they remedy distortions in public political discourse? How can foundations advance pluralism in the face of the homogenizing tendencies of commercial markets? How can they address the issues of inequality that arise within market economies? The test of foundations' role in democratic policymaking resides in questions at this level of analysis and it is only in providing explicit answers to these questions—and demonstrable work in these directions—that foundations will continue to derive their democratic legitimacy.

References

Berle, Adolf A. 1969. *Leaning Against the Dawn*. New York, NY: Twentieth Century Fund.

Blumenthal, Sidney. 1986. *The Rise of the Counter-Establishment: From Conservative Ideology to Political Power*. New York, NY: Times Books.

Bremner, Robert H. 1980. *The Public Good: Philanthropy and Welfare in the Civil War Era*. New York, NY: Alfred A. Knopf.

City Limits. 1997. "Shaking the Foundations." October 1997, pp. 15–17.

Commonwealth Fund, The. 1963. *The Commonwealth Fund: A Historical Sketch, 1918–1962*. New York, NY: Commonwealth Fund.

Covington, Sally. 1997. *Moving a Public Policy Agenda: The Strategic Philanthropy of Conservative Foundations*. Washington, DC: National Committee for Responsive Philanthropy, 1997.

Day, E.E. 1933. "Proposed Social Science Program of the Rockefeller Foundation, March 13, 1933." Rockefeller Archive Center, Record Group 3, Series 910, Box 2, Folder 13.

Dillingham, George A. 1989. *The Foundation of the Peabody Tradition*. Lanham, MD: University Press of America.

Douglas, James, and Aaron Wildavsky. 1978. "The Knowledgeable Foundations," in *The Future of Foundations: Some Reconsiderations*. New Rochelle, NY: Change Magazine Press, pp. 10–43.

Dusenbury, Richard B. 1969. *Truth and Technique: A Study of Sociology and the Social Survey Movement, 1895–1930*. Madison, WI: University of Wisconsin Dissertation.

Eaton, Allen R., and Shelby M. Harrison. 1930. *A Bibliography of Social Surveys*. New York, NY: Russell Sage Foundation.

Embree, Edwin R., and Julia Waxman. 1949. *Investment in People: The Story of the Julius Rosenwald Fund*. New York, NY: Harper and Brothers, 1949.

Ettling, John. 1981. *The Germ of Laziness: Rockefeller Philanthropy and Public Health in the New South*. Cambridge, MA: Harvard University Press.

Ford Foundation, The. 1949. *Report of the Study for the Ford Foundation on Policy and Program*. Detroit, MI: The Ford Foundation.

Fosdick, Raymond B. 1952. *The Story of the Rockefeller Foundation*. New York, NY: Harper and Brothers.

Glenn, John M., Lilian Brandt, and F. Emerson Andrews. 1947a. *Russell Sage Foundation, 1907–46*. New York, NY: Russell Sage Foundation, Volume I.

Glenn, John M., Lilian Brandt, and F. Emerson Andrews. 1947b. *Russell Sage Foundation, 1907–46*. New York, NY: Russell Sage Foundation, Volume II.

Gordon, Kermit A. 1970. "The President's Review." *Biennial Report, 1968–69*. Washington, DC: Brookings Institution.

Lagemann, Ellen Condliffe. 1989. *The Politics of Knowledge: The Carnegie Corporation, Philanthropy, and Public Policy*. Middletown, MA: Wesleyan University Press.

Macdonald, Dwight. 1956 and 1989. *The Ford Foundation: The Men and the Millions*. 1956 New York, NY: Reynal; 1989 reprinted by Transaction Publishers.

New York Times. 1994a. "The Health Care Debate." July 26, 1994.

New York Times. 1994b. "On TV: Horror Stories on the Health Care Front." June 23, 1994.

Nielsen, Waldemar A. 1972. *The Big Foundations*. New York, NY: Columbia University Press, pp. 19–20.

O'Connor, Alice. 1999. "The Ford Foundation and Philanthropic Activism in the 1960s," in Ellen Lagemann (ed.), *Philanthropic Foundations: New Scholarship, New Possibilities*. Bloomington and Indianapolis, IN: Indiana University Press.

Parker, Franklin. 1971 and 1995, revised edition. *George Peabody: A Biography*. Nashville, TN: Vanderbilt University Press, 1971 and 1995.

Rockefeller Archive Center. Record Group 3, Series 900, 1945–46.

Sealander, Judith. 1997. *Private Wealth and Public Life: Foundation Philanthropy and the Reshaping of American Social Policy from the Progressive Era to the New Deal*. Baltimore, MD: Johns Hopkins University Press.

Stanfield, John H. 1987. "Philanthropic Consciousness and Institution-Building in the American South: The Formative Years, 1867–1920," in Jack Salzman (ed.), *Philanthropy and American Society: Selected Papers*. New York, NY: Columbia University Center for American Culture Studies.

4

Private Foundations and Public Policymaking: Latitude Under Federal Tax Law

Thomas A. Troyer and Douglas Varley

The federal tax law provides considerable latitude for private foundations to participate in the formation of public policy. Although special restrictions apply to influencing legislative decisions and to election-related activities, much room remains for foundations to play a significant role in the formation and implementation of government policies. This chapter reviews the applicable federal laws and provides examples of the kinds of work private foundations may support or conduct themselves.[1]

The Lobbying Restriction

All organizations exempt from federal income tax by reason of section 501(c)(3) of the Internal Revenue Code are prohibited from engaging in substantial attempts to influence legislation. Private foundations—a subcategory of section 501(c)(3) organizations—must, however, obey a stricter rule. In contrast to public charities, which can conduct a considerable amount of legislative work, foundations are prohibited from funding or engaging in any "lobbying" at all.[2] Although this prohibition is absolute,

---

[1] This chapter does not address state laws that may apply to foundations that conduct or support advocacy activities. Nor does it discuss the federal Lobbying Disclosure Act, which defines "lobbying" differently from the tax law and may require foundations active in the policymaking arena to register with Congress.

[2] As used here, the term "private foundation" or "foundation" refers to organizations that are exempt from federal income tax under section 501(c)(3) of the Internal Revenue Code that are not "public charities." Public charities are section 501(c)(3) organizations that qualify for more favorable tax treatment because of the activities they conduct or the diversity of their contributors. Both private foundations and public charities are "charities" as that term is used here.

it is also narrow and very clearly defined. In drafting the laws that restrict foundations' work in this area, Congress and the Treasury Department have taken considerable care to ensure that foundations, and their charitable grantees, can spend their resources on a broad array of activities that improve the quality of the legislative process. In addition, it bears emphasis that the federal limitations on lobbying in no way impede foundations' ability to influence actions by executive or administrative branches of governments. Nor do they restrict foundations from litigating in support of policies they favor.

Hence, while there are certain kinds of legislative activity that foundations are strictly prohibited from supporting, there is much room for advocacy work that can affect legislation and other policy outcomes. In addition, by relying on special safe harbor rules, foundations can make grants to like-minded public charities that are engaged in lobbying activities which foundations could not conduct themselves. Thus, foundations frequently can have an even greater impact on the legislative process as funders than they can achieve directly. By paying close attention to the rules discussed here, foundation executives and staff, as well as their legal advisors, can help their organizations advocate government policies that advance charitable objectives while complying fully with their obligations under the federal foundation laws.

HISTORICAL CONTEXT

Congress enacted the ban on foundation lobbying as part of the Tax Reform Act of 1969, which established the current regulatory regime for foundations. Prior to 1969, Congress had paid only episodic attention to foundations. In particular, policymakers gave little thought to the role of foundations in the formation of legislation. Indeed, the most comprehensive assessment of foundations during that period, the Treasury Department Report on Private Foundations, did not mention legislative activities by foundations as an abuse that needed to be addressed (Senate Committee on Finance, 1965). When historical circumstances came together in 1969 for passage of broad-scale foundation legislation, however, Congress added the flat prohibition against foundation lobbying (along with several other restrictions) to the package of reforms the Treasury Department had recommended. The record reveals little about the precise motivation underlying this part of the legislation. Most likely the new, stricter rule for foundations simply reflected the unusually fierce hostility Congress felt toward foundations at the end of the 1960s.

Since that time, legislative activity by foundations has enjoyed the same general lack of congressional attention as before 1969. Although Congress has occasionally taken up the issue of the appropriate level of policy involvement by charities in general—most notably in 1976 when it enacted new rules to encourage public charities to participate in the legislative process— foundations have been largely ignored. Thus, while the specter of the Tax Reform Act of 1969 and the threat of congressional retaliation looms large in the minds of foundations (and their legal advisors), in fact in the more than thirty years since 1969, Congress has not once tightened the 1969 rules for foundations.

PENALTIES FOR FOUNDATION LOBBYING

Private foundations are subject to a 10 percent penalty tax on any expenditure for an attempt to influence legislation at the federal, state, or local level (IRC § 4945(d)(1)). Making a lobbying expenditure also triggers an obligation to "correct" the violation—that is, to recover the expenditure if possible and take whatever additional corrective action the IRS requires. Failure to meet this correction obligation results in a larger second-level penalty tax. As noted above, a private foundation may lose its tax-exempt status under section 501(c)(3) if attempting to influence legislation constitutes a "substantial part" of its activities during any tax year. As far as the authors are aware, this more draconian sanction has never been imposed on a private foundation and, since 1976, only very rarely on public charities.

What Constitutes Lobbying: General Definitions

Under regulations adopted in 1990, whether an activity is "lobbying" depends on the content of the communication and the identity of the recipient. In short, the law applies an objective "magic words" test to determine whether an activity violates the no-lobbying prohibition. Prior to the appearance of these regulations, foundations and other charities confronted considerable uncertainty about the activities they could conduct in connection with the formulation of legislation. To remove this uncertainty and, thus, provide section 501(c)(3) organizations the ability to participate in the policymaking process as Congress intended, the Treasury Department developed a set of clear, bright-line definitions that put all parties on notice about what is, and is not, lobbying.

As the law stands today, it is what the foundation *says* that matters, not its subjective intent in expressing its views. In the technical language of the regulations, an activity is lobbying for purposes of the private foundation rules only if it involves either a "direct lobbying communication" or a "grassroots lobbying communication." Both of these terms have quite narrow and, in certain respects, rather counterintuitive definitions. Foundations' ability to take full advantage of the possibilities these rules provide for supporting policy-related activities depends on understanding these definitions and their application.

DIRECT LOBBYING

A direct lobbying communication is a statement to a legislator or legislative staff member that: a) refers to specific legislation and b) reflects a view on that legislation (Treas. Reg. § 53.4945-2(a) and § 56.4911-2(b)(1)(i)).[3] This definition immediately excludes from the set of prohibited activities all efforts to influence legislators' views on matters other than specific legislation. Hence, the legal rules permit foundations to discuss policy issues with legislators or staff even if those issues are the subjects of pending legislation, provided the foundation does not refer to that legislation (Treas. Reg. § 53.9945-2(c)(2)).

The signal benefit of this rule is that a foundation does not have to stop expressing its views to legislators on a broader policy issue just because there is a pending piece of legislation that addresses an aspect of that policy.

> *Example:* A foundation, or its grantee, prepares a brief paper summarizing the need for scientific research on sources of renewable energy. The paper does not reflect a view on any specific legislative proposal, though there is legislation pending in Congress that would provide tax credits to encourage scientific research of the sort the foundation supports. Under the basic definition of direct lobbying, giving the report to a member of Congress would not violate the prohibition against foundation lobbying.

A similarly important aspect of the lobbying definition is that attempts to influence actions by administrative agencies are not lobbying no matter how pointedly the foundation expresses its views on the specific action in question. Accordingly, while a foundation cannot send letters to members

---

[3]For purposes of this definition, recipients of a lobbying communication may also, under quite limited circumstances, include executive branch personnel involved in the legislative process, and the term "specific legislation" includes not only acts, bills, resolutions, and legislative vetoes, but also specific legislative proposals that have not been introduced; ballot initiatives and referenda; and proposed treaties that must be submitted to the Senate for ratification—but only after negotiations have begun. Treas. Reg. § 56.4911-2(d)(1).

of Congress expressing support for a bill that would limit mining on public land, it can press officials at the Department of the Interior for regulations that would have the same effect. Since the impact of executive and agency decisions can be as far-reaching as legislative action, this rule offers foundations a very significant opportunity to participate in the formation of public policy.

> *Example:* In January of 2001, the Clinton administration issued the Roadless Area Conservation Rule, which barred virtually all road building on 58.5 million acres in national forests. This rule was the result of three years of work and hundreds of meetings where nonprofit organizations, funded in part by foundations, met with White House and agency officials to press for adoption of the rule. None of these meetings were "lobbying" because the roadless rule is not legislation.

> *Example continued:* The timber industry filed suit in federal court to have the roadless rule set aside as illegal. Nonprofit groups, again with foundation support, met with officials at the Department of Justice to encourage the agency to defend the rule vigorously. The meetings were not lobbying because the Department's decision is not legislation.

The legal rules provide additional protection for foundations working to affect administrative actions by stating expressly that a communication with an executive branch official will not be lobbying unless the primary purpose of the communication is to influence legislation (Treas. Reg. § 56.4911-2(b)(1)(i)(B)). Thus, under the primary purpose standard, foundations need not worry that efforts to influence nonlegislative decisions will be recharacterized as lobbying merely because legislation is mentioned in the course of exchanging information with an executive branch official.

> *Example:* A foundation program director meets with a senior official at the Environmental Protection Agency to urge tightening of the clean air regulations. During the course of the conversation, they discuss incidentally possible legislative responses to the new regulations. Since discussing legislation is not the primary purpose of the meeting, it is not lobbying.

> *Example continued:* Later the program director meets with the same EPA official with the primary purpose of asking her to testify before a congressional committee in support of reauthorizing the Clean Air Act. The meeting is lobbying, because the primary purpose of the meeting is influencing action by Congress.

GRASSROOTS LOBBYING

The foundation rules are even more generous with respect to efforts to influence public opinion on policy issues, including legislation. The law defines prohibited "grassroots lobbying" as a communication with the public that: a) refers to specific legislation; b) reflects a view on that legislation; and c) includes a "call to action" that encourages the recipient to contact a government official about the legislation (Treas. Reg. § 56.4911-2(b)(2)).[4] Under this definition, public communications—including television and radio spots, web pages, and mass mailings—that forcefully state a position for or against pending legislation will not violate the ban on foundation lobbying if they do not overtly encourage contact with legislators or other government officials who participate in the formation of legislation.

> *Example:* A foundation makes a grant to pay for the following radio spot. "The state assembly is considering a bill that would make gun ownership illegal. If this egregious legislation passes, you and your family will be criminals if you exercise your constitutional right to protect yourselves." The ad is not lobbying because it does not encourage listeners to contact a government official (see Treas. Reg. § 56.4911-2(b)(5)(iv), Example (4)).

There are two exceptions to the general rule that a communication with the public will not be lobbying unless it includes a call to action. The first involves paid mass media advertisements on "highly publicized legislation."[5] Under a special rule, a paid ad concerning such legislation is presumed to be grassroots lobbying if it runs within two weeks of a vote on the legislation, even if it does not encourage contacting government officials.

> *Example:* Assume the radio spot on the gun bill described above runs within two weeks of a vote on the gun legislation and that the legislation is "highly publicized." The ad will be presumed to be lobbying because it refers to the bill.

The second exception to the "call to action" arises in the narrow case of referenda and ballot initiatives. The foundation rules treat communications with voters about these measures as direct lobbying (Treas. Reg. § 56.4911-2(b)(1)(iii)). Accordingly, no call to action is necessary for such a communication to violate the ban on foundation lobbying. Simply expressing a view on the initiative or referendum will be sufficient.

---

[4]Under these rules, a communication includes a "call to action" only if it: 1) tells the recipient to contact a government official about the legislation; 2) provides the address or telephone number of a legislator (or employee of a legislative body); 3) provides a petition, tear-off postcard, etc. addressed to a government official; or 4) specifically identifies a legislator who will vote on the legislation as opposing the legislation, as being undecided, as being a member of the committee considering the legislation, or as being the recipient's representative. Identifying the sponsor of the legislation is not a call to action. Treas. Reg. § 56.4911-2(b)(2)(iii).
[5]Whether legislation is highly publicized depends on the level of media coverage it receives and the extent to which the general public is aware of the legislation. Treas. Reg. § 56.4911-2(b)(5)(iii).

Despite the more restrictive rules that apply in the case of referenda and ballot initiatives, there remains a significant role for foundation-funded activities in this area. First, as for any communications with members of a legislative body, it is perfectly permissible for foundations to provide the public with information about the general subject of a referendum or initiative so long as there is no reference to the measure itself.

> *Example:* In the weeks before the public votes on bonds that will provide funds for public schools, a foundation pays for television spots that emphasize the importance of education for children of all income levels. The ads do not refer to the bond initiative. Therefore, they are not lobbying.

> *Example:* A mid-sized city has placed on the ballot a measure that would authorize fluoridation in the city's water. Around the same time, a local health foundation takes out an ad in several newspapers explaining the benefits of fluoride for oral health. As long as the ads do not refer to the ballot measure, they are not lobbying.

In states where items are placed on the ballot through a petition process, it is clear under the tax rules that an initiative or referendum is not "specific legislation" until its proponents begin collecting signatures (Treas. Reg. § 56.4911-2(d)(1)(ii)). Consequently, foundations can be confident that activities that occur earlier in the process—such as research to design an initiative or polling to test its viability—will not be lobbying.

EXCEPTIONS TO THE DEFINITION OF LOBBYING

Even if an activity satisfies the definition of direct or grassroots lobbying, it nonetheless is permissible for foundations if it falls within an exception to the basic definition. The most important exception excludes the preparation and distribution of "nonpartisan analysis and research." This exception permits foundations, or their grantees, to offer legislators, executive branch officials, and the public materials that make forceful, substantive arguments for or against specific legislation, provided the materials present a sufficiently full and fair exposition of the legislation to allow the recipient to form his or her own conclusions (Treas. Reg. § 53.4945-2(d)(1)).[6] Although the lobbying regulations do not specifically define the "full and fair" standard, the available authority indicates that the fundamental requirement is that the material provides a factual basis for its conclusions and argues for them in a reasoned fashion (see Rev. Proc. 86-43, 1986-2 C.B. 729). Foundations have relied on

---

[6]In addition to satisfying the "full and fair" exposition standard, nonpartisan analysis and research must also be distributed to persons on both sides of the legislation addressed.

this exception to hold policy briefings on Capitol Hill, to invite legislators and staff to symposia where substantive legislative analyses are presented, and even to produce documentary films on legislative topics.

Traditionally, the exception for nonpartisan analysis and research has been the principal vehicle through which foundations have gotten their views before policymakers. As major funders of scholarly and scientific research, foundations have supported much of the primary intellectual analysis that informs the national policy debate in many areas. The nonpartisan analysis and research exception allows foundations to package that work as forceful, reasoned briefs for the legislative outcomes they desire and give them to legislators.

A second useful, though more limited, exception to the basic lobbying definition excludes oral or written responses to written requests for technical assistance from a legislative committee, subcommittee, or other governmental body (Treas. Reg. § 53.4945-2(d)(2)). In order to qualify for this exception, the written request must come on behalf of the legislative body itself, not from an individual legislator asking on his or her own behalf. Where such a request solicits the foundation's views on the legislation, it grants foundation executives broad ability to state their organization's full analyses of, and conclusions on, proposed legislation directly to legislators.

A third exception allows foundations to communicate with government officials involved in the legislative process about specific legislation that could affect the foundation's existence, powers, duties, tax-exempt status, or right to receive tax-deductible contributions (Treas. Reg. § 53.4945-2(d)(3)). Relying on this exception, foundations have pressed Congress for favorable changes to the tax code provisions that regulate them, including reductions in the tax they pay on their investment income and the ability to provide donors a deduction equal to the value of publicly traded stock. Of broader relevance, this "self-defense" exception has permitted foundations to fund advocacy against attempts to curtail the advocacy rights of charities.

Finally, a narrow exception to the lobbying definition allows foundations to present information to government officials about a program that is, or may be, funded by both the foundation and the government, provided the communications are limited to the jointly funded program (Treas. Reg. § 53.4945-2(a)(3)). Although this exception is not relevant to foundations interested only in changing substantive laws, it can be enormously useful to foundations seeking government funding for particular projects. Thus, while discussions between a foundation and a legislator about appropriations legislation are generally prohibited, under this exception a foundation can ask a legislator's assistance in obtaining an appropriation for a project the foundation is supporting. Obvious examples involve foundations seeking government funding for a public facility, like a hospital or park, the foundation is supporting.

WORKING WITH PUBLIC CHARITY GRANTEES THAT LOBBY

As noted above, the law allows public charities to engage in a significant amount of lobbying.[7] Consequently, these organizations can generally be more effective advocates for, or against, legislation than the foundations that fund them. Hence, while there is much that foundations can do themselves, for most foundations the principal means of participating in the legislative process is supporting public charities working to achieve changes the foundation favors.

The regulations provide two safe harbors for foundation grants to public charities that prevent attribution of the grantee's lobbying to the foundation even if the grantee, in fact, uses the foundation's funds to lobby. These rules have enabled foundations to fund advocacy campaigns that include lobbying on topics as diverse as tobacco taxes, criminal sentencing, funding for after-school programs, and campaign finance reform.

The first safe harbor provides that a private foundation can make a general purpose grant to a public charity engaged in lobbying activities without risking any tax penalty. As long as the grant is not "earmarked" for lobbying, it will not be treated as a lobbying expenditure by the foundation even if the grantee uses some or all of the funds to pay for lobbying expenses (Treas. Reg. § 53.4945-2(a)(6)(i)).[8] For these purposes, a foundation grant is "earmarked" if there is an agreement between the foundation and the grantee that the funds will be used to support specific activities. The mere fact that the foundation knows the organization will be engaged in lobbying during the grant period does not constitute earmarking and will not cause a general support grant to be a lobbying expenditure for the grantor. Hence, this protective rule allows a foundation to identify public charities that advocate legislative positions it wants to see adopted and to provide those organizations general operating support, thereby increasing their ability to promote the foundation's policy agenda.

[7]Under section 501(h) of the Internal Revenue Code, public charities may spend up to 20 percent of the first $500,000 of their program budget on lobbying. For organizations with larger budgets, the permitted lobbying percentage decreases as the size of the budget increases, reaching a maximum lobbying expenditure limit of $1 million for organizations with charitable budgets of $17 million or more. Lower limits apply to grassroots efforts to mobilize the public.

[8]It is worth noting that the foundation will be protected even if the grantee loses its tax-exempt status because of excessive lobbying. Treas. Reg. § 53.4945-2(a)(7).

In practice, foundations make relatively few general support grants, preferring instead to fund specific projects. The second safe harbor in the foundation rules addresses this kind of grant. The federal regulations state explicitly that a private foundation can make a grant to a public charity for a specific project *that will include lobbying,* provided the amount of the grant is no more than the amount budgeted by the grantee for non-lobbying expenditures (Treas. Reg. § 53.4945-2(a)(6)(ii)). Absent earmarking, such a grant will not be a prohibited lobbying expenditure for the grantor even if the grantee spends more on lobbying than projected and uses the foundation's grant to pay these costs. Thus, the rule for project grants creates an opportunity for foundations to target their grants on activities that directly advance their legislative objectives.

> *Example:* A public charity submits a proposal seeking support for a project to protect an environmentally significant watershed. The project will include three activities: (1) researching and compiling information documenting the significance of the watershed and the risks to it; (2) running non-lobbying media advertisements lacking a call to action that will educate the public about this issue; and (3) meeting with legislators and staff to urge passage of legislation restricting development in the area. The budget for the project indicates that the grantee expects to spend $80,000 on activities that will not be lobbying and $20,000 on activities that will be lobbying. The foundation can safely make a grant for the project of up to $80,000.[9]

In sum, notwithstanding the ban on foundation lobbying, the law leaves foundations able to conduct or fund an expansive set of advocacy activities. These rules are technical and complex, but once a foundation understands them, it can safely include support for legislative advocacy among the strategies it uses to achieve its charitable objectives. Given the centrality of government action in protecting and promoting the public good in our system, it is not surprising that foundations find this strategy to be among the most potent means of advancing their broader purposes.

A Note about Electioneering

Federal law prohibits all organizations exempt under section 501(c)(3), including private foundations, from intervening in any political campaign on behalf of (or in opposition to) any candidate for public office (IRC § 501(c)(3)).[10] The rules in this area contrast markedly from those that apply to lobbying. Most importantly, where the lobbying analysis is informed

[9]Again, loss of the grantee's tax-exempt status will not alter the legal consequences of the grant for the foundation.
[10]For private foundations, this prohibition is backed up by the same penalty tax as applies to lobbying expenditures. IRC § 4945(d)(2).

by bright-line definitions that clearly distinguish lobbying from permitted advocacy, the prohibition against campaign intervention involves a vaguer "facts and circumstances" analysis. There is no "magic words" test here.

Consequently, planning advocacy activities that will involve, or merely occur proximate in time to, an election frequently calls for the careful exercise of informed judgment. This difficulty is compounded by the seriousness of the potential penalties for violating the electioneering ban. In contrast to lobbying, where foundations face only a small penalty tax for activities that are "insubstantial," the penalty for any electioneering is, theoretically at least, loss of the foundation's tax exemption. Hence, foundations generally should seek advice of experienced tax counsel before conducting or funding activities associated with an election.

Although due caution is appropriate, the electioneering ban does not mean that foundations are prohibited from conducting advocacy and voter education activities simply because an election is near. In fact, foundations both fund and conduct a range of activities that take place around elections. For example, foundations have funded or conducted national voter education programs distributing information about candidates—the Markle Foundation's Web White and Blue site being a notable example—paid for research into how election campaigns are financed, and supported advocacy activities designed to call attention to particular policy issues during the election season. The touchstone for distinguishing these permissible activities from prohibited electioneering is that all the foundation's efforts must be strictly nonpartisan in both form and substance.

In determining whether an activity meets this standard, the IRS will consider any evidence that the organization had a partisan motive in conducting the activity as well as whether the organization should reasonably have foreseen that its efforts would benefit one candidate over another. Hence, an activity may be characterized as partisan even though it does not involve an explicit endorsement of a particular candidate or party. In this way, the campaign prohibition is broader than the "express advocacy" standard that the Supreme Court has applied under the federal election laws.[11]

Nonetheless, the IRS has stated explicitly that the law does not require organizations to refrain from the activities they regularly carry on simply because an election is near (Kindell and Reilly, 2002). In particular, the IRS

---

[11]Foundations conducting issue advocacy around elections will want to consult their advisors about the election law reforms dealing with this topic enacted as part of the Bipartisan Campaign Reform Act of 2002.

does not expect charities to stop advocating for policy positions they support close to an election, provided their efforts serve a legitimate nonpartisan purpose and are not being carried out to benefit a particular candidate. Moreover, the IRS recognizes that electioneering requires more than just a positive or negative correspondence between the charity's position on an issue and a candidate's position. Rather, a charity violates the prohibition only if its issue ads contain an overt indication that the organization supports or opposes a particular candidate or slate of candidates. That is, the IRS is concerned about ads that use issue labels like "conservative" or "pro-choice" as code words to describe a candidate. Hence, as long as a foundation or its grantee does not link its position on issues with a particular candidate or party, its issue advocacy should not run afoul of the electioneering ban.

In addition to nonpartisan issue advocacy, the IRS has identified a number of voter education activities that foundations may safely support or conduct themselves. Specifically, charitable organizations, including foundations, can sponsor candidate debates, publish candidates' responses to questionnaires, and distribute candidate voting records. Detailed restrictions apply to each of these activities, intended to ensure that the event or publication is strictly neutral among the candidates. Finally, private foundations can fund nonpartisan "get out the vote" drives and, under more stringent requirements, voter registration drives. A detailed recounting of the legal requirements for those activities is beyond the scope of this paper.

Conclusion

Private foundations are subject to special restrictions that limit their ability to lobby and participate in election campaigns. Despite these restrictions, foundations can and do play a significant role in formation of public policy. In particular, foundations can support a wide array of activities that — while not "lobbying" under the federal foundation rules — have a direct and important impact on the legislative process. Moreover, the foundation rules include broad safe harbors that allow foundations to fund public charities conducting the relatively narrow set of lobbying activities. Finally, the special rules that bar all charities from attempting to influence election results need not constrain foundations from promoting nonpartisan issue agendas even during the campaign season. Thus, foundations willing to invest the effort necessary to understand the legal rules that govern them can safely include seeking policy change as a potent means of furthering their charitable objectives.

References

Senate Committee on Finance, 89th Cong., 1st Sess. (1965).

Kindell, Judith, and John Reilly, Election Year Issues, Exempt Organizations Technical Instruction Program for FY 2002, 334, 345, IRS.

5

Critical Junctures: Philanthropic Associations as Policy Actors

Lucy Bernholz

Introduction

Foundations are infamous individualists. Separate in nature, spawned from a family, a community, or a corporation, they are known to be "lone wolves." This image has much truth to it, but it also belies the fact that formal associations of foundations are abundant, proliferating, and maturing, with several marking or moving past their fiftieth anniversaries.

These associations have varied histories, purposes, and structures. Some are formal, funded, membership associations seeking to represent the industry of philanthropy to national policymakers. Others are temporal and oriented toward a specific issue. Others (most) are hybrids of these two extremes, focusing on some subsection of institutionalized grantmakers defined by region, issue, identity, structure, or some combination of these.

The recent growth in the numbers of foundations has been matched by a parallel growth in foundation associations. While many of the existing associations added members, foundations seemed almost as likely to create new associations as to join existing ones. The state of the research on foundation philanthropy is itself an emerging field. Our understanding of these associations, their roles, responsibilities, and viability as actors in the industry, is almost nonexistent.[1]

---

[1] Ralph Hamilton wrote a paper for the Funders Network on Smart Growth and Sustainable Communities that also outlines various types of foundation collaboration. *See* Hamilton, 2002.

It stands to reason that groups of foundations acting together have the potential to influence the way philanthropy works, the relationship between private funders and the public sector, and the public perception of institutional philanthropy. Foundations and their associations work in many ways to address the policy spheres that directly shape philanthropy (what we will call philanthropic policy) as well as the policy issues that directly connect to their programmatic areas of interest (what we will call public policy).

Several foundation associations have specific interests in influencing both philanthropic and public policy. This chapter first draws a landscape of foundation associations. It then presents brief examples of foundations working together on issues of philanthropic and public policy, posits initial observations about the relationships between associations and effective policy work, and identifies areas for additional research and discussion.

A Landscape of Foundation Associations

Foundation staff and board members develop associations or networks that fall into one or more of the following categories:

- Industrywide

- Regional

- Issue-oriented

- Identity-oriented

- Structural

The Council on Foundations, a fifty-two-year-old nonprofit membership association representing more than 2,000 private, community, and corporate grantmakers, holds the most prominent industrywide position. The Council serves as a general purpose membership association, providing educational, outreach, professional development, legislative, and legal services, and an array of publications to its members.

In 2002 the regional associations numbered twenty-nine, and covered a variety of regions in the country. Some are organized around metropolitan areas (e.g., Chicago), others serve parts of a state (e.g., Northern California), several are statewide (e.g., Michigan), and still others serve multiple-state regions (e.g., twelve states in the Southeast). Even within this range of configurations, regional associations tend to provide an array of common services such as education, publications, networking, joint grantmaking opportunities, professional development, and local outreach. Their focus on philanthropic or public policy varies widely.

Foundations also organize themselves around issues, such as education, sustainable growth, the arts, or AIDS. There are at least thirty issue-specific associations of foundations that have also signed on as affinity groups of the Council on Foundations. There are several dozen additional associations with less formal structures. The work of these groups ranges from joint grantmaking to issue advocacy, and it is in this last arena that these issue-specific groups can and do act within the policy arena.

Another slice of the associational pie includes groups of foundations organized by the identity of the members. These include racial and ethnic groups (e.g., Hispanics in Philanthropy, Black Foundation Executives) and gender-specific groups (e.g., Women in Philanthropy). These associations often have both institutional and individual members, so they may include one foundation that funds Native American issues and a Sioux staff member of another foundation.

Finally, there are associations of foundations dedicated to serving different structural types of grantmakers. Leagues of community foundations, associations of unstaffed foundations, and organizations to serve family foundations have all appeared in the last decade. Some of these operate on the national level and others focus within certain regions of the country.

These categories of associations make up the general landscape. Many associations cross these categories, such as state associations of community foundations or regional chapters of identity-based associations. In addition, there are several alternative and informal types of foundation associations. These, which may be focused on a single project or joint funding effort, or merely represent like-minded colleagues gathering for a meal and idea exchange, are not to be discounted within the overall landscape. These are important incubators for established associations to come (almost all regional associations of grantmakers got their start as informal luncheon groups). They also provide potential networks of contacts for policy influence or other action.

Two Landscapes: Philanthropic Policy and Public Policy

Foundations associate in many ways for many ends. Our focus is on the ways in which they address philanthropic and public policy. This paper employs two broad but distinct classifications of policy: first, philanthropic policy defined as the set of regulations and laws governing charitable giving. Second, public policy, a term we will use to encapsulate the public legislation, regulation, or oversight within the issues of concern to philanthropy, such as the environment, social justice, community development, education, or health care.

PHILANTHROPIC POLICY

Institutional philanthropy is regulated as part of the federal tax code; it is subject to oversight by state departments of corporations and attorneys general and, in many if not all states, is subject to state tax law as well. The first myth to be dispelled is that of the independent, unregulated industry— institutional philanthropy falls within the purview of the legal and regulatory statutes overseeing tax-exempt organizations.

The exemption from federal income tax that applies to public charities is further refined and additional limitations set for the operation of private foundations. These restrictions fall within the broader tax exemption frame, and include limitations on self-dealing, requirements on annual distributions, limitations on private business holdings and investments, and provisions that the organization's expenditures are to advance the foundation's tax-exempt mission. In addition to the above, there are public reporting requirements, excise tax issues for private foundations, and public support tests for public grantmaking charities (Mancuso, 2001, pp. 17–18).

State laws also regulate foundations, and can vary significantly on issues such as compensating board members or having family members on the staff of a family foundation. Just as commercial entities do, many individual foundations carefully select the state in which they incorporate to assure the most favorable regulatory structure to achieve their purpose.

Given this web of regulations, it is clear that grantmaking foundations, which exist as a product of the public policy framework and as entities in the public trust, have a strong vested interest in an array of public policy issues. However, even this web is really only a piece of a larger puzzle.

New Actors

Much has been written about the changing nature of philanthropy, the advent of commercial competitors offering charitable options, and the rise of ePhilanthropy.[2] While we tend to view these charitable vehicles as tools for individual philanthropy, they are, in effect, bringing new institutions onto the playing field of organized giving. With these new players comes the need to consider a broader array of philanthropic policy issues. For example, the growth of commercial financial service products aimed at charitable giving has been a focus of decisionmaking at the Internal Revenue Service for the last decade. Traditional philanthropy, including community foundations, fundraising professionals, and private foundations, eagerly responded to calls for public comment on the regulations of these entities.

At the same time, the financial services firms also rallied their industry associations to the call, seeking to influence a regulatory decision favorable to their growing businesses. This is just one well-known example of the entry of new viewpoints into the public policy debate about philanthropy. It heralds an important change in the field—the divergent public policy and regulatory agendas of the different factions in the philanthropic industry.

These divergent viewpoints come into play on some of the key policy issues now lurking on philanthropy's horizon. These include proposed new regulations on financial need of charity recipients, the role of the public sector in advising or requiring philanthropic coordination, the relationship between excise taxes and administrative expenses, the elimination of the itemization requirement for tax deductions on charitable giving, and the proposed new eligibility for faith-based institutions as publicly funded social service providers. However, organizing the interested parties to these changes is not easy.[3]

Individuals and Institutions

In addition to the new organizational actors, philanthropy is increasingly a mix of individual and institutional action. Personal charitable giving has always dominated the landscape, often accounting for more than 70 percent of all donations. Foundations account for only a small piece of the giving pie (xx percent). This imbalance has led many foundations to design grant programs with the express purpose of securing additional funds for sustaining

---

[2]*See*, for example, ePhilanthropy v2.001: From Entrepreneurial Adventure to Online Community, The W.K. Kellogg Foundation, available at www.actknowledgeworks.net.
[3]*See* Senate Bill 1300, Foundational and Corporate Charitable Giving Incentives Act of 2001, introduced by Senators Santorum and Lieberman.

the effort from individuals. Such strategies often require new ways of sharing information with new audiences.[4] These new relationships between individual giving and foundation giving were only recently recognized by the industry (see Bernholz, 2001). They are important from a policy standpoint for a number of reasons.

First, donors are creating foundations while they also use other tax vehicles for their giving. In analyzing charitable gifts to universities in 2000–2001, the Rand Corporation noted that "…an important point to make about personal giving over all…. Each year, more and more of it is filtered through organizations such as foundations, charitable gift funds, and the like" (Strom, 2002). Many individual philanthropists have a lifetime of giving ahead of them. During that time, they will strive to match their giving vehicles with distinct charitable purposes. In doing so, they will view their foundations as only one piece of a portfolio of giving. From a policy perspective it is important to remember that donors vote. Foundations do not. Any individual donor's support may be strongest for legislation that maximizes overall individual tax benefits, not necessarily those that benefit foundations.

Second, the relationship between individual and institutional tax law becomes increasingly important. There is a universe of estate tax law that is coming into play for institutional philanthropy. Savvy philanthropists are carefully employing individual tax strategies to maximize their efficiency in creating new foundations. For example, extremely large bequests to foundations are now being siphoned through charitable trusts for a period of time to allow adequate time for staffing and strategy development before foundation "payout" requirements kick in.[5] This effectively broadens the policy landscape of concern to foundations.

Third, increasing public awareness of institutional philanthropy raises the stakes on public reporting by foundations, indeed on all tax-exempt organizations. The list of interested audiences for reports from foundations and nonprofits includes current and potential donors, wealth advisers, media, government officials, community activists, nonprofit managers, and the general public. The Internet has created a general societal expectation about information access that calls for faster and easier availability in all sectors. At the same time, high-profile corporate bankruptcies, coupled with front-page nonprofit scandals about uncoordinated relief efforts and potential

[4]For example, many foundations help their nonprofit partners add "donate now" capability to their web sites, others expressly seek to build the nonprofit's capacity to increase individual giving, and other private foundation initiatives are set up through community foundations with the express purpose of raising ongoing support from the community foundation's donor base.
[5]*See*, for example, the Gordon and Betty Moore Foundation in San Francisco.

reallocation of funds, only increase skepticism about nonprofit organizations and foundations and fuel moves for greater industry oversight. Currently, the public reporting requirements for individual and institutional giving are quite different. As public awareness, scrutiny, and expectations all increase, state and federal policies regarding reporting requirements (type, frequency, and availability of information) for both institutional and individual giving are likely to be challenged.

FOUNDATION ASSOCIATIONS AND PUBLIC POLICY

Foundations are one focus of philanthropic policy. A web of policies at the national, state, and local level influences individual giving and foundation structures, strategies, and rate of proliferation. In contrast, public policy is one possible focus for philanthropic investment. Within the context of their attempts to improve health, education, or the environment, for example, foundations may invest in policy research, public awareness or education, and joint action on policy development.

Associations of foundations can assist in addressing public policy in several ways. They may serve as information clearinghouses on current and pending regulatory issues in land use, pollution credits, or financing for jails. Some associations have developed robust online databases to allow members easy access to updated information on national and state policies relevant to their work. Other associations routinely host workshops or roundtables with policy experts or researchers to help their members stay current on these issues. Foundation networks also can serve as direct conduits of grants to work with school district leaders, state health officials, or other policy leaders. Associations also may provide a joint funding pool for public awareness campaigns or for the development of new school or transportation policies within a municipality.

Aligning Associations and Policy Mechanisms

Foundation philanthropy is a regulated industry. As such, foundations, like media companies, auto manufacturers, toymakers, and medical professionals, have banded together to represent the interests of their constituent members before the regulating bodies. For the most part, this work occurs at the national level, and representation of the industry to Congress, the IRS, and other lawmakers has been the purview of the Council on Foundations.

The Council has a major investment and focus on policy issues, fielding a government relations staff and managing a legislative affairs network.

The regional associations, on the other hand, vary tremendously in the degree to which they address policy issues in formal ways. Some regional associations of grantmakers (RAGs) are quite active on matters of policy or legislative relations. For the most part, however, policy is a secondary concern for regional associations.[6]

Though the national and regional associations share similar missions of promoting effective philanthropy, the degree of focus on public policy is significantly different at the national and regional levels. This divergence in mission from the national level to the regional level has made sense in the past because much of the legislation and regulation that mattered to foundations has been federal in nature.

While the IRS remains a key regulatory body, state tax boards and legislatures are increasingly important players in the operation of philanthropy. This trend accelerated in the past decade through the course of development of conversion foundations, which were addressed by state attorneys general and departments of corporations. State laws regarding charitable operation and charitable exemptions also have been changing recently, with more and more states offering charitable tax deductions, changes in laws regarding community philanthropy, and state-level regulation of financial service firms' charitable products.[7] Recent tragedies in Oklahoma, New York, Virginia, and Pennsylvania also highlight the role that state attorneys general can— and will—play in regulating philanthropic giving and working to ensure coordination, public reporting, and adherence to standards.[8]

Although the Council on Foundations is the only existing membership association focused on philanthropic policy, it does have peer organizations in the broader nonprofit sector. Other organizations, such as Independent Sector, the National Council of Nonprofit Associations, and the National Center for Responsive Philanthropy, and others, also maintain active policy initiatives.[9] However, these organizations (even those with statewide

---

[6] A quick scan of the web sites for the RAG members of the Forum on RAGs reveals that only six of them highlight public policy, government relations, or legislative affairs as part of their work. The six that note these services at the top level of services provided are Associated Grantmakers of Massachusetts, Donors Forum of Ohio, Council of Michigan Foundations, Northern California Grantmakers, Philanthropy Northwest, and Washington Regional Association of Grantmakers.

[7] North Carolina and Montana, for example.

[8] For more on the role of the state attorney general in overseeing charitable giving following the September 11 tragedies, see *The New York Times*, 2001 and Barstow, 2001.

[9] There are still additional organizations that need to be considered. Some of these, such as the Foundation Center and the Aspen Institute, are primarily research organizations. Others, including academic research centers such as the USC Center on Philanthropy and Public Policy, are also taking on more prominent profiles within the landscape.

affiliates) are primarily focused on the national level. As states become ever-more important actors in regulating philanthropy, the question arises: is the landscape of philanthropic policy agents out of alignment with the policy arenas in which representation matters?

A Panoramic View

> One can describe a landscape in many different words and sentences, but one would not normally cut up a picture of a landscape and rearrange it in different patterns in order to describe it in different ways. Because a photograph is not composed of discrete units strung out in a linear row of meaningful pieces, we do not understand it by looking at one element after another in a set sequence. The photograph is understood in one act of seeing…. (Meyrowitz, 1985)

The vitality of the philanthropic industry may depend most on considering the landscape of foundation associations as a whole, and not by its constituent pieces. The landscape as it relates to policy contains all of the types of associations noted earlier, as well as the independent organizations that focus on policy, and the temporal issue-based coalitions of foundations. As we try to understand the overall story of foundation associations, it is this broadest picture—the widest view—that will be most important. This is because we know that many foundations are members of many associations, that most foundations are members of no associations, and that we cannot, at this time, account for either the duplicates or the non-participants. This broadest view allows us to consider the overall role of associations regarding philanthropic policy.[10]

However, in trying to better understand the relationships between types of associations and philanthropic policy, we are going to slice through the photo in two ways to provide greater detail. First, we will take panoramic snapshots at the levels of the three major policy arenas: national, state, and local. We will then "zoom in" on each of these levels to look closely at examples of associations working on policy issues.

The National Perspective

At the national level, the landscape is dominated by industrywide organizations, structurally specific associations, and identity- or issue-based collectives. Key industrywide players on the national landscape include the

---

[10]This question of how to overlay the totality of foundation associations with the universe of foundations is a preeminent research question. Simply mapping the universe of associations—who they are and who are their members—is a critical first step to take.

Council on Foundations, the Foundation Center, and Independent Sector. These three provide data and research on the industry, advocacy on the national level, and key trade publications. Of the three, only the Council on Foundations limits its membership to grantmaking organizations or operating foundations. The Foundation Center's key audience is nonprofit organizations, and Independent Sector has both nonprofit and foundation members. Together, these groups are sometimes referred to as the infrastructure of philanthropy.

Also operating at the national level are several structurally specific organizations, such as the Association of Small Foundations, the National Center for Family Philanthropy, and Community Foundations of America. All three of these organizations were formed in the 1990s, and all serve constituencies once (and still) served by the Council on Foundations. Fueled by recent growth in these subsectors, each of these organizations developed to serve the specific needs of their membership. The Association of Small Foundations, which was both the fastest growing membership association and became the country's largest group in the late 1990s, serves foundations with few or no staff. These are estimated to constitute the majority of all foundations in the United States and to provide half of all American foundation grant funding. The National Center for Family Philanthropy is a resource center for donors, donor families, and family foundations.

The national level also supports issue-based and identity-based associations. Affinity groups of the Council on Foundations usually draw members from across the country. At least two national associations serve foundations that share common philosophies. The Philanthropy Roundtable serves a membership of foundations, trust officers, and individuals who value a vibrant private sector for its contributions to both voluntary service and wealth creation (www.philanthropyroundtable.org). At another point on the political spectrum, the National Network of Grantmakers is a membership association for individuals (many from foundations) who fund economic and social justice.

The Regional Perspective

RAGs have been part of the philanthropy landscape for decades, dating back to the late 1940s. Many got their start as informal networking associations of foundation executives. Their services now include networking, professional development, grantmaker directories, joint funding opportunities, and in some cases, policy analysis and advocacy on behalf of their membership.

A formal network of these associations, called the Forum of RAGs, operates at the national level. The Forum has twenty-nine members, and coordinates national programming such as the New Ventures in Philanthropy Initiative, an effort to promote philanthropy through RAGs.

The variety of configurations within the regional associations, however, diminishes the degree to which public policy can be a focus of their work. Only those that operate at the level of a single state are actually aligned with any meaningful public policy structures. Multistate and substate regional associations tend to have either too much territory to cover to actively work with state policymakers or too small a voice to be heard at the state capital.

The Local Perspective

At the local level, associations tend to be temporal, issue-specific, and structured as collaborative efforts, not membership groups. Examples of these efforts include a coalition of private and community foundations jointly addressing naturalization needs, or the Seattle area September 11 Task Force, which brought together foundations and individual philanthropists to share information, coordinate strategies, and assess needs related to three areas of interest following the terrorist attacks.

These groups often operate underneath any existing radar screen. Some of them, such as the Funders' Learning Community within the Bay Area School Reform Collaborative, are dedicated to a single issue. Their work may focus on joint funding or initiative development. Through this issue-based work, policy matters specific to the task at hand are often considered. One of the key strengths of these joint funding collaboratives is their expanded ability to consider and work on policy issues, a task that is often beyond the capacity of individual foundations.

Though they are not formal associations, understanding the role of these groups in the policy landscape is important for other reasons as well. First, they are trust-building resources. Foundation staff, board members, and individual philanthropists build their networks through these efforts. Second, they are seed grounds for future, more formal associations. Third, the expanded capacity of the group can reinforce a foundation's commitment to other groups, help them to recognize the power of the collective, and alert them to policy issues (philanthropic and otherwise) of which they might not otherwise be aware.

Many of these temporal, issue-based collectives have some connection to a RAG. Many are housed within the RAG, some emerge and move out of the RAG, and others manage their giving or arrange "pass-through" grants using the RAG infrastructure. The degree to which the RAGs control these groups, or even recognize the organizing potential that they represent, is uneven. The potential exists for these kinds of groups to add tremendously to a RAG's capacity, to help build membership, and to form the basis of a constituency should policy issues call for mobilization. Unmanaged, however, these groups also have the potential for "eating up" a RAG from within, siphoning off the energy of members, and actually growing up through and taking over part of the RAG's membership.

Another rapidly expanding feature of the local landscape is the proliferation of Social Venture Partnerships (SVPs). Started in Seattle, these now number more than twenty and can be found in metropolitan areas around the nation. They operate independently, but also are joined through a national federation coordinated out of the Seattle office. In addition to the formal SVP networks, there are several other giving circles operating in other ways, such as Social Ventures Silicon Valley (SV2), which operates out of the Silicon Valley Community Foundation.

These local giving circles are primarily focused on donor development and education. However, as they have grown in size and scope, they have become viable and active members of certain local philanthropic communities, holding places at the "local funders' tables." They also tend to be very well organized, make effective use of technology for communications purposes, and have individual members with both business and occasionally policymaking backgrounds. The proliferation of these groups calls on us to consider them as part of the landscape, and to learn more about how they may or may not participate as policy actors.

One key exception to the structures noted above are the substate RAGs, which we are defining as local in nature. These RAGs share much in common with their peers at the statewide or multistate level, and the Forum of RAGs considers them all of a type. We have separated them out from the statewide and multistate RAGs because of the differences a substate regional focus places on the RAG's capacity to act on policy issues. Clearly, a metropolitan area RAG has the potential to galvanize local funders and connect them with local policymakers. Whether or not a substate RAG can work effectively on state tax or regulatory issues (especially if there is more than one RAG in a state) raises other questions.

Table 1 displays the relationships between the focus of the work of foundation associations and the arena of that work (or the area from which the group draws membership). Groups or associations indicated in each category are intended as examples only. This is not an inventory.

Table 1. The Landscape as a Whole

Arena of work/membership		
Focus of work	**National**	**Regional (statewide or multistate)**	**Local (substate region)**
Industrywide	Council on Foundations Foundation Center Independent Sector		
Regional	Forum of RAGs	Regional Associations of Grantmakers	Several RAGs
Issue-based	Affinity groups (the arts, education, health)	Foundation Consortium for School Linked Services	Bay Area School Reform Collaborative, Midwest Community Ventures
Identity-based	Ethnic, race, gender	Chapters of some identity-based groups	Chapters of some identity-based groups
Structural	Association of Small Foundations National Center on Family Philanthropy SVP International	League of California Community Foundations	Social Venture Partner Networks

Zooming in

To better understand the ways in which associations act in policy arenas it helps to consider three examples. This section focuses in on three organizations, each operating at a different policy arena—national, regional, and local (substate)—and provides a brief introduction to their philanthropic policy activities.

National—The Council on Foundations

The Council on Foundations' status as the "grandmother" of all foundation associations can be seen in its longevity, its consistent representation of more than 50 percent of all foundation assets, and its role as birthplace for many of the other newly formed national associations. It also serves as the coordinating point for dozens of issue-based or identity-based affinity groups.

The Council has a dedicated focus on philanthropic policy. It is located in Washington, D.C. primarily because of its commitment to government relations on behalf of grantmakers. Its membership covers all structural types of foundations and includes some international representation. It does not include individual philanthropists as members.

The Council provides its members with legislative analysis, legal counsel, policy advocacy, and a seat at the table with policymakers and the associations that represent the broader nonprofit industry. It manages its policy work through a professional staff, board committees, a Legislative Action Network of members, and policy briefings for its members. It takes positions on legislative, regulatory, and tax issues on behalf of its members. The Council often submits comments for congressional review, responds to requests for public input on regulatory proposals, and briefs individual members of the House and Senate.

Regional—The Council of Michigan Foundations Public Policy Initiative

The Council of Michigan Foundations (CMF) is one of only ten single-state, statewide RAGs in the Forum of RAGs network. In addition to the member services, professional development, publications, and joint funding opportunities that it offers its members, CMF also provides an array of services focused on policy issues. These services include the Michigan Public Policy Initiative, Annual Capitol Hill visits, workshops and briefings for legislators and policymakers, and philanthropic policy research such as a study on foundation payout. The Council also provided a statewide download site for the White House Conference on Philanthropy in 2000. As part of another effort, "legislative connections," the Council helped foster one-to-one relationships between foundation staff or board and state representatives.

The Michigan Public Policy Initiative is an effort to educate newly elected term-limited legislators on the public policy issues that directly impact

Michigan's nonprofit organizations (www.cmif.org/legislativepage.htm). At various points in the past (although not currently), CMF also has organized meetings between foundation representatives and the State Attorney General. The Council is known for being proactive where policy matters are concerned. It recognized the educational challenges for policymakers that term limits create, and activated its network to build relationships with new legislators. The Council is active at the national level through the Forum of RAGs and also takes advantage of numerous opportunities to engage in international exchange as well.

The Michigan experience with public policy grew into a four-state effort focused on policy and economic development. In 2006, foundations and regional associations from Michigan, Ohio, Illinois, and Indiana came together to create MidWest Community Foundation Ventures. The project aims to use the collective knowledge, networks, and influence of community foundations to improve the communities and economies in the region.

Local—The Bay Area School Reform Collaborative

The Bay Area School Reform Collaborative (BASRC), now known as Springboard Schools (www.springboardschools.org), was one of several "Annenberg Challenges" around the country. The Bay Area version, led by both the Annenberg and Hewlett Foundations, focused on school reform in several counties bordering San Francisco Bay. While much of the work was focused on direct change efforts within individual schools, the collaborative also emphasized reform of school district and county education policies. As such, it had three main areas of activity: informing BASRC schools and funders about state policy, helping to create policy contexts that assist the implementation of BASRC school reforms, and informing policy leaders about successful school change strategies.

BASRC maintained several learning communities, one of which focused on funders. This community, which included representatives from dozens of foundations, hosted learning sessions on system reform, jointly investigated school improvement strategies, and held occasional institutes for the broader Bay Area philanthropic community. This local network served as an information source on local school policies. Its links to the national network of "Annenberg Challenge" communities also provided members with resources on federal education policy and initiatives nationwide.

The work of the Collaborative did not directly focus on philanthropic policy. In this way it was quite representative of most local funder networks. What it did do is help create relationships between the sectors, facilitate an understanding of the process and priorities on both sides of the table, and educate foundation executives about public policy related to schools. It also provided a robust network of grantmakers with experience considering public policy as part of their work. These same characteristics can be found in networks focused on the environment, community development, sustainable growth, health, and other issues.

Associations and Public Policy

These three levels of analysis—national, state, and local—plus an international lens, are important for considering the role of foundation associations and public policy. Several of the strategies identified above regarding philanthropic policy are also key to associations' work on public policy: information gathering and dissemination; pooled funding; meetings with researchers, policy experts, and policymakers; and public awareness campaigns. Associations offer individual foundations interactions with policymakers that they may not be able to access on their own. Associations and networks of funders also represent greater potential resources for the issues at hand than any single foundation brings to a discussion.

Critical Junctures

The last decade has seen tremendous change in the simple national/ regional structure of foundation associations. At the national level, several new associations formed in the 1990s. At the regional level, the growth of formal and informal associations also has been quite rapid. Accurate data on subnational associations are very hard to find. Anecdotally, we know that applications for membership in the national network of regional associations (the Forum of RAGs) have been on the increase and also reflect a wide variety of institutional structures and maturity.

What is striking about this growth and diversification of associations is that it represents both a coming together and a fragmenting of the foundation industry. Foundations band together, but they seem to be doing it in ever more specific (and perhaps temporal) ways. Large umbrella associations such as the Council on Foundations have experienced splintering efforts that have led to new organizations for community foundations, small foundations, and family foundations.

In addition to the splintering process that marked the 1990s, each of the regional associations and national organizations has several subgroupings within their bounds. Many RAGs, for example, host working groups on certain issues, or have identity-based subgroups. This type of subassociation is interesting, as they seem to be the groundwork for splinter groups down the road.

Even as the number of associations expands, their cumulative reach does not seem to extend very far. While disaggregated data on membership across all associations are not readily available, we estimate that formal associations of all types noted above account for probably no more than 10,000 separate foundation members.[11] This means that, taken together, known associations represent less than 20 percent of all foundations in the country. Since there are more than 70,000 foundations in the United States, no single association can claim to speak for the majority of the industry. Even taken as a whole, the associations of foundations are barely representative of the universe of foundations.[12]

Geographic Alignment

Just as policymaking occurs at national, state, and local levels (see Chapter 1), foundation associations come in a variety of geographic constructions. On issues of philanthropic policy, we have noted a proper alignment of significant policy monitoring and analysis capacity at the national level, in line with the role of the U.S. Congress and the Internal Revenue Service in philanthropic regulation.

We also have noted that there is much less capacity for this work at the state level, even though all states have some regulatory oversight of philanthropic giving. Of the six regional associations of grantmakers that emphasize policy, government relations, or legislative action in their own materials, only three are organized to serve a single, entire state. Two others serve multistate regions and the fifth serves a substate area. Foundations in forty-seven of the fifty states are either being served by associations that do not

---

[11]This is a very generous estimate, as the duplication of membership from RAGs to the Council to affinity groups, and even other structural associations, is estimated to be significant. This figure, 10,000, represents a simple addition of available membership lists and does not attempt to account for the expected duplication. Noting the likely duplication, the actual number of foundations that participate in these associations would be lower.
[12]This observation tends to be countered by the larger associations who measure their representational level by value of foundation assets held in their membership. For the Council on Foundations, which has as its members a significant number of the nation's largest foundations, this measure is quite high, generally the Council's membership represents approximately 60–70 percent of all foundation assets.

emphasize policy or by RAGs that are not aligned with the current state-level policy arena.[13]

While most philanthropic policy is enacted at either the national or state levels, there are municipal decisions and policies that can profoundly influence the actions of local philanthropies. This influence is most likely to fall within a program area, not within the realm of overall philanthropic operations. For example, a dedicated city department with mandated funds for children's issues may influence the activities of funders in that county regarding youth services. City arts taxes may shape the ways local funders allocate arts dollars. Both of these examples are also indicative of the role funders can play in local policymaking. In both such instances, it is also possible that local foundations can influence the creation of these municipal supports.

Table 2. Aligning Associations with Philanthropic Policy

National level	Philanthropic policy body	Alignment issue
COF, NCFP, ASF, CFA	IRS Congress Executive Branch	Fragmentation
State level		
10 statewide, single-state RAGs	50 State legislatures 50 Governor's offices 50 Attorneys General 50 Tax boards	Insufficient coverage
Local level		
Issue-based and hybrid funder associations	Few governing bodies	No jurisdiction on philanthropic policy

[13]There is a growing movement toward regional thinking and policy action. In California, for example, the California Policy Forum brings together regional leadership initiatives, policymakers, citizens, and others to address land use, transportation, fiscal, and governmental policies that cannot be addressed adequately at either the local or state level. This type of work is funded by foundations, but is not being conducted by their formal associations. Ironically, the growing awareness of regional thinking may eventually work to the advantage of the existing associations of grantmakers. However, it is hard to imagine rapid change if we expect the policy arenas to become more regionally structured faster than the existing regional associations could change their structures. (Data from Forum of RAGs.)

These same issues of alignment need to be considered vis-à-vis foundation associations and public policy. The alignment of governing bodies and associational presence will vary from issue to issue. In education, for example, local bodies that can work directly with district or state officials may offer more impact for foundation associations. On climate or water resource issues, an international perspective may be necessary.

Why Associations Matter

Associations are potentially important tools for foundations as policy players because of the limitations on individual foundation action. As Ferris and Mintrom (2001) explain, individual foundations are prohibited from lobbying. Associations of foundations, however, are generally organized as 501(c)(3) nonprofits, and therefore have broader latitude for advocacy and lobbying.

However, traditional membership associations are not the only options. As noted above, foundations also support organizations such as Independent Sector or the National Center for Responsive Philanthropy that maintain active policy monitoring roles. Some foundations may join as members, others provide direct operating support. While these organizations have members, they are less focused on member services and more centered on policy and research as their core activities.

It is critical to consider different types of associations—independent organizations and temporal, issue-based foundation networks—and their potential as policy actors. Independent organizations have dedicated voices and resources to address policy issues. They will be the ones with the longer-term legislative and regulatory knowledge and relationships.

Issue-based networks have shown great resourcefulness in acting on various public policy issues. Issue-based associations of foundations are the greatest in number now, and seem to be growing most rapidly.[14] They are the forums in which the foundation board and staff meet on programmatic issues of concern, and may "cut their teeth" on collaborative work and policy analysis. They are often the groups that new funders seek out first.[15] They are the basis of trust-building and network creation that foundations will need to employ when it comes time to act on pending legislation or regulatory change.

---

[14]More research is needed. This conclusion drawn from initial research conducted for the Forum of RAGs.
[15]Again, more research is needed, but the issue subroups of RAGs have many new funder members—many join the larger philanthropic community through this programmatic interest doorway.

While we are not currently aware of non-membership-based associations of foundations focused on philanthropic policy, they have come and gone in past moments of public oversight or attention. As the industry diversifies, it is not difficult to imagine the creation of a network of foundations—or a more representative set of private grantmakers—that will take on philanthropic policy as its focus.

Degrees of Influence

It is important to determine where the potential for foundation associations lies as far as becoming policy actors. On the face of it, an association clearly expands on the ability of individual foundations simply by bringing to bear on an issue "the power of many." However, the proliferation of foundation associations may cause a backlash effect, as policymakers need to determine which association speaks for which elements within the philanthropic industry. The very existence of so many associations—coupled with the cumulative low penetration rate of all membership associations—may diminish the power of all, for clearly no one association represents the entire industry.

For an association to be an effective policy actor, the commitment to policy analysis and representation will have to be at a high level and have a consistent focus. Relationships need to be built with policymakers, staff capacity in analysis supported and developed, and membership interests defined and articulated. Associations that do not make these commitments of focus and persistence may find that their only real role in the policy sphere is as an address book or e-mail list to reach the potential constituents.

It also is important that the sphere of influence of any given association be aligned with the policy arena in which it portends to have influence. Substate RAGs may wield great influence at the municipal level, and be able to draw together funders and county-level government leaders very quickly. Such strengths make them viable players in helping their membership address issue-based policy matters. However, the municipal level is rarely a factor in affecting philanthropic policy. Even local arts taxes or children's funds affect the issues on which foundations work more than the regulatory nature of their industry.

Statewide RAGs are best aligned with the policy arena of attorneys general, departments of corporations, and state tax boards. National organizations are best aligned with the IRS and congressional committees with oversight of the tax and reporting codes. Having a properly aligned infrastructure will be key for the industry as major policy and regulatory challenges come along. This was true in the 1990s during the rapid growth of conversion foundations. It may be true in the twenty-first century if major challenges to reporting requirements or payout come along, new types of conversions start to take hold, or the growth of the commercial philanthropic sector continues to attract regulatory scrutiny.

The Limits of Associations

While the power of many may seem, at first glance, to outweigh the power of the few, this may not always hold true for membership associations. Membership associations must, by definition, serve their members. As they are often dependent on dues for revenue, growing the membership base is a key goal of most membership associations. As their memberships grow, the ability to serve the different types or to find a common policy voice becomes increasingly difficult. This is especially true in an industry as disparate as philanthropy, with many structural types, areas of focus, and operational preferences.

Membership associations that align with policy arenas affecting philanthropic policy and that have made significant commitments to building their capacity as policy actors can succeed. In other instances, there may be other types of associations that can move more quickly or employ policy tools other than just the representative voice of a membership group that have roles to play in shaping philanthropic policy. For example, the ability of a select group of foundations—dedicated to acting on certain policy issues—may be more effective because the group can speak with a single voice, its members may be able to acquire the access they need to key policymakers, and they can remain focused.

Another challenge for foundation associations is the interdependent nature of philanthropy. It is part and parcel of the nonprofit universe. Its members work across every facet of social concern and in every corner of the civic, scientific, educational, environmental, and health worlds. Many of its practitioners remain active in professional and corporate spheres. It is, in essence, interconnected in many ways and in many directions, and determining the limits of the policy realm is no easy task.

This interdependence also can be seen in the (changing) relationships between individual and institutional philanthropy. Individual donors may not favor policy programs that benefit foundations over those that benefit a broader range of charitable vehicles, because the individual may have vested interests in all of the vehicles. As commercial firms grow ever more active in the philanthropic sphere, they bring to bear not only their expertise in product development, marketing, and customer service, but they are also likely to be supported by the commercial firm's government relations staff or the political connections of top management.

The Future of Associations

Several foundation associations have taken time to consider the future. National organizations, regional associations, and groups formed along both identity and issues have been actively involved in "futuring" and strategic planning. Associations outside of philanthropy, and even associations of associations have been trying to identify key leverage points for the future work.[16]

In work done with several foundation associations over the course of 2001, Blueprint Research & Design identified several key trends that these organizations need to consider as they move into the next century. These include the rapid growth and diversification of philanthropic organizations, changing expectations about information and communication, the role of the media and growing levels of public awareness, and the growth in secondary industries (research organizations and consultants) serving foundations (Bernholz, 2000a and 2000b; see also Blau, 2001). As the types of organizations actively involved in philanthropy continue to diversify, the types of associations will also change. For example, in 2008 there were enough online giving marketplaces that they were regularly meeting to discuss their common issues—which include policy issues focused on Internet commerce, nonprofit reporting, international giving, donor intent, and disclosure practices. We now have an industry that has several clusters of associations of like organizations—what we may be headed toward are associations that truly cut across the sector—connecting commercial vendors to private foundations, giving marketplaces to the social entrepreneurship movement, and so on.

---

[16]See, for example, the American Society of Association Executives' (www.asaenet.org) work on the Digital Now, which takes a look at the implications of the information age on associations. ASAE also conducts research on demographics, communications, and other trends of import to associations.

Driven by these trends, existing foundation associations are altering business as usual, and new associations are coming into play. Foundation associations are considering alternative forms of revenue beyond membership dues. They are investing heavily in knowledge-sharing tools and communications models, and some are opening their doors to new types of members.[17] Based on preliminary research conducted for the Forum of RAGs and the Charles Stewart Mott Foundation, it also appears that temporal, issue-based associations of foundations are rapidly developing, giving circles of individual donors are proliferating, and blended associations that include individual donors, foundation grantmakers, consultants, and financial advisors also are appearing on the horizon.[18]

While the changing nature of associations noted above may respond to some of the change drivers, they raise questions about the ability of these associations in the policy arena. Temporary and fluid focus and membership may not prove to be an asset when policy issues arise. On the other hand, if foundations grow used to "associating for a cause" and then moving on, this might allow them to mobilize more quickly, provide more intense focus, and capitalize on other relationships to address policy challenges.

Research Opportunities

In considering the role of philanthropic associations in policymaking, this chapter opens up a new field of inquiry within foundation studies. As such, it asks many more questions than it answers. The following list of potential research topics reaches beyond the policy roles of associations, and asks several more basic questions about the landscape itself. Answers to these questions will further our ability to consider the roles for associations in policy.

The Landscape of Associations

- What types of associations are most prevalent? How old are most associations? How are they structured? What is their geographic reach?

- Why do foundations join associations? Why do they not join?

- Which types of associations are growing fastest? Why?

[17]For examples of each of the above, see the consulting work at Philanthropy Northwest, the post-September 11 work of the New York Regional Association of Grantmakers, and the information services at the Donors Forum of Chicago, and the membership lists of Philanthropy Northwest.
[18]Contact the Forum of RAGs for this research. For examples of each of these kinds of groups, consider the HIV Funding Collaborative, AOL Giving Tree Circles and SVP, and the Legacy Group.

- What is the membership reach of existing associations? How far do they reach? What types of philanthropic organizations do they include?

- Do new philanthropists seek existing associations or create new ones?

- How do these new associations interact with established associations?

Foundation Associations and Policymaking

- What associational structures facilitate policy work?

- What can we learn from new network analytic tools and methods that could inform, improve, or accelerate these pursuits?

- Are different types of associations more effective at different levels of policy?

- Who else, besides membership associations, plays active roles in philanthropic policy? How do the associations work with (or against) these players?

- Which associations do foundations expect to conduct policy work?

- What knowledge do public policymakers have of foundation associations?

- What strategies are effective in changing philanthropic policy?

- How does association action on policy issues influence individual action (and vice-versa)?

Conclusion

In the work that they do regarding philanthropic and public policy, associations provide important connections—critical junctures—between the public and private sectors. As an industry, we know very little about the nature of these associations. We have no complete inventory of them; know little about the common lifecycle, and even less about the reasons some foundations join and others do not. While research exists on the relationship between associational structure and effectiveness in policy work, we are unaware of efforts to apply this analysis to philanthropy.

There is a great deal of research to be done. Given the tremendous change underway in institutional philanthropy, the time is right to consider how the current infrastructure fits the new industry participants and where change may soon be felt. This chapter raises some initial questions about the levels of alignment between existing associations and policy arenas, about the fragmentation of the associational landscape, and about the estimated reach of associations into the industry. Each of these issues is part of understanding how the industry works now, where it is headed in the future, and how it will shape and be shaped by public policy.

References

AAFRC Trust for Philanthropy. 2001. "Total Giving Reaches $203.45 Billion as Charitable Giving Contributions Increase 6.6 % in 2000." Press Release, May 23, 2001, available at www.aafrc.org/press3.html.

Barstow, David. 2001. "Victim's Families Lack Voice in Effort to Coordinate Relief," *The New York Times*. December 14, 2001, A1, B7.

Bernholz, Lucy. 2001. *Collective Wisdom*, Washington, D.C.: The Forum of RAGs and Blueprint Research and Design, Inc. available at www.rag.org.

Bernholz, Lucy. 2001. *Comparison Shopping*, Washington, D.C.: The Council on Foundations.

Bernholz, Lucy. 2000. *The Future of Foundations*, Los Angeles; University of Southern California, available at http://www.usc.edu/schools/sppd/philanthropy/forum/papers.

Blau, Andrew. 2001. *More than Bit Players*, New York, NY: Surdna Foundation, 2001, available at www.surdna.org.

Ferris, James, and Michael Mintrom. 2001. *Foundations and Public Policymaking: A Conceptual Framework*, Los Angeles, CA: University of Southern California.

Hamilton, Ralph. 2002. "Moving Ideas and Money: Issues in Funder Collaboration," prepared for the Funders Network, Chicago, IL: Chapin Hall Center for Children.

Mancuso, Anthony. 2001. *Eguide: Nonprofit Corporations: Qualify for Federal Income Tax Exemption*, Berkeley, CA: Nolo Press, Inc., May 2001, pp. 17–18.

Meyrowitz, Joshua. 1985. "The Blurring of Public and Private Behaviors," in *No Sense of Place: The Impact of Electronic Media on Social Behavior*, Oxford University Press.

New York Times, The. "Collaborative Charity," *The New York Times*. October 15, 2001.

Senate Bill 1300. 2001. Foundational and Corporate Charitable Giving Incentives Act of 2001, introduced by Senators Santorum and Lieberman. 107th Congress, 2001–2002.

Strom, Stephanie. 2002. "Universities Report Record in Private Contributions," *The New York Times*. March 22, 2002.

W. K. Kellogg Foundation, The. 2001. ePhilanthropy v2.001: *From Entrepreneurial Adventure to Online Community*, available at www.actknowledgeworks.net.

6

The Role of Foundations in Shaping Health Policy: Lessons from Efforts to Expand and Preserve Health Insurance Coverage

Thomas R. Oliver and Jason Gerson

Introduction

> More than any other societal institution, foundations are positioned to promote and foster innovation in improving the health and well-being of individuals, families, and communities. The remarkable independence they enjoy as a result of their legal status and endowments makes it possible for them to set aside considerations of popularity or profitability and move beyond preexisting agendas to promote social progress as they define it.
> (Prager, 1999, p. 1)

Foundations, according to their proponents, are not just another form of charity (Rogers, 1987). Instead, foundations are vital institutions that exercise private power for the public good (Lagemann, 1989; Knott and Weissert, 1995). Terrance Keenan of the Robert Wood Johnson Foundation (RWJF) asserted that foundations are dedicated to "underwriting the quest for solutions to basic problems affecting the common good" (1998, p. 1). In theory, then, there is a strong connection between the responsibilities and activities of foundations and those of government. The real test of their effectiveness is not solely what gets done with their grant money, but what they persuade others to do—especially government (Keenan, 1998, p. 2; Beatrice, 1993, p. 187).

Lauren LeRoy and Anne Schwartz of Grantmakers in Health have argued that any foundation can play a role in policy development. Yet philanthropic involvement with public policy is inconsistent and often tentative. A few foundations make public policy an integral part of their work; in many others, it is tangential to what boards and staff see as their core mission (LeRoy and Schwartz, 1998, p. 230). There are many reasons for this state of affairs. First, foundations generally believe that they should not relieve government of its responsibility to finance and implement social policy (Keenan, 1998, p. 2). Second, for many foundations the intrinsic conflict and controversy in public policy is uncomfortable. Third, foundations often interpret rules against lobbying on pending legislation as prohibiting their involvement in many other forms of advocacy. Dennis Beatrice, a former vice president of the Kaiser Family Foundation, has suggested that, "Foundations need to realize that advocating for attention to reform, filling information gaps, and educating policymakers and the public are perfectly acceptable foundation activities in the eyes of the Internal Revenue Service" (1993, p. 186).

Beatrice also argued that foundations tend to stay away from public policy because of their organizational history, habits, and staffing. Working with government is not their traditional mission and they are more used to working with health care institutions, community groups, or program demonstrations. Foundation officers without experience in government can be frustrated by unpredictable shifts in the policy process and lack of measurable progress toward their grantmaking goals. Most fundamentally, foundations have a different relationship with government than with grantees. To the degree that foundations can shape governmental agendas—a basic issue for this study—they must do so through persuasion since they have no formal authority (Beatrice, 1993, p. 186).

Foundations do bring important resources to the policy process. Although their funds amount to only 0.1 percent of all governmental health spending, their legitimacy and access to policymakers greatly extend the potential influence of their activities (Knott and Weissert, 1995, p. 150). They also develop significant expertise and information on the issues of the day. Foundations have been key participants in the "politics of knowledge," helping create new fields and institutions that influence policy decisions (Lagemann, 1989; Smith, 2002, p. 5).

Perhaps the most critical asset of foundations is their nearly complete freedom to select the issues they wish to address and the means of addressing them. According to David Rogers, the first president of RWJF, it is this independence of choice that makes foundations "unique and precious institutions in our cultural and social order" (1987, p. 194). Unlike governmental officials who must confront a wide range of issues and typically take a conservative posture, foundations can focus quite narrowly on a problem and inquire into radical solutions without direct constraints. Foundations have no explicit constituency—no stockholders, customers, or voters they must answer to (Weissert and Knott, 1985, p. 276). Compared to virtually any other institution in modern society, they are able to look beyond momentary conditions and take risks in their approach to social problems. If foundations have the appetite for risk and patience to fund projects in public policy, then regardless of the policy outcome, a guaranteed benefit is an added vitality to the democratic process (David, 2002).

This study seeks to highlight the commonalities as well as the distinct interests, resources, and strategies of foundations in the area of health policy. Grantmakers in Health is supported by more than 200 foundations and this analysis will not attempt to document the full range of their activities. It will instead review and compare the activities of a select number of national foundations, a new breed of state health foundations, and some local foundations that consciously participate in health policy matters.[1] Since the field of health policy is extraordinarily broad, this paper will focus its analysis on foundation activities aimed at expanding or protecting health insurance coverage. The issue is serious, persistent, and provides valuable insight into the connections between philanthropy and public policy.

Foundation Involvement in Health Policy Issues

Health is a priority area of focus for U.S. foundations. Based on a sample of over 1,200 of the largest foundations in the U.S., more than nine out of ten funders award grants in the health field. Foundations, nonetheless, account for only a tiny fraction of the more than $1.5 trillion spent annually on health services and programs in this country. Historically, this was not always the case. In the 1920s, spending by newly organized foundations was about 90 percent of federal government spending on health; by 1973 it fell to 16 percent; and by 1991 it amounted to only 0.4 percent of federal health spending (Weissert and Knott, 1995, p. 277).

[1]This study focuses on foundations that share the view that health insurance is a critical social good, and that the large and growing population of uninsured Americans is a serious problem that both warrants and requires governmental intervention. The study does not survey foundations or think tanks supported by philanthropy that approach the issue of health care coverage as, primarily, a question of the underlying values of our society and political system and that seek to minimize the responsibilities of government versus those of individuals and voluntary institutions. The allocation of philanthropic resources and strategies of actors on the more conservative side of this issue appear to differ significantly from those identified in this study.

The disproportionate weight of government funding as compared to foundation funding is evident even in California, which has large, prominent foundations dedicated to health grantmaking. Mark Smith, president of the California HealthCare Foundation (CHCF), points out that the $48 million the foundation spends in a year pursuing its mission to improve the health of Californians is less than the amount the state's Medi-Cal program spends every hour (M. Smith, 2001). So the main issue for foundations is how to leverage their comparatively limited resources in the health field (Grantmakers in Health, 2000; Ferris and Graddy, 2001).

As LeRoy and Schwartz (1998) observe, foundation support for health policy activities is only a small part of their overall interest in improving health and health services. The vast majority of health grantmaking goes directly to biomedical research, health care providers, and work on specific diseases (Beatrice, 1993; Atienza, 2008). Interest and funding commitments for health policy are increasing, however.

Grantmaking for health policy, like other issues, is concentrated among a small number of foundations. The top twenty-five funders of health policy in 2002 awarded 90.8 percent of the health policy grant dollars, basically unchanged from 1995. On its own, RWJF awarded 62.8 percent of all giving in health policy in 2002, up markedly from 44.6 percent in 1995. RWJF gave more than seven times the policy-related funding provided by the second-largest funder, the California Endowment (Lawrence, 2004). This study suggests that the leverage of foundations depends on much more than their financial assets. For example, the actual grants awarded underestimate foundation resources devoted to health policy, since several foundations have large, full-time professional staffs or program administrators active in health policy research, analysis, communications, and sometimes direct involvement in activities such as legislative testimony. In addition, the cumulative impact of an increasing number of small foundations dispersed across many communities is greater than a few large foundations with equivalent funding capacity.

Health Insurance Coverage: A Paramount Challenge for Philanthropy and Public Policy

This chapter focuses on the role of foundations in efforts to protect and expand health insurance coverage. Foundations that engage this issue have moved into a complex, controversial area that is far different from making charitable grants to health care providers. The amount of resources needed to provide all citizens with health insurance coverage is enormous, and the role of governmental policy in this area is a matter of considerable dispute. Because health care is provided through both private insurance markets and public programs, this study examines foundation activities aimed at improving employer-sponsored coverage as well as activities aimed at bolstering public programs such as Medicaid and the State Children's Health Insurance Program (SCHIP).[2]

THE IMPORTANCE OF HEALTH INSURANCE

Insurance, of course, is neither the beginning nor the end of the road to good health. Many factors other than health services determine individual and population health status, including economic inequality, stress, childhood development, work status, social support, nutrition, and environmental hazards (e.g., Amick et al., 1995; Wilkinson and Marmot, 2000). Nonetheless, health insurance coverage is a significant private and public good. Insurance coverage, whether from a public or private source, is a critical step in assuring equitable access to health services (Schoen et al., 1997; Berk and Schur, 1998; Institute of Medicine, 2001). The uninsured make fewer visits to the doctor, use emergency room care more frequently, and are more often hospitalized for chronic conditions than their insured counterparts (Blumberg and Liska, 1998). The uninsured are also several times more likely than insured individuals to lack a usual source of care, delay or not receive needed care, or fail to fill a prescription due to the costs. Compared to insured individuals, fewer of the uninsured report that they are in excellent or very good health and more report that their health is only good, fair, or poor (Kaiser Commission, 2002, pp. 5–6).

The costs of going without health insurance manifest themselves in many ways. The uninsured have later intervention and poorer outcomes from cancer, cardiovascular disease, diabetes, and other specific diseases. Babies born to uninsured mothers have lower survival rates. Being uninsured reduces the use of medical care by as much as 50 percent and, if individuals are uninsured for long periods of time, they have a significantly higher risk of dying (Institute of Medicine, 2003; Dorn, 2008). Since individuals in poorer health suffer reduced productivity and earnings, health insurance coverage also has general economic benefits (Hadley 2002).

---

[2]Although it is beyond the scope of this study, prescription drug benefits emerged as a complementary and, at times, a competing issue in health care coverage after 1999. In recent years, prescription drug costs have risen dramatically and become a major focus of reform efforts for private insurers, for state programs, and for the federal Medicare program. The issue gained its own place on the policy agenda and, in some ways, diverted attention and resources away from those without any form of health insurance (Oliver, Lee, and Lipton, 2004).

HEALTH INSURANCE COVERAGE: THE POLICY CONTEXT

In the fifteen years since President Clinton sought to secure health insurance for all Americans, coverage has generally moved in the opposite direction intended by the president and underlying public opinion (Jacobs and Shapiro, 1995). In response to the growing problems many Americans have in obtaining or maintaining health care coverage, political leaders continue to feel pressure to address the issue (Calmes, 2007). The scope and methods of health insurance reform are considerably different than in 1993, however. Incremental and largely bipartisan proposals and reforms with far lower expectations have replaced the comprehensive, often partisan initiatives seen from the late 1980s until the downfall of the Clinton plan.

Despite these incremental initiatives, the ranks of uninsured Americans grew for twelve consecutive years prior to 1999 and then, after a brief hiatus, continued to rise almost inexorably. Between 1994 and 1998, the number of uninsured rose from 39.8 million to 43.9 million before declining to 42.1 million in 1999 (Hoffmann and Pohl, 2000, p. 5). A combination of tight labor markets, rising incomes, and expanding enrollment in SCHIP further reduced the number of uninsured to 39.8 million between 1998 and 2000. In that period, 2.6 million additional low-income Americans below 200 percent of the poverty level—including 1.6 million children—became insured (Holohan, 2002). Then, as the economy slowed, the trend reversed itself and the uninsured population rose in 2001 to 41.2 million (Mills, 2002, p. 2). Despite an improving economy, 3.4 million more Americans became uninsured between 2004 and 2006 (Holohan and Cook, 2008). By 2006, nearly 47 million individuals were uninsured at any given time, and 89.6 million—one out of every three Americans under age 65—had no health insurance for some or all of the two-year period from 2006–2007 (Families USA, 2007).

Certain populations are especially at risk of being uninsured. An estimated 30 percent of young adults age 19–29 (Collins et al., 2006), 31 percent of the poor, 33 percent of Hispanics, 19 percent of Blacks, and 18 percent of Asian and Pacific Islanders were uninsured in 2005. In contrast, 11 percent of children (age 0–18), 11 percent of Non-Hispanic Whites, and only 0.8 percent of older adults (age 65 and older) were uninsured (DeNavas-Walt et al., 2006). More than 50 percent of the uninsured are adults without dependent children (Kaiser, 2007).

There is also considerable variation in insurance coverage across states. In the period between 2003 and 2005, the percentage of residents who were uninsured ranged from about 9 percent in Minnesota to nearly 25 percent in Texas (DeNavas-Walt et al., 2006). Some observers of state health policy have concluded that only a small number of states have the necessary combination of economic capacity and political will to make significant steps toward universal health insurance without major financial support from the federal government (Oliver and Paul-Shaheen, 1997; Holohan and Pohl, 2002). Even if a large number of states were able and willing to provide insurance for the "gap" population—those who depend on Medicaid, SCHIP, or state-subsidized coverage—it would have to include the right states to "move the needle" on overall coverage (Colby, 2002). Over 40 percent of uninsured Americans live in just four large states—California, Texas, New York, and Florida (Dubay et al., 2003).

Where there are low numbers of uninsured individuals, there is almost certainly a strong base of employer-sponsored coverage. But over time, there has been relative erosion in private sector coverage. During the late 1990s, marginal gains in private insurance coverage occurred in the midst of the strongest economy and tightest labor market in over three decades. The national unemployment rate fell to 4.1 percent in late 1999, less than half the rate of a decade earlier. Yet, the proportion of the nonelderly population insured through employer-sponsored health plans decreased overall in the 1990s and continued to decline even more rapidly after 2000 (Fronstin, 2000, p. 1; Kaiser, 2007). Periods of strong economic growth and employment have not translated into substantial reductions in the number of uninsured because even workers who maintain employer-sponsored coverage have been forced to shoulder a larger proportion of health insurance costs (Schroeder, 1999, p. 10; Fronstin, 1998; Levitt et al., 1999, p. 4). In addition, the increasing gap in the wages of skilled and unskilled workers corresponds to a parallel gap in health insurance coverage (Kilborn, 1999; Kaiser Commission, 2002). Increasing enrollment in public health insurance programs, particularly Medicaid and SCHIP, has not fully offset the erosion of employer-sponsored coverage.

FOUNDATIONS AND SOLUTIONS FOR THE UNINSURED

A key problem facing the policy community, including foundations concerned with gaps in insurance coverage, is that many individuals do not take coverage offered to them in private or public programs. Thus, foundations are faced with two basic challenges. First, they must support strategies to improve take-up rates for existing programs. Second, they must also help develop initiatives to provide insurance coverage for individuals who do not currently qualify for employer-sponsored or public programs.

As veteran health policy entrepreneur Paul Ellwood has noted, there is no single button to push to change the American health care system (Oliver, 2004). The vast majority of health care organizations and clinicians are in the private sector, not in government. In 2001, 177 million Americans had employer-sponsored insurance while fewer than half as many, 71 million, had coverage through Medicare, Medicaid, and other public programs (Mills, 2002). Even though initiatives that encourage small employers to offer and contribute to their workers' insurance coverage repeatedly have disappointing results, most Americans' faith in employer-sponsored coverage remains unshaken (Gusmano et al., 2002; National Public Radio, 2002).

In addition, within the public sector the policy environment is fragmented, with some major programs at the federal level (Medicare, veterans, military, Indian Health Service) and others shared between the federal government and the states (Medicaid, SCHIP). There is clearly an expectation that states will continue to have significant authority in the design and implementation of health insurance programs (Thompson, 2001; Dubay et al., 2003). A major focus of this chapter, therefore, is to understand how foundations decide to allocate their resources to private or public initiatives, and whether they give priority to policies and programs at the national, state, or community level.

Finally, when funders take on the issue of health insurance, they face the political challenges inherent in economic redistribution and governmental regulation. On the face of it, health insurance is an important and popular issue. In October 2002, when asked which was the most important health issue for the president and Congress to deal with, 35 percent of poll respondents answered "increasing the number of Americans covered by health insurance" (Kaiser Health Poll, 2002). The issue received considerably more support than helping seniors pay for prescription drugs (23 percent), financially bolstering Medicare (21 percent), or protecting patients' rights in HMOs (10 percent).

Expanding health insurance, however, requires that the healthier and wealthier members of society subsidize less fortunate members. And, programs to accomplish such an end are inevitably accompanied by a host of rules regarding eligibility for the subsidies, methods of holding down the costs of services for the newly insured, financial accountability for the transfer payments, and so forth. Because redistributive and regulatory policies are highly contentious (Lowi, 1964; Wilson, 1973, 1980), foundations and others advocating for policy change must be prepared for organized resistance, controversy, and long-term commitment if they wish to deliver solutions for the persistent problems of the uninsured. In addition, they must accept the loss of control that comes with entering a bigger arena with more uncertainty (Schwartz, 2003).

In the end, most foundations find themselves funding a combination of activities—public and private, and at different levels of the system. Some grants support policy or program development aimed at long-term systemic change, while other grants support the delivery of discrete, short-term services (California Endowment, 1997; Schacht, 1998; Schwartz, 2003). While this chapter focuses on foundation efforts to change public policy, it is important to recognize that support for direct services may at times be a logical complement and not a competitor to systemic solutions.

Allocation of Foundation Resources

Foundation resources include money, knowledge, personal connections, leadership skills, and prestige. In other words, the capacity of foundations to influence public policy extends well beyond their financial assets. Yet in their written reflections or in direct conversations, foundation leaders demonstrate an acute awareness of the limits of their own organization's resources. They recognize quite clearly that the strategic choices of board members and staff can multiply or diminish the impact of foundation programs on social problems. The term they invoke most often is "leverage." For foundations that monitor public policies and programs, what are the strategies that can leverage their modest resources into new courses of action and better system performance? James Ferris and Michael Mintrom (Chapter 2) and Grantmakers in Health (2000) suggest a number of activities that foundations can engage in:

- Generate and disseminate data and policy analysis

- Improve public understanding of health issues

- Educate current and future policymakers and issue experts

- Support development, implementation, and evaluation of demonstration programs

- Serve as a builder of policy networks and convener of participants

- Provide a voice for vulnerable groups

- Collaborate directly with governmental agencies

- Shape policy implementation

- Support direct services

These diverse activities fit into three basic strategies for shaping public policy:

1) Educate the public and members of the policy community.

By definition, the issues that come before government have not been solved through private transactions or by voluntary collective efforts. They are complex and it is often the case that solving one part of a problem creates other, unintended problems (e.g., Oliver, 1999).

Information is critical, therefore, for the purposes of what Lawrence Brown (1991) calls "documentation," "analysis," and "prescription." It is needed to accurately define the full scope and magnitude of a problem—for example, how insurance coverage varies by family income, the size of firms, or type of industry. It is also important in analyzing the likely outcomes of policy proposals—for example, are subsidies adequate or will people who are eligible for public coverage still not enroll due to stigma. Finally, in the political marketplace where preferences are not fixed but instead depend on the available "products" (Riker, 1986; Jones, 1989), policy proposals themselves are an important form of information and education.

Foundations are influential, some argue, if they supply accurate and balanced information for health care purchasers, governmental officials, and ordinary citizens in a market that is dominated by large, commercial interests (Altman, 1998). Their research and analysis can validate or invalidate the claims of self-interested parties and encourage debate to rely more on facts and experience than on ideology. A foundation must earn credibility through well-designed work, but it has the advantage of being viewed as "a broker of objective information … with no axe to grind, no turf to defend" (Van Dusen and Nash, 2000).

2) *Invest in the development and demonstration of new institutions and policy options.*

Students of the policy process have long observed that the prospects for governmental action increase dramatically when there is an available, worked-out solution to the problem as it is defined (Walker, 1977, 1981; Eyestone, 1978). Many foundations see a primary role for themselves in "product development" for government, especially on politically charged issues where public officials are reluctant to take the first steps (Beatrice, 1993). Since foundations are viewed as being more nonpartisan than other prominent sources of policy proposals, such as interest groups or think tanks, their ideas may have more face validity to wary policymakers.

A proposed solution must adequately meet the tests of technical feasibility, economic feasibility, and political feasibility (Kingdon, 1984). Policymakers are far more likely to support a given proposal if they see there is substantial consensus among experts on its technical feasibility. Since there is usually considerable disagreement among experts on complex issues in health policy (Walker, 1981; Brown, 1991), real-world demonstrations can help push an innovation forward.

Foundations are often able to develop an idea and put it to the test long before government is ready to sponsor a demonstration of its own; as "venture capitalists," foundations "run interference" or "prime the pump" for future policy development (Weissert and Knott, 1995; Keenan, 1998; Davis, 1999). RWJF, for example, supported the creation of several state health care commissions in the late 1980s and early 1990s, which provided elected officials with carefully developed proposals that combined major expansions of insurance coverage, cost controls, revenue sources, and regulatory oversight into packages that had a realistic chance of enactment under the right political conditions (Schoen, 2002; Oliver and Paul-Shaheen, 1997, pp. 739–40).

Demonstrations are typically the most expensive form of product development for public policy; they are also the most difficult to organize, operate, and evaluate. But a 1993 survey of congressional, federal agency, and interest group staff found that all participants valued the results of demonstrations more highly than those of commissions or other policy reports (Weissert and Knott, 1995, p. 282).

3) Support capacity-building and advocacy efforts.

As noted earlier, foundations are prohibited from lobbying on pending legislation. This is a relatively narrow restriction on their activities, however, and many leaders have expressly committed themselves to other forms of advocacy work. Typically, they provide funds and technical assistance to enable other organizations to build coalitions, coordinate strategy, and pressure public officials for changes in policy and program budgets (Holton, 2002).

Foundation staff may also work directly with governmental agencies charged with program implementation, or support groups monitoring governmental performance and even mounting legal challenges to policies and program decisions. Most commonly, foundations act as patrons of individual advocacy groups (Walker, 1991; Knott and Weissert, 1995) or help convene different groups to build networks and coordinate resources devoted to their priority issues (Prager, 1999, p. 13; Ferris and Mintrom, 2002, p. 21).

The three basic strategies are not mutually exclusive, and foundations often use all three when they mount major initiatives to address problems as daunting as improving health insurance coverage. In many cases, the strategy or mix of strategies that will yield the greatest return on foundation investments is not self-evident (Schroeder, 1998, p. 212).

Foundation Strategies for Shaping Public Policy on Health Insurance Coverage

The analysis that follows is based on in-depth profiles of twelve foundations that were actively engaged in the issue of health insurance coverage during the late 1990s and early 2000s. Five of the foundations operate at the national level: Commonwealth Fund, Henry J. Kaiser Family Foundation, W.K. Kellogg Foundation, David and Lucile Packard Foundation, and Robert Wood Johnson Foundation (RWJF). Three relatively new foundations operate primarily at the state level: the California Endowment, the California HealthCare Foundation (CHCF), and the California Wellness Foundation (TCWF). Four foundations operate primarily at the local level: Alliance Healthcare Foundation of San Diego, Consumer Health Foundation of Washington, D.C., Rhode Island Foundation of Providence, and Rose Community Foundation of Denver.

The profiles describe the distinctive philosophies, strategies for shaping health policy, and selected initiatives of each foundation to protect or expand health care coverage. Along with different strategies for program development, the foundations exhibited tremendous variation in terms of their resources, staff size, organizational structure, management style, and approach to grantmaking.

Taken together, the foundation activities described in this study establish a fairly comprehensive range of strategies for influencing public policy. The following sections examine what patterns emerged from the allocation of foundation resources and what those patterns suggest about foundation preferences and capabilities for improving health insurance coverage. They present an overview of the choice of issues, audiences and partners, jurisdictions, and stages of involvement in the policy process. Table 1 provides a summary of foundation strategies and priorities in the policy arena.

CHOICE OF ISSUES

A fundamental element of foundation strategy is the selection of issues to address. Jack Knott and Carol Weissert (1995) suggest that allocating resources among issues is the most troublesome part of decisionmaking for foundations and other participants in the policy process. They highlight two important dimensions to this selection process: 1) timing of entry into an area; and 2) consistency of funding in that area once it's selected as a foundation priority. They characterize foundations as "pioneers," "explorers," "ranchers," or "itinerants," based on the issues they focus on and the timing and duration of their funding.

It is clear that most if not all of the foundations included in this study became "ranchers" and put down stakes on this issue for the long run. They are doing so because, as Steven Schroeder, former president of RWJF argued, universal health insurance coverage is "central to the values and moral character of a country" (Iglehart, 2002, p. 246). They are also doing so because the scope and magnitude of the uninsured population and the spillover effects on health status and economic well-being make it "a problem you can't ignore" (Laws, p. 2002). Among the major national foundations with a historical commitment to health policy and problems of the uninsured in particular, the Pew Charitable Trusts is the only one that has left the issue to others and moved on to a new strategic agenda (Rimel, 1999; Byrnes, 2000).

All of the national and state foundations in this study have, to varying degrees, decided to take a leadership role in keeping the issue of health care coverage alive. The RWJF Covering the Uninsured campaign, the Commonwealth Task Force on the Uninsured (transformed into the Program on the Future of Health Insurance in 2005), the Kaiser Commission on Medicaid and the Uninsured and its public opinion polling, and funding by TCWF and the California Endowment of annual reports on insurance coverage in California are all examples of foundations' long-term commitment to substantial reductions in the uninsured. Ruth Riedel, former president and CEO of the Alliance Healthcare Foundation in San Diego, said that it chose to focus on the uninsured specifically because of a lack of political leadership on the issue. Every foundation has been involved in different activities aimed at improving coverage in existing insurance programs—the "maxing out" strategy described by David Colby of RWJF.

All of the foundations also committed themselves to working through both the private and public sectors. This, too, is pragmatic: Cathy Schoen of Commonwealth pointed out that their grantmaking priorities do not necessarily reflect a philosophy that employer-sponsored coverage is better, but that the system still works reasonably well for the majority of Americans and shifting large numbers of people into public insurance programs would require explicit new revenue sources to replace the existing tax expenditures for employee health benefits (Schoen, 2002). Some of the "strange bedfellows" in the RWJF campaign hold the premise that success in expanding coverage would require both larger enrollment in public programs as well as tax credits or other inducements for individuals and employers. The initiatives funded by national, state, and local foundations such as those in Rhode Island, San Diego, Ventura, and Denver all sought to increase the number of employers who offered coverage and the number of their employees who took up the offer of coverage for themselves and their families.

Even if foundations are sometimes reactive in their issue priorities—for example, their nearly universal efforts to facilitate enrollment in SCHIP—their grantmaking style is often highly proactive. All of the foundations included in this study are engaged to a considerable degree in strategic grantmaking; that is, creating initiatives with dedicated funding and carefully chosen partners rather than primarily responding to unsolicited proposals. Kaiser, Commonwealth, and the CHCF provide only modest amounts of funding for projects outside their established initiatives.

It is not necessarily the case, however, that all foundations become more directive as their assets, expertise, and experience grow. TCWF has in fact pulled back from strategic grantmaking, opting instead for a "responsive grantmaking" approach, in which projects are initiated primarily by community and advocacy groups.

CHOICE OF AUDIENCES AND PARTNERS IN THE POLICY PROCESS

Lucy Bernholz has observed that foundations are "infamous individualists" in their grantmaking priorities and strategies (see Chapter 5). Ferris and Mintrom (see Chapter 2) argue that individualism is a liability for foundations that want to find points of leverage in public policy. To accomplish their objectives, they must cultivate relationships and establish their credibility and reliability with a wide range of audiences and partners. These can include the general public; trade associations, advocacy groups, and community leaders; governmental agencies and officials; mass media; and other foundations.

General Public

Of the national foundations, RWJF, Kellogg, and Kaiser most clearly consider the general public as an audience for their initiatives. RWJF intentionally structured the series of six reports it commissioned from the Institute of Medicine (IOM) to increase the amount and scope of coverage of the IOM's findings in the mass media. It also sponsored ad campaigns and, in 2003, it mounted a Cover the Uninsured week to increase public awareness. The Kaiser Health Polls and general coverage of health insurance issues through Kaisernetwork.org were intended to reach the general public when health-beat reporters around the country pick up information and pass it on to their local readers and listeners. Kellogg's work with the National Leadership Coalition on Health Care used social marketing techniques to raise awareness about the uninsured in general; and the institute it established at the Joint Center for Political and Economic Studies uses opinion polls, public forums, and other means to focus attention on insurance coverage for African Americans and other minorities. TCWF used its annual report on The State of Health Insurance in California as a "hook" to gain media coverage across the state; advocates at the local level then take advantage of the coverage to give the issue a local spin (Holton, 2002).

All four of the local foundations viewed the general public as an audience for their initiatives. The Alliance Healthcare Foundation's San Diegans for Health Coverage was explicitly committed to informing and educating the public about health insurance issues using opinion polls and media campaigns. The Rose Community Foundation's Colorado Consumer Health Initiative, the Rhode Island Foundation's support of the Ocean State Action Fund, and much of the Consumer Health Foundation's grantmaking involved consumer-oriented projects that made educating the public a key goal.

Observers and advocates for the uninsured might question why foundations will spend significant amounts of their resources on general public education, when the debate over health insurance tends to fall apart in the politics of policy formulation. When foundations have the ability to throw their weight around with tens or even hundreds of millions of dollars to help move the issue forward, public education appears to be an indirect and timid use of those resources.

Advocacy Groups

Trade associations and other advocacy groups are a primary audience for all of the national foundations. The reports of the Commonwealth Task Force on the Future of Insurance were aimed at these groups as well as at researchers, legislative staff, and program specialists in government agencies. They are an important constituency for the Kaiser Commission's reports and Kaisernetwork.org news summaries, poll findings, and webcasts of health policy events. The California HealthCare Foundation's Small Business Health Insurance Resource Center and its daily online California Healthline newsletter were targeted primarily at the business community, health care organizations, and advocacy groups.

Public policy scholars have noted how foundations are important "patrons" of interest groups (Kingdon, 1984; Walker, 1991). The activities of foundations in the area of health insurance coverage indicate that there is often a much stronger relationship, with foundations and advocates joining forces as strategic partners on specific initiatives. In its work on children's health insurance, Packard established a number of such relationships, including national organizations such as Families USA and the Center for Budget and Policy Priorities, as well as state organizations such as Consumers' Union and Children Now. Kellogg also engaged Families USA to provide technical assistance in many states and alert policymakers to options for expanding Medicaid coverage to uninsured parents. Kellogg's major partnerships, however, have been with community-based institutions and organizations in its Community Voices program. The RWJF Covering the Uninsured campaign established ongoing partnerships with the Health Insurance Association of America, Families USA, the U.S. Chamber of Commerce, labor unions, and other major interest groups.

The California Endowment and TCWF, far more than the national foundations, have conducted their efforts on health insurance through advocacy organizations. TCWF developed strong partnerships with statewide groups such as the Western Center on Law and Poverty and the Children's Partnership on monitoring public health insurance expansions and developing the "express lane eligibility" program for Medicaid and SCHIP. The Endowment's 100% Campaign for universal coverage of children in California was led by three nonprofit advocacy groups. TCWF, like Kellogg, puts far more emphasis on true grassroots activity than the average foundation. It exerted influence on national, state, and local policies through its support of the interfaith Pacific Institute of Community Organizations (PICO) and its thirteen local chapters. The California HealthCare Foundation brought together representatives from state business groups but ultimately did not get much assistance from them in its campaign to expand insurance coverage for small firms and self-employed individuals. Ruth Holton, former policy director of TCWF, argued that, in California at least, the most effective strategy for advocacy is to link the technical expertise and professional connections of statewide organizations with community-based, grassroots organizations who can "put a face on the issue" for state legislators or county boards of supervisors (Holton, 2002a, p. 16).

Establishing partnerships with advocacy groups is a primary strategy for all four local foundations. The Consumer Health Foundation, like TCWF and Kellogg, has carried out most of its work on health insurance through advocacy organizations. It supported virtually all of the advocacy groups working on health care issues in the D.C. region as a way of improving access and coverage in the area. The Rhode Island Foundation's Leadership Roundtable on the Uninsured and its support for the Ocean State Action Fund involved partnerships with consumer, provider, and health advocacy groups, as well as union and business leaders. The Rose Community Foundation supported the Colorado Consumer Health Initiative, a diverse coalition of more than fifty local and statewide consumer-based organizations aimed at strengthening the consumer voice in health policy discussions and decisions.

The relationships that foundations develop with advocacy groups are sometimes quite complex. Successful relationships take time to develop and run two ways. Grantmaking, therefore, must be viewed as building up political capital, not a series of independent, one-time expenditures. Eugene Lewit of the Packard Foundation observed that, "The advocacy groups have to be there when you need them.... You have to have relationships with them because nobody wants to feel used. So you can't just fund them when you need them." The fact is, however, that a given organization may be right for one initiative but not another. Foundations are also aware that long-term partnerships may be perceived as unfair to groups that did not receive funding the first time around. TCWF is sensitive to the shaky finances of most nonprofit advocacy groups and requires that a group can be funded for only two consecutive grant cycles, then it must let others compete for scarce dollars (Holton, 2002b).

Another challenge is that advocacy groups—like other grantees—have their own way of doing things and resist hands-on direction from a foundation. Lewit said that Packard, for example, recognized the importance of creating a vibrant advocacy community: "There's a strong sense that advocacy groups are important for keeping these issues alive." At the same time, its board has focused on concrete results like insuring every child in Santa Clara County. So it is natural to want to steer grantees in a direction that foundation staff think will most quickly turn a promising process into real results. Margaret O'Bryon of Consumer Health Foundation also acknowledged that working with grassroots community-based organizations is long-term work. In some situations, advocates can be dogmatic and, through their inflexibility, actually prevent progress in policy formulation or implementation. In many states, for example, advocates for children are unalterably opposed to scaling back Medicaid benefits to afford an expansion of coverage to adults or to children with higher family incomes.

Governmental Officials and Agencies

Governmental officials and agencies are both an audience and active partners for foundation initiatives to expand health insurance. In addition to funding reports and newsletters that circulate throughout the health policy community, Commonwealth, Kaiser, RWJF, and the California HealthCare Foundation all have sponsored briefings in Washington through the Alliance for Health Reform, National Health Policy Forum, National Conference of State Legislatures, and other nonpartisan organizations that specialize in educating issue experts on Capitol Hill and in the federal agencies. They have underwritten study panels by the National Academy of Social Insurance and the Institute of Medicine that often generate explicit policy recommendations. The Urban Institute project on Assessing the New Federalism, funded by all of the national foundations included in this study except Kaiser, has provided regular data and evaluation for federal and state officials on Medicaid, SCHIP, and welfare reform. Through the National Health Policy Forum, Packard supported site visits for congressional staff to acquaint them personally with the Santa Clara Children's Health Initiative. In Sacramento, the National Conference of State Legislatures established a support center for legislators and staff with a grant from the California HealthCare Foundation.

Several foundations have worked directly with governmental officials or agencies as partners in their health insurance initiatives. Packard provided funds to the National Governors' Association and the National Academy of State Health Policy to provide technical assistance to state SCHIP directors, for example. Packard also invested heavily in a partnership with the federal Agency for Healthcare Research and Quality to evaluate the outcomes of SCHIP. The RWJF State Coverage Initiative built on planning grants from the federal Health Resources and Services Administration to state health agencies. The purpose of the RWJF grants was to push state coalitions and officials to move past the planning phase into actual expansions of health insurance coverage. Kaiser and Commonwealth, because they see themselves as information sources and not promoters of specific policy initiatives, do not have formal partnerships with government agencies. Their presidents are both former governmental officials, though, and they and other foundation staff regularly communicate with legislative and executive officials and are called upon to provide formal testimony to congressional committees.

Among the California health foundations, TCWF established a collaborative of nonprofit organizations to work with the state health department on implementation of Medicaid managed care reforms. More recently, TCWF, Packard, and the California Endowment started working with health, education, and social services agencies at the state and local levels to develop and implement "express lane eligibility" for enrollment of school lunch recipients in Medicaid and SCHIP. The Health-e-App technology developed by the California HealthCare Foundation in collaboration with Medi-Cal was designed to help streamline enrollment not only for children but all applicants for the state's health insurance programs.

To varying degrees, all four of the local foundations see government as an audience for their health insurance initiatives. The Rose Community Foundation's Hot Issues in Healthcare is the most explicit example, its primary goal being to directly educate state legislators through briefing sessions and other activities. Alliance's San Diegans for Health Coverage also aimed to educate policymakers, though its activities were somewhat more diffuse. Two of the local foundations have worked directly with government as partners in health insurance initiatives. The Rose Community Foundation worked with Colorado state officials to establish Child Health Advocates in order to take on administration of the state's SCHIP. The Rhode Island Foundation worked with state officials and agencies on a number of projects, most notably through its support for the Providence Smiles dental program and its purchase of the Neighborhood Health Plan of Rhode Island. Interestingly, the two foundations that have partnered with government have also tried to establish themselves as neutral, credible actors who are not pushing particular solutions or approaches.

Mass Media

All of the national and state foundations in this study have recognized the need to use the media to communicate messages about their priority issues to the public, industry, policymakers, or specialists in the field. The fundamental purpose of Kaisernetwork.org is to greatly expand the dissemination of policy-relevant information through a variety of media channels. According to Larry Levitt, the mass media improve the flow of information not only to the public and interest groups but also to governmental officials—who might miss another data-laden foundation study but must react to news coverage of policy issues in their home districts. RWJF has relied heavily on the mass media in its Covering the Uninsured campaign, especially the week of saturation coverage in 2003. RWJF and the California Endowment, for example, also allocated resources to "coach" their grantees to be media-savvy and effective in policy advocacy. Ruth Holton said that TCWF staff attempted to avoid the media spotlight and routinely referred the media to its grantees rather than comment on policy issues themselves.

Kaiser is the only national health foundation that had developed explicit partnerships with mainstream media organizations. It conducted opinion polls in collaboration with the *Washington Post* and National Public Radio, for example. It set up health programming on the major television networks, as well as Black Entertainment Television and MTV. Finally, it established programs to improve the quality of reporting on health policy and increase the number of minority journalists covering health issues.

Among the local foundations, two made modest but important investments in partnering with media organizations. Alliance provided ongoing support for a health reporter at the local public radio station, while the Rhode Island Foundation cosponsored a local public radio station to create a five-day program examining health care issues.

Other Foundations

The foundations in this study have a mixed record of collaboration with each other on health insurance initiatives. In general, Kaiser and Kellogg have not put a lot of effort into joint projects. Other foundations, including RWJF, claim to have been more commonly involved and enthusiastic about joint initiatives. David Rogers argued that, throughout its history, RWJF has valued collaboration with other foundations: "We were frequently most successful and our programs most durable if we collaborated with other partners in developing and following many of our major grantmaking efforts…. Our programs have often gained strength, legitimacy, and visibility through such collaborations." (1987, pp. 82–83)

Collaboration among funders increases the complexity of planning and decisionmaking, but according to Marcia Sharp it also has a number of advantages. An increase in financial support obviously increases the potential scale of the enterprise. Another advantage is that joint sponsorship provides a "safe haven" for the individual foundations who reduce their financial risk and increase their political cover by bringing on partners (Sharp, 2002; Hughes, 2002).

RWJF did not collaborate with other funders in planning its Cover the Uninsured Week, but it actively sought contributions to expand the impact of the initiative. As the lead organizer as well as underwriter, it even developed procedures to accept donations from other organizations—not something it is accustomed to doing (Colby, 2002). RWJF did team up with Packard and the Atlas Foundation to develop administrative options to expand children's health insurance coverage in California. Other initiatives in California are noteworthy for the involvement of several foundations. TCWF, California Endowment, and Packard all had important roles in the "express lane eligibility" program—first in its development, then in funding partial implementation during the state's budget crisis. The Endowment has underwritten the broader use of the online Health-e-App developed for Medicaid enrollment by the California HealthCare Foundation. While there is still competition among the California health foundations, collaboration was steadily increasing. The presidents were meeting quarterly and the policy directors were meeting informally on a monthly basis. In addition, TCWF and the Endowment began a partnership to support regional policy and advocacy training for their grantees.

Perhaps the most significant collaboration among foundations has taken place on local initiatives. The Alliance-led FOCUS program in San Diego to provide subsidized health insurance to low-income workers resulted in collaboration with the Endowment, the California HealthCare Foundation, and Commonwealth. Packard, the Endowment, TCWF, and the local Santa Clara Family Foundation worked together on the Santa Clara Children's Health Initiative to achieve universal coverage of all children in the county, regardless of immigration status. Kaiser supported case studies of the Santa Clara program's development. The Consumer Health Foundation helped to establish the Health Working Group of the Washington Regional Associations of Grantmakers to pool the resources of local funders to promote programs leading to "100% access, 0% disparity" throughout the region.

CHOICE OF JURISDICTIONS

As the section on foundation audiences and partners suggests, none of the national foundations included in this study have had an exclusive preference for activities in only one level of jurisdiction. Even those foundations with systematic preferences—Kaiser at the national level and Kellogg at the local level—have funded projects to generate information, policy development, or advocacy in other jurisdictions.

The Kaiser Commission and the Commonwealth task force focused their research and evaluation primarily on the national level, and the RWJF campaign on covering the uninsured was a national effort as well. The work that RWJF has sponsored at the Institute of Medicine and the Economic and Social Research Institute is intended to promote national models for expanding insurance coverage. Packard's work on children's health insurance included involvement with federal agencies as well as state program directors.

David Colby of RWJF observed that the nature of the issue and the current policymaking environment determine where foundations think they can make the most difference. In recent years, comments by their leaders confirmed that national foundations have devoted more resources to state- and community-level activities (LeRoy and Schwartz, 1998, p. 230).

RWJF and Kellogg created large national programs to support efforts by states and communities to expand insurance coverage. The RWJF Covering Kids program helped create advocacy coalitions in all fifty states; and its State Coverage Initiatives program supported state health agencies in implementing new proposals for insurance coverage. Kellogg's Community Voices program supported coalition-building and demonstration programs in thirteen local "learning laboratories" across the U.S. Commonwealth has sponsored evaluations of many state and local initiatives to expand employer-sponsored coverage. Kaiser created its State Health Facts Online database even though its leadership believed that universal coverage can come only through federal action. In addition to their strategic initiatives, all of the national foundations except Kaiser have a funding program focused on their home base—New York City for Commonwealth, New Jersey for RWJF, Michigan for Kellogg, and a number of Bay Area counties for Packard.

The California health foundations also have been active in all three jurisdictions—national, state, and local. They recognized that both private and especially public health insurance programs like Medicaid and SCHIP are creatures of federalism; thus, there are important policy levers in the nation's capital as well as in Sacramento and throughout the California business community. For example, the grassroots letter-writing campaign inspired by TCWF applied pressure on HHS Secretary Tommy Thompson to approve California's waiver application to use SCHIP funds to cover parents. The California HealthCare Foundation has featured California health issues, including insurance coverage, through its partnership with the National Health Policy Forum. All three foundations have supported state-level advocacy campaigns, like the California Endowment's 100% Campaign to cover all the state's children or the joint effort to develop and implement "express lane eligibility" for Medicaid and SCHIP. Much of the health foundations' efforts, however, have been devoted to capacity-building and coverage expansions at the community level. These include the insurance demonstrations in Santa Clara and San Diego, as well as support for community clinics throughout the state. TCWF and the Endowment, in particular, see community-based organizing as a critical complement to communications with political insiders.

The preponderance of local foundation activities occurs at the local and state level. The Rhode Island Foundation and the Rose Community Foundation have supported statewide advocacy campaigns, like the latter's Colorado Consumer Health Initiative. The Rose Community Foundation initially had a rather tight focus on the greater Denver area and still requires that funded projects have an impact on the Denver metropolitan area. Yet much of its health insurance coverage work (Child Health Advocates, Hot Issues in Health Care) is carried out at the state level. The Consumer Health Foundation's work is more regional in focus, with activities taking place across D.C., Virginia, and Maryland. The Rhode Island Foundation has a statewide focus and, given the state's small size, the state/local distinction on matters of health insurance coverage is largely insignificant. Though the Alliance Healthcare Foundation's initiatives are carried out exclusively within the San Diego region, it participated in a national network of foundations and other organizations to advocate for the proliferation of "3-share" insurance models like its FOCUS program.

There is ample evidence from this study that state and even local foundations are pushing their resources up the federal hierarchy. If most foundations—even those with very limited resources—are devoting attention and energy to policymaking outside their principal jurisdictions, they must believe that spreading their resources will have short- or long-term payoffs. Further research could clarify when and where this particular form of diversification in foundation programming is most productive.

STAGES OF THE POLICY PROCESS

As foundation leaders interviewed for this study clearly understand, the policy process is fraught with peril even for initiatives put forward by the most powerful participants. The constitutional design of the U.S. government and most state and local governments makes defending the status quo immensely easier than promoting policy innovation (Hayes, 1992; Steinmo and Watts, 1995). Nonetheless, many scholars recognize an important, proactive role for leadership; Bryan Jones refers to the stages model when he describes the tasks of leaders as "defining a policy problem, recommending a policy proposal, mobilizing supporters, and shepherding the proposal through a complex policy process characterized by uncertainty and ambiguity" (Jones, 1989, p. 11). The following section examines whether foundation strategies for improving health insurance coverage target certain stages of the policy process more than others.

Problem Identification and Definition

Foundations now invest heavily in generating and disseminating information to the policy community. Brown (1991) argued that information generated by health services researchers—often supported by foundations—is most influential in providing "documentation" of problems for policymakers. Jack Walker (1974) noted that the identification of "performance gaps" was an important catalyst for governmental action. In a similar analysis, John Kingdon (1984) found that several factors—dramatic change in social indicators, "focusing events," feedback on program performance, or conceptualizing an event or behavior in a new way—were all important in helping the public and their political representatives define problems and their significance.

Foundations have put a lot of effort into defining a very heterogeneous population of people without health insurance as "the uninsured" and then tracking trends in their absolute numbers and rates among selected target groups. Media reports on this issue tend to emphasize increases in the total number of uninsured, missing the point that due to overall population growth the total number of insured persons has also increased. They also raise awareness among the middle and upper classes that the vast majority of the uninsured are employed, which establishes them as a more sympathetic group than welfare recipients, for example. Kaiser's primers, fact sheets, and online data on insurance coverage; the IOM reports sponsored by RWJF, and the foundation's accompanying public relations campaign; and TCWF's and the California Endowment's annual report on insurance coverage in California are all activities aimed at influencing problem definition. The literature review and survey conducted by the California HealthCare Foundation helped to better specify the weakest parts of the small group insurance market; its work also concluded that evidence could not support claims that offering health insurance was a profitable business strategy for small employers.

Developing and categorizing information and statistics are seldom sufficient to produce quick, demonstrable results, but those activities may accelerate the process of agenda-setting by building an evidence base, developing "causal stories" of responsibility for social problems (Stone, 1997), and influencing legislative testimony. Like other participants in the policy community, foundations cannot generate focusing events, but they can be ready to respond to either "problem-driven opportunities" or "politics-driven" opportunities for policy innovation (Oliver and Paul-Shaheen, 1997).

Among local foundations, the Rhode Island Foundation's support for Kids Count has helped develop a rich set of data on child health indicators for state officials. The Alliance Healthcare Foundation has sponsored local studies on the lack of coverage among employees of small businesses as a way of establishing the importance of programmatic intervention.

Agenda-setting

John Kingdon (1984) found that governmental agenda-setting is largely top-down, controlled by elected officials and their top political appointees. As such, it is not heavily influenced by foundations or other actors outside of government. James Smith (Chapter 3) observes, "a foundation's policy opportunities are largely shaped by external circumstances and sometimes battered by unforeseen contingencies. There are no formulas to assure success." Unexpected events, unpredictable interest and participation in policy debates, and leadership turnover are among the many factors that can open "windows of opportunity" in the policy process and alter what policy options receive serious consideration. According to prominent scholars, issues rise on the governmental policy agenda when a given problem can be coupled with a feasible policy alternative and favorable political conditions (Walker, 1981; Kingdon, 1984; Polsby, 1984).

Foundations are active and at times influential in problem definition, as noted above, and in the generation of policy alternatives. Agenda-setting depends on the availability of alternatives that policymakers judge to be technically and politically feasible—and in an era still dominated by budget concerns, alternatives must be affordable both now and as initiatives are "scaled up" in the future. So demonstrations and evaluations of existing programs in other jurisdictions feed the professional consensus that is critical, in Kingdon and Walker's view, to policy innovation. Much of the work of the Commonwealth Fund task force and Kellogg's Community Voices program has been devoted to identifying workable programs that governmental officials could adopt today if there was political will to do so. In addition, Commonwealth's efforts in policy modeling have provided more consistent and sophisticated analysis of the likely impacts on coverage and costs of different approaches—information that policymakers place a high value on when they begin to formulate actual legislation.

The important trend identified in this study is the increasing effort of foundations to "keep the issue alive" in the political stream through activities such as regular opinion polls, media campaigns, building interest group coalitions, and educational forums for policymakers. Kaisernetwork.org and its poll reports are helpful for tracking what Kingdon calls the "mood of the country" toward health issues. RWJF's "strange bedfellows" campaign has been primarily devoted to agenda-setting. But just as what Kingdon calls "focusing events" and "windows of opportunity" can unexpectedly push the health insurance issue higher on the policy agenda, similar phenomena in other issue areas can create significant distraction for policymakers and the public. This was the unfortunate situation for the Cover the Uninsured Week in March 2003, which came just as the nation's leaders were campaigning for public endorsement of a war against Iraq that began the following week. In contrast, the potential contribution of foundations in what Kingdon calls "softening up" the political stream is made clear by the work of TCWF on "express lane eligibility" for public health insurance and the Endowment's 100% Campaign for universal children's health insurance in California.

Fostering effective policy networks is also a crucial aspect of agenda-setting. Mark Smith of CHCF explained that,

> Foundation business is the relationship business. People outside foundations see us as holders of money and givers of grants and that is fundamentally what we do. But the amount of money is really trivial compared to the federal government, the state government, even a good-sized hospital. So the key is knowing how to spend the money—on what issue, at what time, with what tactic, on whom—and that's based on knowing people. . . . The question is always who's interested in this, who cares about this . . . and what is their capacity to act on this information once it's produced. So that's a question of knowing our constituencies, knowing consumers of information well, and having enough of a sense of the political, economic, and social environment to know when an issue can move and what is likely to move it.

Tom David, formerly executive vice president at TCWF, viewed its advocacy work in the same light; it is essential not just for influencing pending decisions but for preparing for decisions to come: "There is also an ongoing need to keep the policy infrastructure staffed and active even in 'fallow' periods, because a breaking news event or election result can change the policy climate overnight. If advocates are not prepared to act when the timing is right, a critical opportunity may be missed" (Holton, 2002a, p. 1).

Foundations are capable of playing a more active and comprehensive role in the policy process in their community-based initiatives. At the national or state level it is difficult if not impossible for participants outside of government to create "windows of opportunity," but at the local level there are many examples of "entrepreneur-driven opportunities" for policy innovation. The capacity for innovation is greatest when leaders gain support for their ideas across government, business, and civic organizations (Oliver, 1991, 1996). David Rogers argued that RWJF funding for demonstration projects "often served as a powerful catalyst to bring together the necessary actors in communities that would otherwise have been unknown to us. It also helped make the process more democratic by allowing many to compete for funds" (1987).

Local foundations have themselves contributed to putting the issue of health insurance coverage on the agenda, chiefly through coalition-building and improving the packaging of information for policymakers. The Rhode Island Foundation's Leadership Roundtable on the Uninsured brought all the major public and private sector actors to the table to begin to explore coverage for the working uninsured. The Hot Issues in Health Care project created by the Rose Community Foundation and Alliance's San Diegans for Health Coverage project attempted to provide intelligible, usable information to government officials and opinion leaders. Both the San Diego FOCUS program and the Santa Clara Children's Health Initiative are examples of state and local foundations that established the policy agenda with their financial resources and, more importantly, creative partnerships with a variety of public and private organizations.

Policy Formulation

Though policy formulation is usually the domain of elected officials, political appointees, and staff, foundations can still exert some influence through issue briefs, testimony, and analysis of pending legislation and rule-making. In an earlier era, foundation-sponsored commissions closely collaborated with governmental officials and agencies in developing detailed programs of action to reform parts of the health care system (Feldman et al., 1992). The contemporary policy process has many watchdogs, however, and the relationship between foundations and policymakers is closely monitored—especially by their ideological opponents.

James Smith tells the cautionary tale of RWJF's involvement in the Clinton administration's health care reform effort in 1994. RWJF president Steven Schroeder recalls that the attack on the foundation for hosting four community forums on behalf of President and Ms. Clinton made his board and staff "much more sensitive about politics and how to avoid getting caught in the middle of highly partisan issues" (Iglehart, 2002, p. 247). In its campaign on covering the uninsured, David Colby stressed that, "We have been very careful to be sure we are not identified with a *solution*." RWJF and Kellogg have focused on injecting different proposals for expanding coverage into the process, or publicizing existing state and community initiatives, instead of supporting any one model (Colby, 2002; Kellogg, 2002). Commonwealth has had the same approach, but in 2003 as it sensed growing anxiety about health insurance across the country, it came forward with its "consensus framework" of what it advertised as a politically balanced set of incremental initiatives (Davis and Schoen, 2003). The intent was not to advocate for a specific program, but to indicate common ground for people on different sides of the debate to move toward and thereby facilitate policy formulation (Schoen, 2003).

Having a role in policy formulation is less discomfiting to the California foundations. While they are careful to avoid any direct lobbying on legislation, their strategy includes core support for groups that are intimately involved with the drafting of legislation and program implementation. Funding from TCWF enabled PICO's local chapters to mount a campaign that produced 50,000 hand-written letters sent to the U.S. Department of Health and Human Services urging approval of a California SCHIP waiver. Thousands of PICO members traveled to Sacramento to lobby the governor and legislators for $50 million in additional state support of health services for the uninsured. The California HealthCare Foundation distances itself from most forms of advocacy, but its development of Health-e-App combined technical assistance and direct formulation of a simplified application process for the state Medi-Cal program.

Policy Implementation

Foundations are appropriately interested in policy implementation because the translation from legislative or judicial decisions is never easy. A substantial amount of literature confirms that there are often profound gaps between the stated intentions of government and the actual performance of its policies and programs (e.g., Palumbo and Calista, 1990; Ingram, 1990). Problems in implementation occur for many reasons: flaws in the underlying theory of action, inadequate resources, breakdowns in coordination between different organizations and levels of government, noncompliant target populations, or a lack of strong leadership (Bardach, 1977; Sabatier and Mazmanian, 1981).

In the implementation stage of the policy process, foundations typically build partnerships among stakeholders, and work in collaboration with governmental agencies or nonprofit organizations to address gaps or provide funds for technical assistance to implement reforms. The Packard Foundation, for example, gave core support to the National Academy for State Health Policy and the National Governors' Association to provide states with technical assistance in SCHIP implementation. The RWJF national program on Covering Kids created state and community coalitions to monitor and assist state governments with SCHIP implementation. In California, all three state health foundations supported implementation of children's health insurance in different ways. The state health foundations have also focused on Medicaid. California HealthCare Foundation has produced data with county-by-county comparisons of Medi-Cal performance. Throughout the Health-e-App initiative, CHCF worked closely with state and county agencies to maneuver through research and development, pilot testing, and approval of statewide adoption of the new process. Several of the California foundations, as well as Packard, have supported administrative advocacy and oversight of program implementation to prevent excessive delays in the "express lane eligibility" initiative to combine enrollment in school lunch and state health insurance programs.

Three of the four local foundations have supported projects related to SCHIP implementation. The Rose Community Foundation took the boldest approach by creating Child Health Advocates, a nonprofit organization that was responsible for the marketing, eligibility, and enrollment and administration of Colorado's SCHIP. Both the Consumer Health Foundation and the Rhode Island Foundation worked with RWJF to bring the Covering Kids initiative to their respective geographic areas.

Policy Evaluation

This study confirms that most large foundations pay close attention to the performance of both ongoing governmental health programs and new initiatives at the national, state, and even local level. They regularly support projects for evaluating public programs, which may be conducted by independent investigators or done in collaboration with governmental agencies. In addition, they may invest substantial resources in evaluation of their own efforts to develop viable models for new public programs.

The national foundations in this study have a long track record of conducting careful evaluation of public policies and their own demonstration projects. According to David Rogers, the first president of RWJF:

> The decision to initiate independent objective evaluations as part of almost every one of our major national programs has been perhaps our most widely recognized contribution to modern philanthropy. . . . Through the difficult process of evaluating many programs, we have learned painfully how hard it is to make meaningful progress in human affairs no matter how well-intentioned we are, and how often unexpected results that run counter to conventional wisdom can occur. But by publishing the results of these evaluations of our grants, we fulfilled what staff and trustees viewed as a public responsibility—reporting on our successes and failures. We have had our share of both. (Rogers, 1987, p. 82)

The Packard Foundation went to great lengths to initiate and implement a national network for research and evaluation of SCHIP. In addition, it worked with state agencies to evaluate the expansion of SCHIP in California. Several of the foundations funded the Urban Institute's National Survey of America's Families and its evaluation of the impact of welfare and Medicaid reforms as well as SCHIP. The Commonwealth task force put a great deal of resources into evaluating potential models for the expansion of private health insurance. Kellogg advertised the thirteen local coalitions in its Community Voices program as "learning laboratories" both for its network of participants and for other efforts to expand and protect access to care for vulnerable populations (Kellogg, 2002).

In California, foundations took the lead in supporting and managing the evaluation of the major local initiatives to expand health insurance. The California HealthCare Foundation devoted considerable resources to evaluation of the San Diego FOCUS program and Packard has done likewise in the Santa Clara Children's Health Initiative.

Not all foundations require elaborate evaluations of their own initiatives. Evaluations sponsored by the California HealthCare Foundation range from formal controlled studies by professional evaluators to grantees' own reporting of their activities and outcomes. The caliber of the evaluation depends on the level of interest and level of funding. Sometimes the project is important to the field: "In that case, you've got to show that it works. There are other times you [evaluate] based on the notion that it's a good thing to do, and you're not interested in spending a lot of money in order to prove what you think you already know" (Smith, 2002).

The local foundations included in this study do not devote a significant amount of their own financial and staff resources to evaluation of public policies or their own programs. Because many of their programs are of interest to other communities and national policymakers, several of the local foundations have participated in evaluations sponsored by Commonwealth, Kellogg, Packard, RWJF, or the California HealthCare Foundation.

Whether foundations invest too many or too few of their resources in policy evaluation is a difficult question to answer. Clearly, the policy process goes on with or without evaluations because policymakers tend to use research and analysis to support their positions, not to alter them (Weiss, 1989; Brown, 1991). Foundations, like other participants in the policy process, are driven by their values as well as empirical findings; as Mark Smith suggests, they will invest in some programs they think are worthwhile regardless of evaluation results. Finally, the impact of policy evaluation is further limited by common failure to produce definitive results. Reflecting on his years at RWJF, Steven Schroeder put the foundation's serious efforts at evaluation in the context of a greater struggle:

> Despite our efforts, our quest for performance measurement remains incomplete. In part this is because it is so difficult to establish causality when we are working on complex social issues, often alongside many others. For example, during the past decade we have invested heavily in programs to reduce the number of Americans who lack health insurance. Despite our efforts, the number of uninsured has resumed its upward climb. Should we accept some blame for that lack of progress? Did our efforts prevent worse outcomes? How can we know? . . . We often feel more like Sisyphus than Sir Edmund Hillary. Still we remain enthusiastic and committed, because of our mission, our focus, our realism and our culture. (Schroeder, 2001)

Assessing the Outcomes of Foundation Strategies to Shape Health Policy

This report has reviewed the basic strategies and types of activities that were employed by a dozen foundations in their efforts to improve health insurance coverage. Due to the nature of health care financing and delivery in this country, all of the foundations have devoted resources to improving private insurance coverage as well as protecting and expanding public sources of coverage. All of the foundations, however, accept the premise that governmental action is critical to solving the problems of more than forty million uninsured Americans and they view public policy as a way to leverage the relatively limited resources they can devote to this issue.

Across all twelve foundations, what patterns can be identified and what lessons can be drawn from the wide range of their activities to shape health policy?

LESSON 1

Foundations are not strictly leaders or followers on the issue of health insurance coverage.

On a broad scale, foundations often react to the policy agenda. Nearly all of the foundations in this study committed substantial resources to improving enrollment in the new State Children's Health Insurance Program, even though its maximum target enrollment was five million and several million more children and adults are eligible but not enrolled in Medicaid. Nonetheless, RWJF, Kellogg, TCWF, the Endowment, and several local foundations promoted major expansions of coverage at a time when few federal or state policymakers are receptive to those proposals. It would be difficult to reject the conclusion that foundations have helped keep the issue alive and make it attractive to Democratic presidential candidates and an increasing number of other policymakers.

Foundations are often innovative in their means rather than their ends. In some very practical areas, such as enrollment of children and families in public insurance programs, foundations identified solutions and succeeded in having them adopted by government. The Health-e-App technology developed under the auspices of the California HealthCare Foundation and the Express Lane Eligibility program initiated by TCWF and then piloted with the assistance of the California Endowment and Packard Foundation are significant examples of foundation-inspired innovation. The Alliance Healthcare Foundation in San Diego and the Rhode Island Foundation were instrumental in designing, attracting financial and organizational assistance, and implementing entirely new insurance programs for low-income individuals. Kaiser's efforts to build unconventional partnerships with media organizations and vastly expand online sources of information on federal and state health policies have been innovative as well.

LESSON 2

While foundations can adopt different strategies in the public policy arena, those strategies become less differentiated for foundations with greater resources and for foundations focused on state or local initiatives.

There are several strategies foundations can employ to achieve their policy goals. Most foundations have invested in a very broad set of activities around all three basic strategies: 1) educate the public and members of the policy community; 2) invest in the development and demonstration of new institutions and policy options; and 3) support capacity-building and advocacy efforts. Only Kaiser, Commonwealth, and the California HealthCare Foundation self-consciously adopted a niche role emphasizing one or both of the first two strategies. Their primary goal was to improve the quality and availability of information for policymaking. Kellogg took a greater interest in national and state policymaking, but its main role was to facilitate community-based change. RWJF, with its substantially greater assets, has been able to pursue all three basic strategies to expand insurance coverage and access to care. Except for the California HealthCare Foundation, all of the state and local foundations have pursued each of the three strategies and place a heavy emphasis on capacity-building and advocacy work.

The pattern of activities identified in this study suggests that, relative to other participants operating at their level in the policy community, both state and local foundations have substantial resources and access to policymakers. As a result, they are able to expand their activities into more direct forms of influence in the policy process. In addition, state and local foundations have chosen to push their issues up the federal hierarchy, working with higher level governments and also foundations. The California Endowment, for example, became a principal sponsor of RWJF's national Cover the Uninsured Week. The Rose Community Foundation became a central actor in development of the Colorado SCHIP program, for example, and the California HealthCare Foundation worked closely with the National Health Policy Forum to keep federal officials aware of developments and emerging issues in the California health care system. The Alliance Healthcare Foundation attracted significant support from both California's new health foundations and national foundations such as RWJF and Commonwealth. The Rhode Island Foundation actively sought out partnerships with national foundations such as RWJF and the Annie E. Casey Foundation.

Finally, most of the state and local foundations made a major commitment to expand access to care by supporting direct services as well as insurance coverage. Denis Prager (1999) argued that one of the central tensions facing foundations is whether to deal with the root causes of problems or respond to the symptoms of those problems. The California Endowment and TCWF, in particular, have argued that there is a great need to do both short-term and long-term work and that supporting the health care safety net is complementary to their policy initiatives. The same philosophy has guided Kellogg's Community Voices program, which has addressed the needs of the uninsured by strengthening community-based services and promoting policies to expand insurance coverage.

LESSON 3

It is necessary but not sufficient for foundations to develop expertise in health policy.

Foundations that wish to shape public policy must develop both policy expertise and personal connections in the policy community. Influence is impossible without expertise; leaders at Kaiser, Commonwealth, and the California HealthCare Foundation all stress the importance of being an authoritative source of information. But influence depends even more on being a familiar and reliable source of assistance for policymakers and their staff, advocacy groups, and media organizations.

This requires foundations to hire individuals who know government and governmental programs and are able to bridge the two cultures of philanthropy and politics. Kaiser, Commonwealth, and RWJF have done this to a considerable degree. Packard's work on children's health evolved from emphasizing internal staff analysis to cultivating relationships with agencies and officials in all jurisdictions—federal, state, and local. Even though the California Endowment and TCWF believe strongly in grassroots action, they each strengthened their capacity in the policy arena by bringing in staff who understand the levers of power and effective tactics in advocacy work. Ultimately, foundations gain influence by connecting knowledge with power through their relationships with leaders inside and outside of government.

LESSON 4

Foundations must clarify whether they can best meet their goals as investors or as entrepreneurs in the policy process.

The process of policy innovation requires the collaboration of different types of leaders—inventors of policy ideas, investors, promoters, and managers. But it also typically requires "policy entrepreneurs" who take the lead in that collaboration. Policy entrepreneurs "recombine intellectual, political, and organizational resources into new products and courses of action for government" (Oliver and Paul-Shaheen, 1997, p. 744). The most distinguishing trait of these leaders is their singular focus on a specific idea for new governmental procedures, organizations, or programs, and the significant professional and often financial stakes they place in those ideas. Policy entrepreneurs can and often do come from positions outside of government, even though their success depends on recruiting government insiders who have key positions and the political capital to move their proposals forward.

Foundations are clearly capable of becoming entrepreneurs in the policy process. Alternatively, foundations may choose the role of investor, providing financial support, technical assistance, access to decisionmakers, and prestige to one or more groups promoting their own ideas for improving public policy and public health. Or they may avoid taking specific policy positions at all and serve only as a generator and broker of policy-relevant information. The issue is whether information alone is sufficient to avoid "market failure" in politics of policymaking, or whether the inequality among interests is so great that additional voices need active representation. In other words, is advocacy in a fairly direct form and for a specific purpose necessary for foundations to achieve the maximum leverage for their initiatives in the public policy arena?

There is a fundamental difference in these roles and important implications for the allocation of foundation resources. In general, the national foundations in this study consciously avoided endorsing particular solutions to the problems of the uninsured. Kaiser has refrained from funding projects involving the development or advocacy of specific initiatives, although it has supported dissemination and analysis of others' proposals. RWJF and Commonwealth have supported the development of many model solutions and, even though Commonwealth at one point announced its "consensus framework" to advance discussion of specific policy options, neither foundation has directly promoted any policy option in a selective way. The indirect support of advocacy by RWJF on the issue of health coverage is in sharp contrast with its creation and support of the Campaign for Tobacco-Free Kids, a leading source of advocacy in tobacco control, and the Partnership for Solutions, a program that promotes specific policies to improve health care for people with chronic health conditions. Similarly, Packard has been a strong supporter of the overall SCHIP program, but has assisted in the development and implementation of many different state models. Only in its involvement with the Santa Clara Children's Health Initiative did Packard adopt a more comprehensive, entrepreneurial role. Kellogg treated the thirteen sites in its Community Voices program as "learning laboratories," but the foundation itself did not explicitly promote any of the alternative models that emerged in the course of the program—the lessons and best practices were supposed to emerge from formal evaluation and informal dialogue among leaders in the different communities. Overall, these foundations have played a general investment role in highlighting problems of the uninsured and keeping the issue alive politically. They initiated a diverse and complex set of activities, most of which were carefully conceived within the limited role they chose for themselves. None of the foundations, however, have moved beyond that role to invest heavily in a specific solution or take on the broad tasks of policy entrepreneurship.

In contrast, nearly all of the state and local foundations selected—indeed, sometimes created—particular policies or administrative arrangements that they wanted government to adopt. From its inception, TCWF has viewed advocacy of policy change as a core part of its mission. The California Endowment stepped up its advocacy efforts. While both foundations prefer that other groups provide leadership, political skills, and mobilization of constituencies, neither shies away from taking policy positions or recruiting groups for specific policy initiatives. The Express Lane Eligibility program to combine enrollment in school lunch and state health insurance programs was created through work coordinated by TCWF. Even the California HealthCare Foundation, which sees its primary role as a source of information, moved further into advocacy and even entrepreneurship on selected issues. Its Health-e-App initiative is a hallmark example of successful policy entrepreneurship.

Due to their more limited resources, local foundations appear to focus their health policy efforts on one principal initiative at a time. Regardless of whether a foundation actually initiates the local program or not, it becomes part of the entrepreneurial team and its leaders have critical responsibilities for organizing, funding, implementing, and sustaining the program. Alliance and the Rhode Island Foundation unquestionably served as policy entrepreneurs in expanding health insurance in their communities, and the Rose Community Foundation played a similar role in implementing and expanding the Colorado SCHIP program.

There are many possible reasons why foundations would shy away from the role of policy entrepreneur and prefer that of investor. The choice involves practical issues of the amount of resources available to address an issue and the proximity of the foundation to key actors in the policy community. The choice also depends on whether the foundation's board and staff are willing to commit themselves to a specific initiative for a lengthy period of time. Packard, for example, estimated that in Santa Clara County alone it would take five to ten years to get 95 percent of children enrolled in a health insurance program. The likely collapse of the FOCUS program in San Diego showed that successful entrepreneurship in establishing a new program does not ensure its long-term stability if state or federal governments are unable or unwilling to underwrite that model of coverage. Given the political and fiscal conditions in Washington and in most states, foundations and others interested in improving health insurance coverage may believe it is fruitless to focus on a single solution when real progress toward universal coverage may be years away.

Nonetheless, at whatever scale and in whatever manner foundations pursue an expansion of health insurance, they must confront the question of whether they might increase their effectiveness by not only helping develop products for policymakers but engaging in more selective, forceful advocacy of their preferred products. The evidence from this study suggests that focused advocacy efforts might well be put to greater use in foundation efforts to protect and expand health insurance across the nation.

LESSON 5

The test of foundations' capacity to solve critical social problems lies in their collective contributions, not their individual roles in the policy process.

Many foundation leaders make the argument that pluralism in the world of philanthropy is a good thing. It is an appealing argument, since it confers nearly absolute freedom on any individual foundation in how it pursues its values and goals in public policy. As noted above, the twelve foundations included in this study essentially share the same values and goals regarding health insurance coverage but they have emphasized different strategies in their efforts to expand coverage. A few foundations, particularly those operating at the national level, adopted a highly specialized role in health policy. Kaiser, the California HealthCare Foundation, Commonwealth, and RWJF have almost completely avoided funding projects that involve advocacy of specific solutions to the large-scale crisis in health care coverage.

It may be reasonable for foundations, both individually and collectively, to adopt highly specialized roles if that enables each organization to be more effective in its chosen role. But the impact of philanthropy on public policy will suffer if support for any of the three basic strategies highlighted in this study is insufficient. The overall ecology of foundations and public policy is what matters.

The limited progress toward universal coverage can hardly be attributed to foundation boards and staff wary of political controversy. As a number of foundation leaders have pointed out, a few billion dollars of philanthropy does not go far in a $1.5 trillion health care system. Nonetheless, the potential impact of foundations might be more highly leveraged through stronger, more selective advocacy and also through stronger collaboration among foundations.

If there is a lesson that smaller, more local foundations can teach larger foundations, it is the importance of establishing and sustaining a specific policy design and marshalling resources to support it through close public-private partnerships. Hypothetically, what would happen if, for a few years, RWJF, Kellogg, and other large foundations devoted hundreds of millions of dollars each year to a single cause—universal coverage—and perhaps a single proposal, and then put nearly all of the money into building a social movement instead of developing more proposals and small demonstration projects?

In health insurance initiatives large and small, there can be different forms of collaboration. One approach is to pool resources into a single, foundation-sponsored initiative. This is what RWJF, the California Endowment, and Kellogg did with Cover the Uninsured Week in March 2003. Another approach is to establish informal collaboration in support of a government or community-based initiative. The national evaluation of SCHIP, the development and implementation of Express Lane Eligibility in California, and the two local health insurance initiatives in Santa Clara and San Diego counties are examples of this approach.

Collaboration is primarily a means to an end, not an end in itself. There are two key issues regarding collaboration among funders and their operational partners in any initiative. First, are resources sufficient to meet the agreed-upon goals of the participants? Second, is the combination of activities comprehensive, incorporating each of the three strategies needed to maximize the likelihood of reshaping public policy?

The experience from the FOCUS program in San Diego suggests that, even in a best-case scenario of collaboration, foundations can rapidly approach boundaries to further progress on the issue of health insurance coverage. Without a single, well-endowed source of responsibility or success in persuading governmental officials to adopt the program, even the most skilled policy entrepreneurs within the world of philanthropy cannot sustain expansions of coverage—and fairly modest ones at that—because of their extraordinary financial costs. Advancing toward universal health coverage appears to be more difficult than most other health policy issues, if only for this reason.

The main question confronting foundations who seek to expand health care coverage is, how to move the policy process beyond agenda setting? What is the strategy to move from superficial consensus to active political debate and policy formulation, while maintaining solidarity among the "strange bedfellows"? At all levels of the political system, there will be many opportunities for collaboration among foundations, but significant commitment and communication will be required in addition to major financial resources to work out the most effective configuration of roles and resources for protecting and expanding health insurance coverage across the nation.

Table 1. Foundation Strategies for Improving Health Insurance Coverage

CHOICE OF STRATEGIES	RWJF	Common-wealth	Kaiser	Kellogg
Educate the public and members of the policy community				
Generate and disseminate data and policy analysis	3	3	3	2
Improve public understanding of health issues	3	2	3	2
Educate policy makers and issue experts	3	3	3	2
Invest in the development of new institutions and policy options				
Develop new models and demonstration projects	3	2	1	3
Shape policy implementation	3	3	2	2
Evaluation	3	3	3	2
Support capacity-building and advocacy efforts				
Serve as a builder of policy networks and convener of participants	3	3	3	2
Provide a voice for vulnerable groups	2	1	2	3
Support direct services	2	1	1	3
CHOICE OF AUDIENCES AND PARTNERS				
General public	3	2	3	2
Trade associations and advocacy groups	3	3	3	2
Governmental agencies and officials	3	3 (audience)	3 (audience)	2
Mass media	3	3	3	2
Community leaders and organizations	2	1	1	3
Other foundations	2	2	1	2
CHOICE OF JURISDICTIONS				
National	3	3	3	2
State	3	2	2	3
Local	2	1	1	3
STAGES OF POLICY PROCESS				
Problem identification and definition	2	2	3	1
Agenda setting	3	2	2	2
Policy formulation	3	2	2	3
Policy implementation and program management	3	2	1	3
Policy evaluation	3	3	2	2
Authors' rankings: 3=Substantial priority 2=Moderate priority 1=Little or no priority				

Table 1, continued

CHOICE OF STRATEGIES	Packard	CHCF	Endowment	TCWF
Educate the public and members of the policy community				
Generate and disseminate data and policy analysis	3	3	2	2
Improve public understanding of health issues	2	2	3	3
Educate policy makers and issue experts	3	3	3	3
Invest in the development of new institutions and policy options				
Develop new models and demonstration projects	3	2	3	3
Shape policy implementation	3	2	3	3
Evaluation	3	3	2	2
Support capacity-building and advocacy efforts				
Serve as a builder of policy networks and convener of participants	3	3	3	3
Provide a voice for vulnerable groups	2	1	3	3
Support direct services	2	1	3	3
CHOICE OF AUDIENCES AND PARTNERS				
General public	2	2	3	3
Trade associations and advocacy groups	3	2	3	3
Governmental agencies and officials	3	2	2	2
Mass media	2	2	2	2
Community leaders and organizations	3	1	3	3
Other foundations	3	3	3	3
CHOICE OF JURISDICTIONS				
National	3	2	2	2
State	3	3	3	3
Local	3	2	3	3
STAGES OF POLICY PROCESS				
Problem identification and definition	2	3	2	2
Agenda setting	1	3	3	3
Policy formulation	2	3	3	3
Policy implementation and program management	3	2	2	3
Policy evaluation	3	2	1	2

Authors' rankings: 3=Substantial priority   2=Moderate priority   1=Little or no priority

Table 1, continued

CHOICE OF STRATEGIES	Alliance	Consumer Health	Rhode Island	Rose
Educate the public and members of the policy community				
Generate and disseminate data and policy analysis	2	1	2	2
Improve public understanding of health issues	3	2	3	3
Educate policy makers and issue experts	2	1	3	3
Invest in the development of new institutions and policy options				
Develop new models and demonstration projects	3	1	3	3
Shape policy implementation	1	2	3	3
Evaluation	1	1	1	1
Support capacity-building and advocacy efforts				
Serve as a builder of policy networks and convener of participants	2	3	3	3
Provide a voice for vulnerable groups	2	3	3	3
Support direct services	3	3	3	3
CHOICE OF AUDIENCES AND PARTNERS				
General public	3	2	3	3
Trade associations and advocacy groups	2	3	3	3
Governmental agencies and officials	2	1	3	3
Mass media	2	1	2	2
Community leaders and organizations	2	3	3	3
Other foundations	3	3	3	3
CHOICE OF JURISDICTIONS				
National	2	1	2	2
State	2	3	3	3
Local	3	3	3	3
STAGES OF POLICY PROCESS				
Problem identification and definition	2	1	2	2
Agenda setting	3	3	3	3
Policy formulation	2	1	3	2
Policy implementation and program management	2	2	3	3
Policy evaluation	1	1	1	1
Authors' rankings: 3=Substantial priority 2=Moderate priority 1=Little or no priority				

References

Altman, Drew E. 1998. "Foundations Today: Finding a New Role in the Changing Health Care System." *Health Affairs* 17 (March–April): 201–5.

Altman, Drew E. 2002. Personal interview with president, Henry J. Kaiser Family Foundation, 1 October.

Amick, Benjamin C., III, Sol Levine, Alvin R. Tarlov, and Diana Chapman Walsh. 1995. *Society and Health*. New York, NY: Oxford University Press.

Bardach, Eugene. 1977. *The Implementation Game*. Cambridge, MA: MIT Press.

Beatrice, Dennis F. 1993. "The Role Of Philanthropy In Health Care Reform." *Health Affairs* 12 (Summer): 185–192.

Berk, Marc L., and Claudia L. Schur. 1998. "Access to Care: How Much Difference Does Medicaid Make?" *Health Affairs* 17 (May–June): 169–80.

Blumberg, Linda, and David Liska. 1998. *The Uninsured in the United States: A Status Report*. Washington, DC: The Urban Institute.

Brown, Lawrence D. 1991. "Knowledge and Power: Health Services Research as a Political Resource." In *Health Services Research: Key to Health Policy*, ed. Eli Ginzberg. Cambridge, MA: Harvard University Press.

Byrnes, Maureen K. 2000. "Strategic Philanthropy: Principles Put Into Practice." *Health Affairs* 19 (May–June): 241–244.

California Endowment. 1997. Annual Report. Woodland Hills, CA: The California Endowment.

California Endowment. 2001. Annual Report. Woodland Hills, CA: The California Endowment.

California HealthCare Foundation (CHCF). 2001. *Health Care in California: Improving Delivery and Financing Systems*. 1999–2001 Foundation Report.

Calmes, J. 2007. "Why Health Care No Longer Makes Politicians Leery." *Wall Street Journal - Eastern Edition* 249(125): A1–A13.

Colby, David. 2002. Phone interview with senior program officer, Health Care Coverage, Robert Wood Johnson Foundation, 22 November.

Collins, S. R., C. Schoen, J. L. Kriss, M. M. Doty, and B. Mahato. 2006. "Rite of Passage? Why Young Adults Become Uninsured and How New Policies Can Help." The Commonwealth Fund, Updated May 24, 2006.

David, Tom. 2002. Introduction to *Reflections on Public Policy Grantmaking*. Woodland Hills, CA: The California Wellness Foundation.

Davis, Karen. 1999. "Improving Lives Through Information." *Health Affairs* 18 (March/April): 219–225.

DeNavas-Walt, Carmen, Bernadette D. Proctor, and Cheryl H. Lee. 2006. U.S. Census Bureau, Current Population Reports, P60-231, "Income, Poverty, and Health Insurance Coverage in the United States: 2005." U.S. Government Printing Office, Washington, D.C.

Dorn, Stan. 2008. *Uninsured and Dying Because of It*. Washington, D.C.: Urban Institute, January.

Dubay, Lisa, Christina Moylan, and Thomas R. Oliver. 2003. "Advancing Toward Universal Coverage: Are States Able to Take the Lead?" *Journal of Health Care Law and Policy* 7 (1).

Eyestone, Robert. 1978. *From Social Issues to Public Policy*. New York, NY: Wiley.

Families USA. 2007. *Wrong Direction: One Out of Three Americans Are Uninsured*. Washington, D.C.: Families USA.

Feldman, Penny H., Susan Putnam, and Margaret Gerteis. 1992. "The Impact of Foundation-Funded Commissions on Health Policy." *Health Affairs* 11 (Winter): 207–22.

Ferris, James M., and Elizabeth A. Graddy. 2001. *Health Care Philanthropy in California: The Changing Landscape*. Los Angeles, CA: Center on Philanthropy and Public Policy, University of Southern California.

Fronstin, Paul. 1998. "Features of Employment-Based Health Plans." Employee Benefit Research Institute Issue Brief, Number 201. Washington, DC: EBRI, September 1998.

Fronstin, Paul. 2000. Sources of Health Insurance and Characteristics of the Uninsured: Analysis of the March 1999 Current Population Survey. Washington, DC: Employee Benefit Research Institute, January.

Grantmakers in Health. 2000. *Strategies for Shaping Public Policy: A Guide for Health Funders*. Washington, DC: Grantmakers in Health, January.

Grantmakers in Health. 2002a. Strategies for Shaping Public Policy: Findings from the Grantmakers in Health Resource Center. Unpublished database.

Grantmakers in Health. 2002b. Working for Health Care: Prospects for Expanding Employer-Based Coverage: Findings from the Grantmakers in Health Resource Center. Unpublished database.

Grantmakers in Health. 2002c. Enrolling Children in Public Health Insurance: Findings from the Grantmakers in Health Resource Center. Unpublished database.

Grantmakers in Health. 2002d. Building a Community Response to Access: Findings from the Grantmakers in Health Resource Center. Unpublished database.

Grantmakers in Health. 2002e. Small Group and Individual Insurance Markets: How Philanthropy Can Inform State Debates: Findings from the Grantmakers in Health Resource Center. Unpublished database.

Grantmakers in Health. 2003. *A Profile of New Health Foundations*. Washington, D.C.: Grantmakers in Health, May.

Gusmano, Michael K., Mark Schlesinger, and Tracey Thomas. 2002. "Policy Feedback and Public Opinion: The Role of Employer Responsibility in Social Policy." *Journal of Health Politics, Policy, and Law* 27 (October): 731–72.

Hadley, Jack. 2002. *Sicker and Poorer: The Consequences of Being Uninsured*. Report prepared for the Kaiser Commission on Medicaid and the Uninsured. Washington, D.C.: Kaiser Family Foundation, May.

Hayes, Michael T. 1992. *Incrementalism and Public Policy*. White Plains, NY: Longman.

Hoffmann, Catherine, and Mary Pohl. 2000. *Health Insurance Coverage in America: 1999 Data Update*. Washington, D.C.: Kaiser Family Foundation, December.

Holohan, John. 2002. "What is Happening to Health Care Coverage in the Wake of the Recession and September 11th?" Presentation to the conference on State Efforts to Expand Health Care Coverage: Current Realities, Future Possibilities? University of Maryland School of Law, Baltimore, Maryland, 18 November.

Holahan, J., and A. Cook. 2008. "The U.S. Economy and Changes in Health Insurance Coverage, 2000-2006." *Health Affairs* 27(2): w135–144.

Holton, Ruth. 2002a. *Reflections on Public Policy Grantmaking*. Woodland Hills, CA: The California Wellness Foundation.

Holton, Ruth. 2002b. Personal interview with director of public policy, The California Wellness Foundation, 1 October.

Hughes, Robert. 2002. Phone interview with vice president, Robert Wood Johnson Foundation, 22 November.

Iglehart, John K. 1983. "The Changing World of Private Foundations: An Interview with David E. Rogers." *Health Affairs* 2 (Fall): 5–22.

Iglehart, John K. 1997. "Inside the 'Quiet Giant' with the W.K. Kellogg Foundation's President." *Health Affairs* 16 (September-October): 191–197.

Iglehart, John K. 2002. "Addressing Both Health and Health Care: An Interview with Steven A. Schroeder." *Health Affairs* 21 (November/December): 244–49.

Ingram, Helen. 1990. "Implementation: A Review and Suggested Framework." In Naomi Lynn and Aaron Wildavsky, eds. *Public Administration: The State of the Discipline*. Chatham, NJ: Chatham House, pp. 462–80.

Institute of Medicine. 2001. *Coverage Matters*. Washington, D.C.: National Academy of Sciences.

Institute of Medicine. 2003. *A Shared Destiny: Effects of Uninsurance on Individuals, Families, and Communities*. Washington, D.C.: National Academy of Sciences.

Jacobs, Lawrence R., and Robert Y. Shapiro. 1995. "Don't Blame the Public for Failed Health Care Reform." *Journal of Health Politics, Policy and Law* 20 (Summer 1995): 411–423.

Jones, Bryan D. 1989. "Causation, Constraint, and Political Leadership." In *Leadership and Politics*, ed. Bryan D. Jones. Lawrence, KS: University Press of Kansas, pp. 3–14.

Kaiser Commission on Medicaid and the Uninsured. 2002. *The Uninsured: A Primer*. Washington, D.C.: Henry J. Kaiser Family Foundation, March.

Kaiser Commission on Medicaid and the Uninsured. 2007. *The Uninsured: A Primer*. Washington, D.C.: Henry J. Kaiser Family Foundation, March.

Kaiser Daily Health Policy Report. 2002. "Program to Help Identify Uninsured Children Through School Lunch Program Begins." 2 December.

Keenan, Terrance. 1998. "Purpose and Policy in Private Philanthropy." In *Health Policy Grantmaking: A Report on Foundation Trends*, Loren Renz and Steven Lawrence. 1998. New York, NY: Foundation Center, pp. 1–3.

Kilborn, Peter T. 1999. "Low-Wage Businesses Add to Number of Uninsured Workers." *New York Times*, 3 May.

Kingdon, John W. 1984. *Agendas, Alternatives, and Public Policies*. Boston, MA: Little, Brown.

Knott, Jack H., and Carol S. Weissert. 1995. "Foundations and Health Policy: Identifying Funding Strategies in Health Programming." *Policy Studies Review* 14 (Spring/Summer): 149–160.

Lagemann, Ellen Condliffe. 1989. *The Politics of Knowledge: The Carnegie Corporation, Philanthropy, and Public Policy*. Middletown, CT: Wesleyan University Press.

Lawrence, Steven. 2001. *Health Funding Update*. New York, NY: Foundation Center.

Laws, Margaret. 2002. Personal interview with director of public policy, California HealthCare Foundation, 30 September.

LeRoy, Lauren, and Anne Schwartz. 1998. "Health Grantmakers and Public Policy." *Health Affairs* 17 (September/October): 230–232.

Levitt, Larry, Janet Lundy, Catherine Hoffmann, Jon Gabel, Heidi Whitmore, Jeremy Pickreign, and Kimberly Hurst. 1999. *Employer Health Benefits: 1999 Annual Survey Executive Summary*. Kaiser Family Foundation and Health Research and Education Trust.

Lowi, Theodore J. 1964. "American Business, Public Policy, Case Studies, and Political Theory." *World Politics* 16 (July): 677–715.

National Public Radio/Kaiser Family Foundation/Kennedy School of Government Health Care Survey, May 2002.

Oliver, Thomas R. 1991. "Ideas, Entrepreneurship, and the Politics of Health Care Reform." *Stanford Law & Policy Review* 3 (Fall): 160–80.

Oliver, Thomas R. 1999. "The Dilemmas of Incrementalism: Logical and Political Constraints in the Design of Health Insurance Reforms." *Journal of Policy Analysis and Management* 18 (Fall): 652–83.

Oliver, Thomas R. 2004. "Policy Entrepreneurship in the Social Transformation of American Medicine: The Rise of Managed Care and Managed Competition." *Journal of Health Politics, Policy and Law* 29 (August-October): 701–33.

Oliver, Thomas R., and Pamela Paul-Shaheen. 1997. "Translating Ideas into Actions: Entrepreneurial Leadership in State Health Care Reforms." *Journal of Health Politics, Policy and Law* 22 (June): 721–88.

Oliver, Thomas R., Philip R. Lee, and Helene L. Lipton. 2004. "A Political History of Medicare and Prescription Drug Coverage." *Milbank Quarterly* 82 (June): 283–354.

Palumbo, Dennis J., and Donald J. Calista. 1990. "Opening up the Black Box: Implementation and the Policy Process." In Dennis J. Palumbo and Donald J. Calista, eds., *Implementation and the Policy Process*. New York: Greenwood Press, pp. 3–17.

Prager, Denis J. 1999. *Raising the Value of Philanthropy: A Synthesis of Informal Interviews with Foundation Executives and Observers of Philanthropy*. Report prepared for Jewish Healthcare Foundation, Forbes Fund, and Grantmakers in Health, February.

Renz, Loren, and Steven Lawrence. 1998a. *Health Policy Grantmaking: A Report on Foundation Trends*. New York, NY: Foundation Center.

Renz, Loren, and Steven Lawrence. 1998b. "Health Policy Grantmaking by Foundations in the 1990s." *Health Affairs* 17 (September/October): 216–29.

Riker, William H. 1986. *The Art of Political Manipulation*. New Haven, CT: Yale University Press.

Rimel, Rebecca W. 1999. "Strategic Philanthropy: Pew's Approach to Matching Needs with Resources." *Health Affairs* 18 (May/June): 228–233.

Rogers, David E. 1987. "Some Reflections on Foundation-Building." *Health Affairs* 6 (Summer): 78–84.

Rowland, Diane. 2002. "The New Challenge of the Uninsured: Coverage in the Current Economy." Testimony prepared for the Subcommittee on Health, Committee on Energy and Commerce, U.S. House of Representatives, 28 February.

Sabatier, Paul A., and Daniel A. Mazmanian. 1981. "The Implementation of Public Policy: A Framework of Analysis." In Daniel A. Mazmanian and Paul A. Sabatier, eds., *Effective Policy Implementation*. Lexington, MA: Lexington Books, pp. 3–35.

Schacht, Jennie. 1998. "Creating Partnerships with Clinic Associations to Preserve the Safety Net." *Health Affairs* 17 (May–June): 248–252.

Schoen, Cathy, B. Lyons, D. Rowland, K. Davis, and E. Puleo. 1997. "Insurance Matters for Low-Income Adults: Results from Five-State Survey." *Health Affairs* 16 (September–October): 163–71.

Schoen, Cathy. 2002. Phone interview with vice president for health policy, research and evaluation and Executive Director, Task Force on the Future of Health Insurance, The Commonwealth Fund, 25 November.

Schoen, Cathy. 2003. Personal communication, 25 July.

Schroeder, Steven A. 1991. "New Priorities for The Robert Wood Johnson Foundation." *Health Affairs* 10 (Summer): 185–187.

Schroeder, Steven A. 1998. "Reflections on the Challenges of Philanthropy." *Health Affairs* 17 (July-August): 209–216.

Schroeder, Steven A. 1999. *Understanding Health Behavior and Speaking Out on the Uninsured: Two Leadership Opportunities*. The 1999 Robert H. Ebert Memorial Lecture. New York: Milbank Memorial Fund.

Schroeder, Steven A. 2001. "Reflections: Looking Back at Lessons Learned." President's message, Robert Wood Johnson Foundation 2001 Annual Report.

Schwartz, Anne. 2003. Personal communication, 9 January.

Sharp, Marcia. 2002. "Foundation Collaborations: Incubators for Change?" Paper prepared for forum on "Leveraging Philanthropic Assets for Public Problem Solving," Center on Philanthropy and Public Policy, University of Southern California, May 13–14.

Silow-Carroll, Sharon, Stephanie E. Anthony, Paul A. Seltman, and Jack A. Meyer. 2001. *Community-Based Health Plans for the Uninsured: Expanding Access, Enhancing Dignity*. Prepared for the W.K. Kellogg Foundation.

Smith, Mark. 2001. "Grantmakers Are from Mars; Policymakers Are from Venus: Is There Hope for This Relationship?" Report from the field, Grantmakers in Health, 12 February.

Smith, Mark. 2002. Personal interview with president, California HealthCare Foundation, 30 September.

Steinmo, Sven, and Jon Watts. 1995. "It's the Institutions, Stupid! Why Comprehensive National Health Insurance Always Fails in America." *Journal of Health Politics, Policy and Law* 20 (Summer): 329–72.

Stone, Deborah A. 1997. *Policy Paradox: The Art of Political Decision Making*. New York, NY: W.W. Norton, pp. 188–209.

Thompson, Frank J. 2001. "Federalism and Health Care Policy: Toward Redefinition?" In Robert B. Hackey and David A. Rochefort, eds., *The New Politics of State Health Policy*. Lawrence, KS: University Press of Kansas, pp. 41–70.

Van Dusen, Annie. 2002. Phone interview with senior program officer, Rose Community Foundation, 6 December.

Walker, Jack L. 1974. "Performance Gaps, Policy Research, and Political Entrepreneurs." *Policy Studies Journal* 3 (Autumn):112–16.

Walker, Jack L. 1977. "Setting the Agenda in the U.S. Senate: A Theory of Problem Selection." *British Journal of Political Science* 7: 423–45.

Walker, Jack L. 1981. "The Diffusion of Knowledge, Policy Communities, and Agenda Setting: The Relationship of Knowledge and Power." In *New Strategic Perspectives on Social Policy*, ed. John E. Tropman, Milan J. Dluhy, and Roger M. Lind. New York: Pergamon Press.

Walker, Jack L. 1991. *Mobilizing Interest Groups in America*. Ann Arbor, MI: University of Michigan Press.

Weiss, Carol H. 1989. "Congressional Committees as Users of Analysis." *Journal of Policy Analysis and Management* 8 (3): 411–31.

Wilkinson, Richard, and Michael Marmot, eds. 2000. *Social Determinants of Health: The Solid Facts*. World Health Organization.

Wilson, James Q. 1973. *Political Organizations*. New York, NY: Basic Books, pp. 327–46.

Wilson, James Q. 1980. "The Politics of Regulation." In James Q. Wilson, ed., *The Politics of Regulation*. New York: Basic Books, pp. 357–94.

7

Looking for High Leverage: The Changing Context of Foundation Engagement in Wetlands and Habitat Protection

Walter A. Rosenbaum

Hewlett is looking for high leverage activities that have policy impact. . . . I want to back a winner, not just follow good strategies. Unfortunately, only a few foundations know how to win. . .they need to practice ruthless triage to find what really works.

Hal Harvey
Environmental Program Director,
Hewlett Foundation

Introduction

On May 29, 2002, The David and Lucile Packard Foundation publicly announced a contribution of $6.33 million as the first installment on the purchase of salt ponds in South San Francisco embracing a parcel roughly equal to the size of Manhattan Island. Packard's announcement was part of a media event dramatizing one of the largest wetlands restoration projects ever undertaken in the West —"an unprecedented public/private partnership" noted Packard (David and Lucile Packard Foundation, 2002; Rogers, 2002). The purchase involved a collaboration between the state of California, the federal government, and four private charitable foundations to acquire and restore 16,500 acres of wetlands and endangered species habitat for public domain, at a cost of $100 million. The acquisition, in turn, added a crucial parcel to the evolving CALFED Bay-Delta Program, the nation's largest ecosystem restoration project, embracing more than two-thirds of California's interior and coastal area.

A month later and across the continent, the Nature Conservancy announced its intention to restore 337,000 acres of wetlands and to buy conservation easements to prevent the development of another 300,000 acres along Florida's Kissimmee River, at a total cost of $700 million. Charitable foundations were also expected to underwrite a substantial portion of the expense involved in the land purchases (Newman, 2002). By protecting this vast riverine ecosystem stretching from the headwaters of the Kissimmee River in Central Florida to Lake Okeechobee in South Florida, the Conservancy hoped to improve indigenous water quality to a level essential for the success of another huge national ecological reconstruction effort: the Everglades ecosystem restoration project.

As important for the foundations, but far less publicized, was the political aftermath. A month after Packard's announcement, news services reported that the California Legislature might not approve the state's participation in the salt flats purchase unless "substantial changes" were made in the arrangements and, at the same time, other critics were threatening to challenge the property appraisal in court. In Florida, the Nature Conservancy conceded that it would have to depend upon Congress to allocate almost $500 million over six years from a newly enacted multibillion-dollar farm bill if its project were to succeed. In short, both ecosystem projects were embedded in a matrix of vested political institutions and contingent public policies. The foundations would have to collaborate with other project proponents in further public policy work to assure the success of their investments.[1]

The California and Florida ecosystem projects illustrate notable growth and change in the manner through which U.S. charitable foundations have sought to leverage their influence in environmental policymaking over the past decade and a half. Focusing upon foundation activity in land and habitat conservation illuminates an especially vital and significant domain of this environmental engagement in terms of the foundation resources committed. The CALFED and Everglades restorations are the largest examples of an evolving national trend toward ecosystem planning as a primary conservation strategy and, thus, are particularly useful as centerpiece studies.

[1]The narrative is based upon a diversity of sources. Interviews were conducted between June and December 2002 and again during early 2008 with professional staff and management of many foundations, consulting organizations, and stakeholder groups engaged currently, or very recently, in activities affecting policymaking for both the California and Florida projects (see the interviewee list at the end of the chapter). Other data was provided by the Foundation Center, The Center on Philanthropy and Public Policy, and the Environmental Grantmakers Association.

A Decade of Growth and Change for Environmental Grantmaking

The concurrent participation of charitable foundations in the California and Florida ecosystem projects would be significant if only for the magnitude of institutional investments. However, the two state projects were selected as the setting in which to examine foundation engagement in environmental policymaking because they exemplify a growing foundation commitment to protecting ecologically valuable lands by promoting public or private policy initiatives and an altered array of strategic considerations driving this foundation engagement. Both trends, in turn, illuminate significant transformations in the broader context of environmental grantmaking that have influenced how foundations have sought to influence conservation policies over the last decade.

GROWTH AND CHANGE IN ENVIRONMENTAL PHILANTHROPY

Over the last decade, charitable involvement in environmental grantmaking has significantly changed. Total investments have enlarged, and support for land conservation and land use planning—especially for the preservation or restoration of wetlands and endangered species habitat—has steadily enlarged. In 2007, environmental and animal-related groups ranked tenth in total grants among all grant recipients—most of this for land conservation (*Chronicle of Philanthropy*, 2008).[2] In contrast to earlier decades, this engagement has increasingly supported the development of institutions and policies for land use planning on a very comprehensive spatial and temporal scale—policies of regional or ecosystem magnitude rather than fragmented, smaller land acquisition and management. These broad policy goals have meant a considerably greater foundation presence in public policy development at the state, regional, and local level. In fact, as the California and Florida projects illustrate, foundations often discover they must become politically engaged *before* and *after* the successful acquisition in land and habitat to assure the successful implementation of their land management objectives. In short, the last decade exemplifies a continuing departure among many foundations from a traditional concentration upon purchasing and protecting resources, such as wetlands, wildlife habitat, and forestland, to greater involvement in affecting public policies affecting these resources (Jehl, 2001; Billitteri, 1998; Schwinn, 2007).

---

[2]In the following discussion, "conservation" is the aggregate of six grant categories in the Foundation Center's statistics compiled between 1998–2003: natural resources conservation/protection, water resource conservation, land conservation, forestry services, wildlife protection, animal protection and welfare. Beginning in 2004, "conservation" represents a single category without differentiation in the Center reports.

An Enlarged Environmental Philanthropy

Between 1990 and 2000, foundation spending for the environment and animal protection increased 350 percent, from $200 to $700 million and by 2006 it had reached $1.145 billion.[3] More than 80 percent of these grants have annually been awarded for environmentally related programs.

Foundations have still collectively invested very modestly—about 6 percent of total annual giving—in environment and animal programs when compared, for instance, to the 25 percent in grants for education, health, or arts and culture. And a striking ideological and tactical asymmetry exists between politically liberal and conservative foundations when it comes to environmental policy engagement.

The Enrichment of Conservation Grantmaking

Since 1990, no domain of environmental grantmaking has been more generously supported nor expanded more vigorously than land conservation in all its aspects. During the years since 1990, conservation grants have constituted more than two-thirds of all grant dollars invested in environmental programs. Moreover, the amount of these conservation investments has significantly increased since 1990, reaching more than $601 million in 2006. Conservation grants continue to constitute the largest proportion of all foundation giving for environment and wildlife protection as well (Figure 1).

Figure 1. Natural Resource Conservation Grants: Percent of All Environmental and Total Environmental/Wildlife Grants, 2001–2006

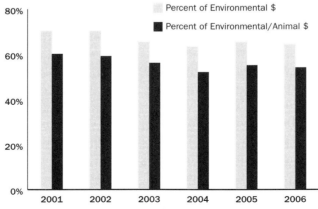

Source: The Foundation Center, *Foundation Giving Trends*, various years.

[3]Grantmaking data from 2000–2006 found in The Foundation Center, *Foundation Giving Trends*, 2008 Edition (New York: The Foundation Center, 2008).

The changing character of philanthropies engaged in land use policymaking is also illuminated by the composite involved in the Florida and California activities. Until the early 1990s, the relatively few foundations actively involved in land use issues were likely to have a predictable mix of characteristics: a long-term commitment to environmental engagement (Surdna, Ford, and Doris Duke) as part of a much broader social agenda, a rank among the larger philanthropies, and a specific commitment to regional or local environmental philanthropy (Beldon, Joyce, Geraldine R. Dodge Foundation). The array of philanthropies currently involved in the same policy domain is now much larger; the number of very active wealthy foundations has significantly increased (as evident, for instance, in the presence of the Turner, Hewlett, MacArthur, and Gates Foundations) along with increased involvement by much smaller, locally or regionally based philanthropies like Florida's Margaret Ordway Dunn Foundation or California's Save San Francisco Bay Association.

Why Wetlands and Habitat Conservation?

The Foundation Center identifies more than sixty-three categories of environmental grantmaking embracing every important domain of state, local, and national environmental policymaking: air and water pollution regulation, toxic waste management, recycling, global warming, energy conservation, and much more. The six categories aggregated in this study under "natural resource conservation," however, account for more than half of all annual environmental grantmaking since 1992.

There are several reasons why land and habitat conservation—in its many dimensions—has such a strong attraction for grantmakers. One attraction is that wetlands, forests, wildlife habitat, and related terrestrial resources are "ecological supermarkets" creating a multitude of expansive ecological benefits achieved by few other environmental investments. The protection of these "supermarkets" is grounded in the ability to manage the lands which contain them. Wetlands are especially valuable, providing water quality protection, wildlife habitat, soil conservation, aquifer recharge, recreation, and floodwater storage (an acre of wetlands can store 1.5 million gallons of floodwater)—all increasingly critical environmental priorities. Wetland-dependent species generated more than $79 billion annually, or about 71 percent of U.S. commercial and recreational fishing revenues in 2000 (U.S. Environmental Protection Agency, 2002). "Species habitat," in turn, is always something more: forest, grasslands, wetlands, aquifer recharge zones, groundwater retention, recreational area, or something else.

Another reason for a conservation priority is that these richly diverse resources are rapidly disappearing. The U.S. has already lost half of its original wetlands: Florida, for instance, has lost 46 percent and California 91 percent of these resources, and an additional 60,000 acres annually disappear across the nation. Thus, securing wetlands or habitat protection materially amplifies the environmental benefits and, thus, the "return" on economic investment. Moreover, acquiring wetlands, forest, and other habitat conservation creates or preserves a tangible environmental amenity, one that may pay immediate dividends in public goodwill and produce tangible, often engaging "results" for foundation officials always keen to demonstrate prudent stewardship of institutional resources. (Some leaders among the cadre of environmentally active foundations complain that land conservation is entirely too attractive, diverting too many resources away from other environmental objectives such as environmental justice and grassroots organizational development (Viederman, 2000; Willman, 2004; Dowie, 2006).

And there are strategic advantages to land conservation. Hooper Brooks, Director of Environmental Grants for the Surdna Foundation, has observed that land conservation encourages stakeholders and the public to become involved in larger systemic issues and thereby promotes a civic environmental education valued by many foundations. The creation of land trusts, moreover, can elicit the support of conservatives and others who mistrust governmental intervention in social problems. Saving private land, noted Brooks, "is a way that doesn't have to involve the government, puts [the trusts] in a place where they have huge potential" (Green, 1999).

The collateral benefits of conservation investment have become especially important to foundation funders when wetlands and habitat protection are integral to ecosystem restoration projects, such as the California and Florida endeavors. This growing interest arises, in large measure, as a response to a major evolution in federal government conservation strategies. In addition to the California and Florida projects, other major federal projects involve the Chesapeake Bay, Platte River, Greater Yellowstone, and Mojave Desert ecosystems.

The Growing Importance of Systemic Ecological Planning

The signal was the Clinton administration's 1993 Reinventing Environmental Management, recommending cross-agency ecosystem planning and management under all federal programs affecting ecosystems. By 2008, more than eighteen federal agencies were engaged in more than fifty ecosystem programs (GAO, 1994).

What distinguishes ecosystem approaches to land management, among other things, is that "the ultimate purpose is sustainability, both ecological and socioeconomic. The overall goal is sustaining ecological attributes and functions into perpetuity. Proponents of ecosystem management consider social and ecological sustainability interdependent" (Cortner and Moote, 1999). In practical terms, this means managing land and water resources on a very vast geographic and temporal scale, explicitly identifying ecological and socioeconomic interdependencies and assessing the impact of change upon all system components and continually adjusting management plans in response to experience with their implementation. Both CALFED and the Everglades Restoration illustrate the vast and intricate scale of ecosystem planning: the Florida project embraces 25,000 square miles reaching from Orlando to Key West, including 14 counties, more than 300 municipalities, the whole Everglades ecosystem itself and its sustaining ecosystems; CALFED includes 61,000 square miles—about 37 percent of the state (Working Group, 1998; CALFED, n.d.). Thus, the management and use of any ecosystem component—river valleys, for example, or forest habitat— has to be determined on the basis of its relationship to other important elements in the ecosystem and must contribute to sustainability of both the natural and built environment.

Some Significant Policy Implications

These trends have had significant implications for the forms of policy engagement by grantmakers over the last decade and, equally important, for the socialization and education of foundation officers and staff concerned with environmental matters.

Thinking More Holistically

Environmental policy discourse among program officers and governing officials exemplifies a growing sensitivity to the systemic relationships implicit in environmental management and the strategic importance of land in this perspective—in brief, to thinking about land and habitat in the context of an ecosystem. This awareness has been further cultivated in recent years by scientific consultants and "consultative groups" who, as we shall shortly elaborate, now assume an important role in "educating" foundations ecologically. An environmental program manager for the Hewlett Foundation described this trend as "learning to think big," rather than focusing on the protection or acquisition of relatively small, and often fragmented, land parcels. Framing environmental investments in terms of their systemic consequences was evident, for instance, in the MacArthur Foundation's decision to purchase large tracts of agricultural lands bordering the Florida Everglades as a contribution to the restoration program evolving there. Ralph Hamilton, former Director of Florida Philanthropy for the MacArthur Foundation, observed:

> It soon became evident to me that the built community and the environment were related, and that we needed to think of environmental issues as regional . . . if we wanted to improve the quality of life in poor communities, we had to be aware of how land was used ... we wanted to encourage local officials and environmental NGOs to think regionally. (Interview, July 30, 2002)[4]

From a broader perspective, this growth of systemic thinking also illustrates the spreading concern among foundations committed to environmental engagement that program decisions be defensible as "sound science." And when environmental science itself seems deficient, foundations, especially the larger ones, are beginning to aggressively invest resources in improving that science. The Moore Foundation, predicted to be among the nation's ten largest grantmakers, has identified as a funding priority an investment in environmental research not funded by the federal government.

Increasing Subnational Governmental Engagement

Today, ecosystem policymaking and management inevitably involves more public and private stakeholders at all federal levels because much of the land and other resources essential to such planning are not federally owned. Nonfederal lands, most privately owned, account for three-fourths of the nation's remaining wetlands and 60 percent of the total habitat of currently listed endangered species. Thus, private property owners, individual or corporate, as well as their local government regulators, become important stakeholders and actors in decisions about the use of such land. One implication, especially, powerfully shapes foundation experience. Land use control historically has been largely a state or, in reality, a local governmental concern. More than 36,000 units of local government currently exercise some land use authority.[5] Consequently, when nonfederal land or other resources are an interest, foundations must expect to engage state and local governmental institutions and actors in dealing with the public policy implications.

---

[4]The term "NGO" in quoted material is synonymous with "nonprofits" used elsewhere in the narrative.
[5]Includes states, counties, municipalities, and townships.

Policy Implementation as a Policy Objective

An important consequence of increasing foundation engagement in conservation policy appears to be a growing awareness among foundation staff of the importance of policy *implementation*, particularly at the state and local level, as an arena for policy influence. Foundation consultants have assumed an important role in emphasizing to foundation personnel that policy implementation is a mode of policymaking. "Lots of foundations don't understand the importance of implementation," noted an attorney for California's Resources Law Group, consultants highly influential in promoting foundation involvement in the CALFED project. "It's a new arena for many foundations and they need to make sure that [governmental conservation] policies are implemented; I try to educate staff to the implementation aspect of policymaking." A strategic problem for foundations promoting the public purchase of land essential to ecosystem planning such as the Everglades or the CALFED projects, for instance, is that funders must often ensure that governmental funding commitments are implemented over the decades that may be required, and to ensure continuing oversight over the implementation of land use designs.

Many foundations have probably focused belated attention on implementation as a potential target of policy influence because environmental policy implementation typically involves highly complex, attenuated, and technical activities, seldom achieving the visibility of agenda-building and policy formulation in governmental institutions. In the Everglades restoration project, for example, the implementation of the restoration plan required the creation of several hundred separate, distinct physical and biological structures. The development of each structure ought properly to be considered a policymaking microcosm involving numerous public and private stakeholders engaged in an ongoing process of *ad hoc* negotiation and bargaining about design and resources. The growing salience of implementation issues was suggested in a response by Surdna's Environmental Program Director, Hooper Brooks, to a question about the kind of environmental policy impacts that were important to the organization: "Yes, we're interested in policy impacts through public education and supporting implementation of programs" (Interview, December 9, 2002).

Such, in broad outline, appear to be some important transformations in the context of foundation environmental grantmaking over the last decade. Their collective impact can be more sharply defined by examining foundation activities related specifically to the California and Florida projects.

The Anatomy of Conservation Policy Engagement: The CALFED and Everglades Projects

The conceptualization created by James Ferris and Michael Mintrom in Chapter 2 to characterize foundation policy engagement provides a useful organizing framework readily adapted to a necessarily concise discussion of foundation involvement in the CALFED and Everglades projects.

Why Are Foundations Engaged?

The foundations engaged in various land use issues related to the CALFED and Everglades projects generally share at least two characteristics: their primary institutional facilities, or significant investments, are located in the state where the projects are sited; and, the foundations have a long-standing commitment to environmental concerns (sometimes to the geographic region of the project), if not to policy engagement explicitly. However, external consultants and environmental nonprofits, as well as foundation staff, may exercise considerable influence on decisions about projects and institutional recipients for grants within the arena of geographic commitment.

Geographic and Environmental Commitments

The Packard Foundation's 1999–2003 Policy Agenda, for instance, declared that a primary objective was "to bring about a fundamental shift in land use planning in the Western United States to limit sprawl and protect important open space and biological diversity" and that one benchmark for program success would be to "acquire land and development and water rights in California." The Turner and MacArthur Foundations, whose grantmaking in support of institutional capacity among environmental advocacy organizations promoting the Everglades restoration supplemented their direct contributions for land acquisition, were both committed to land conservation in the Southeast. Not surprisingly, most of the foundations involved with the two projects also targeted specific regions, such as the Western and Southeastern United States, as priorities. The synergy created by an institutional commitment to both land conservation and *regional* grantmaking undoubtedly magnified the appeal of engagement with the CALFED and Everglades programs and increased the potency of grantee proposals associated with these projects. The relationship between geographic location and project involvement is even greater among the smaller foundations, such as Florida's Elizabeth Ordway Dunn and Munson Foundations (Everglades) and California's Water Education and San

Francisco Bay Foundation (CALFED). Environmental engagement may not necessarily be a primary or priority grantmaking interest. However, many of these foundations discovered that other institutional concerns, such as social justice or better urban planning, could be promoted through environmental engagement also.

Consultants

External consultants and consulting organizations often exercise considerable influence over when and where foundations target environmental grantmaking. One reason for this consulting presence is that foundations, even large ones, often have a "lean" staff with few environmental specialists; smaller funders may have no institutional environmental expertise at all. It is not uncommon for funders to seek the assistance of consultants or for consultants to initiate discourse with funders, about environmental projects.

Examples from the California and Florida restoration work include:

- The California's Resources Law Group (RLG) initiated a series of "briefings" for the staff of several very large state charitable foundations to inform them about the importance of the CALFED project for the state's economic future and to suggest how they could "access" the project planning to exert influence. These briefings subsequently promoted the foundations' funding of seminars for state legislators and public education campaigns to support state funding for land purchases associated with CALFED.

- In 2007, the Resources Law Group collaborated with the Packard Foundation to create a new strategic plan for the development of the Bay Delta after the CALFED coalition dissolved in 2004 as a result of institutional conflicts. The new 2007 strategic initiative, called the Bay Delta Conservation Plan, resulted from a cooperative effort of the state, the RLG, and Packard in which Packard provided much of the initial funding while the RLG drafted a strategic plan, organized the technical support, and assisted with organizational management. With additional funding from the Hewlett Foundation, this broad foundation-consultant alliance has reinvigorated the ambitious wetlands and species conservation objectives originally proposed by the CALFED plan.

- The Everglades Foundation, a small Florida funder, hired a consultant specifically to clarify when and where it could productively support Everglades restoration.

This discourse between consultants and foundation staff, as later discussion will amplify, often is sustained by an infrastructure of recurrent conferences, symposia, and seminars sponsored jointly by consulting organizations and collaborative foundations, such as the Environmental Grantmakers Association, to keep foundations informed on current environmental policy issues.

Affinity Groups: Life Under the "Big Tent"

With few exceptions (mostly involving smaller foundations), grantmakers associated with the California and Florida projects belong to a variety of affinity groups, of which the most important is the Environmental Grantmakers Association (EGA). With over 250 members, the EGA includes almost all of the largest, wealthiest, and most active foundation grantmakers associated with environmental policymaking in the United States.[6] In the environmental policy domain, affinity groups are constituted from members sharing a common set of environmental interests. The Florida-based Funder's Network for Smart Growth and Sustainable Communities, for instance, was created in 2000 to be a learning network for national foundations interested in issues related to sustainable development in Florida and elsewhere; it presently includes sixty-eight foundations. A few affinity groups represent conservative foundations concerned with land conservation policy at state and local levels. The most significant of these appears to be the Free Market Environmental Roundtable, supported primarily by free market and libertarian think tanks, including the Cato Institute, Center for the Study of American Business, Pacific Research Institute, and the Competitive Enterprise Institute. The Roundtable, however, has no obvious role in the public discourse over the CALFED project and commonly assumes a low public profile (it does not, for instance, maintain a web site but cosponsors several others); it primarily facilitates the exchange of ideas and propagation of free market and libertarian principles among ideologically affiliated organizations.

The Environmental Grantmakers Association (EGA), like most affinity groups, conducts a variety of activities intended to provide resources for informing, mobilizing, and facilitating cooperation among member foundations.[7] In addition to an annual conference, EGA sponsors numerous forums and other meetings among small subsets of foundations with particular policy priorities, such as energy conservation, or climate

---

[6]A roster of the Environmental Grantmakers Association can be found at the association's web site: www.ega.org.
[7]See, for example, the EGA's 2002 Fall Retreat Program: "Crafting Alliances, Reweaving Democracy," 2002 Fall Retreat, September 7–11, The Grove Park Inn, Asheville, NC.

warming. It is widely assumed that EGA is a major force in determining which nonprofits and what environmental policy priorities will receive grant support to the point where some critics believe the EGA, together with a few very wealthy and aggressive funders such as the Pew Charitable Trusts, largely determine the environmental agenda and strategies for the domestic environmental movement.

The impact of the EGA upon charitable trusts engaged in the California and Florida ecosystem plans is not well documented and therefore difficult to evaluate, although anecdotal information suggests that that the EGA may be most influential with foundation trustees and directors while the smaller and more specialized affinity groups, focused upon more circumscribed environmental issues, may be more important to program officers.

Not Always "What" But "Who" Is Involved

Foundation environmental agendas sometimes reflect the personal vision and aggressive leadership of particular individuals, often staff environmental specialists, who see an "opening" in the foundation's larger mission for specific regional environmental funding. One example is the major role assumed by Ralph Hamilton, then Director of Florida Philanthropy for the MacArthur Foundation, in the early planning of the Everglades restoration. Hamilton initiated a collaboration with the Florida Governor's Commission for a Sustainable South Florida, the state's Department of Community Affairs, and local officials in Palm Beach County, where the foundation had significant investments, to encourage local development of land use policies compatible with the restoration objectives. Probably more often, the project recruits someone, in the sense that a foundation's environmental mission attracts individuals who actively craft specific funding agendas within the context of a congenial mission statement.

The Influence of Environmental Nonprofits

People in the work know each other, observed a program director for Defenders of Wildlife, a nonprofit active in the South Florida ecosystem project, "and there is a sort of subculture; groups develop reputations for reliability that make them more or less attractive to grantmaking foundations" (Interview, Nicole Rivet, Defenders of Wildlife, July 31, 2002). Subcultures of relationships between funders and grantees clearly exist and influence foundation decisions about grantmaking opportunities in both the South Florida and California projects.

Formal protocols may imply that proposals submitted to grantmakers by environmental nonprofits are solicited by foundation initiative and respond to program objectives crafted by program officers. The reality is more complex. Discussions with both foundation and nonprofit informants suggest that: 1) foundation environmental programs often are created, or the substantive policy goals strongly influenced, at the initiative of nonprofits themselves; 2) foundation program officers sometimes encourage specific advocacy groups to write specific grant proposals subsequently funded by the foundation; and 3) *which* nonprofit is associated with a grant proposal is as important as what the proposal entails, for some NGOs develop reputations for exceptional competence (or pronounced incompetence). These informal understandings are aspects of the subculture whose subtle influence has clearly affected the character of organizational infrastructures promoting specific land use policy initiatives in both Florida and California, even if foundation program officers acknowledge the fact uneasily ("We don't talk about this," observed one such manager of a foundation deeply involved in the CALFED project).

The important role of nonprofits in initiating and crafting foundation land conservation proposals was evident, for example, in the working relationship that developed between the MacArthur Foundation and the Conservation Foundation (a nonprofit) prior to MacArthur's decision to provide financial resources and strategic influence for the purchase of agriculture land bordering the Everglades. According to a Conservation Foundation program manager:

> We worked with the MacArthur Foundation in developing their approach to the South Florida project. We worked with them to think through the whole South Florida system and its ecological relationships and how the foundation could become involved. (Interview, Elizabeth Dowdle, Conservation Foundation, July 25, 2002)

Another example of nonprofit influence in foundation grantmaking decisions is the ongoing collaboration between the Sacramento-based Resources Law Group and the Packard Foundation. The Resources Law Group (RLG) acts as auxiliary staff for the foundation's ambitious, recently initiated Conserving California Landscape Initiative (CCLI), intended to conserve extremely large regional ecosystems and their human infrastructures on the basis of long-term sustainability. The RLG, acting as an intermediary between the foundation and grant applicants for the CCLI program, analyzes and evaluates grant requests for foundation program officers. From the foundation's perspective, this provides the foundation's very small and scientifically limited staff with the legal and scientific resources essential for reviewing grant proposals competently. In broader perspective, the viewpoint of both nonprofit and foundation program managers seems to be that the ongoing, informal discourse often arising before and during the creation of foundation grantmaking programs is an appropriate, even essential, dialogue that provides grantmakers with the technical and scientific guidance needed to make judicious environmental program decisions.

No Right Turns

Foundations in California and Florida presently funding conservation-related policy activity at the state and local governmental level are politically liberal or nonpartisan rather than conservative ideologically. Thus it is, and has been, almost without exception in other policy venues as well. The absence of economically or politically conservative charitable foundations from grantmaking that promotes preservation or acquisition of wetlands and animal habitat, or that advances public policies facilitating such action—indeed, the lack of a conservative foundation presence during most public debate over such policies—is commonplace to foundation observers of all ideological dispositions.

Several explanations have been suggested for this ideological cleavage. First, conservative foundations believe that very few competent nonprofits are available to promote conservative interests at state or local policy levels. Second, conservative foundations find it more appealing to trustees, directors, and corporate funders to underwrite litigation by public interest law firms, such as the Pacific States Legal Foundation, that challenge state and federal regulatory actions affecting property rights. For example, rather than invest money in grants to organizations opposing purchase of land for species habitat, conservative foundations would rather underwrite legal challenges to the use of the Endangered Species Act to limit private use of animal habitat. Moreover, notes Christopher Yabolnski of the Heritage Foundation, "Conservative groups are most likely to be involved with philosophical conservative advocacy, such as the Cato Institute or the Heritage Foundation, and with think tanks promoting such philosophy" (Interview, September 3, 2002). Additionally, many conservative foundations are largely funded by individuals strongly committed to "libertarian" or "property rights" ideologies whose policy agendas move in very different directions of conservation policy.

Foundation Approaches: How Much Collaboration?

Charitable foundations, as Lucy Bernholz notes, have historically been "infamous individualists" whose institutional cultures tolerated only fitful collaboration. However, within the last decade collaboration among grantmakers generally has apparently increased and evidence from the California and Florida endeavors appears to support this conclusion. Some examples:

- Several large California foundations, including Hewlett and Packard, and Surdna joined with some smaller state funders to underwrite a study of ecosystem governance structures that has strongly influenced the evolving design of the CALFED governance process.

- In South Florida, the Surdna and MacArthur Foundations collaborated with local funders to "build receptivity" for the Everglades restoration by sponsoring public education activities and meetings with local public officials to publicize the need for local land use planning to inhibit urban sprawl on the Everglades perimeter.

In many ways, affinity groups such as the Funders Network for Smart Growth (FNSG), the older Environmental Grantmakers Association (EGA), and consulting organizations like the Consulting Group on Biological Diversity have become important catalysts for foundation collaboration by providing for the discussion of common interests which, not coincidentally, also socialize foundation staff into collaborative thinking and create informal communications networks.

One strong incentive for collaboration is the opportunity to create pooled funding initiatives that considerably magnify influence in common policy goals. A frequently cited example is the foundation partnership, noted earlier, whose collective financial contribution was a major inducement for the state of California to contribute to purchasing the San Francisco Bay salt flats. Another incentive to collaboration is the increased political capital—particularly an amplified access and status among public policymakers—that foundation partners may be able to create collectively. Collaborations in both the California and Florida projects, however, tend to be *ad hoc* and contingent upon an ability to bring foundation staff together in a shared conviction about both the environmental benefit of collaboration and the synergy that partnership contributes to each foundation's larger mission.

Consulting Organizations and Catalysts to Collaboration

During the last decade, a number of organizations have formed for the purpose of educating environmental grantmaking foundations about emerging issues of ecological importance, providing them with technical/ scientific expertise about ecological issues, and providing a forum where nonprofits, foundations, and scientific experts can meet to explore opportunities to influence national and international environmental policies. A consultative organization is a hybrid of affinity groups, traditional environmental advocacy groups, charitable foundations, and scientific associations. Although characteristically small in staff and budget, consultative groups have become potent as mediators and catalysts for the development of new environmental policy initiatives and strategies among a frequently large and wealthy array of environmental grantmakers. As consultative organizations have multiplied, their impact magnifies because they create new influence and information networks between various institutional actors involved in environmental policymaking; they link grantmakers and grantees with current scientific discourse; and they identify strategic investment opportunities for environmental grantmakers.

Two consultative groups have been notably important in raising the salience of domestic ecosystem projects, like the Everglades and CALFED endeavors, for environmental grantmakers. The Consultative Group on Biological Diversity (CGBD), created in 1987 by a partnership of US AID with the Pew, Rockefeller, MacArthur, and Ford Foundations, has a present membership of forty-six foundations and US AID. CGBD's most important institutional aspect is the working group constituted of foundations interested in specific environmental issues such as forest conservation or climate and energy. Lynn Lohr, the former CGBD executive director, believed that:

> CGBD is essentially a facilitator between foundations and nonprofits. It can, and sometimes does, initiate ideas to foundations. More often, foundations come to CGBD with ideas, need networking, resources, ideas and such. We also hold conferences on emerging issues to educate foundations on important groups. (Interview, August 20, 2002)[8]

Another consultative group important in the development of foundation interest in the CALFED project, and in the subsequent strategic planning and foundation support for CALFED's institutional successor, is the

---

[8]Environmentalism and politically conservative foundations share a long tradition of disengagement. *See*, for example, Mark Dowie, *American Foundations: An Investigative History* (Cambridge, MA: MIT Press, 2001); and Roger M. Williams, "Sustaining Ideas on the Right," *Foundation*, January/February 2006.

Resources Law Group (RLG) located in Sacramento, California. Although the RLG originated primarily as a public interest litigant in environmental law cases, in recent years it has become far more diversified. Currently, it provides consulting as well as legal services related to land conservation, land use planning, and natural resource restoration, as well as strategic advice to foundations in environmental grantmaking and resources for this purpose. In the last few years, RLG has organized conferences for Packard and other foundations to educate them about ". . . governance issues related to ecosystems, coordinated planning between the Hewlett, Moore, and Irvine Foundations to protect valuable California lands involved in the CALFED Project, and to encourage cutting-edge science and linking it to charitable grantmaking." As an RLG staff lawyer explained, "RLG gave strategic advice to Packard about protecting important California land resources, but we don't ordinarily deal with the legislature."

The rise of consultative groups, with their access to environmental science communities and their ability to fashion new modes of discourse between technical experts and foundation program officers, seems especially responsive to the lack of in-house environmental expertise widely observed among environmental grantmakers. In this respect, the consultative group doubtless alleviates much of the unease grantmakers might otherwise experience when confronting scientifically complex and contested environmental issues as, for example, when foundations want to know which best practices to underwrite for wetlands management or species protection.

STRATEGIC CHOICES: JURISDICTIONS, VENUES, TACTICS

Public policymaking related to ecosystem protection will inevitably implicate federal, state, regional, and local governmental jurisdictions in some significant manner. However, as foundation interest increasingly turns to land and habitat owned privately or corporately, a very substantial engagement with policymaking at the state and local government level occurs, as the ecosystem projects in California and the Everglades exemplify.

Jurisdictions

In both California and Florida, many grantmakers initially were engaged, in varying degree, in promoting congressional authorization and appropriations to initiate the projects. With the projects authorized and underway, grantmakers increasingly appear to be investing considerably more resources and effort to sustain state, regional, and local governmental support for the projects and for "on the ground" implementation of planning objectives.

Why the intensified state and local engagement? Foundations are recognizing (often with considerable prompting by consultants) that these ambitious plans are contingent upon the inclusion and conversion of very large parcels of wetlands and species habitat under the regulatory jurisdiction of state and local governments. Moreover, state and local governments are themselves often attractive as potential underwriters of conservation land purchases. Smaller foundations often limit their engagement to underwriting the purchase of relatively small land parcels by program-related investments (PRIs) to nonprofits like the Nature Conservancy. The larger philanthropies more often support simultaneous engagement in multiple state and local jurisdictions. Another compelling reason for multijurisdictional (and multifora) engagement is that securing governmental or private commitments to conserve land or to change its designated use often requires continued foundation oversight of the policy implementation—funding must be authorized for state commitments to land preservation; infrastructure to support land conservation must also be created; legal challenges to conservation measures may subsequently arise; and much more. Thus, follow-through becomes almost an essential component of foundation program thinking.

One illustration of a multijurisdictional imperative implicit to the Everglades work occurs because the Florida plan assumed that more than 47,000 acres of agricultural land north of Lake Okeechobee (the Everglades Agriculture Area) can be restored from current private and corporate agriculture development to native wetlands (Working Group, 1998). Much of this land is owned by large sugar growing corporations or other corporate farm interests. In some instances, foundations themselves have underwritten the purchase of land parcels. More often, foundations have decided to use their grant resources to encourage municipal, county, and state governments to authorize the purchase of these lands with public money and to make necessary changes in land use regulations to facilitate the new land uses. In California, the Hewlett Foundation supported multiple strategies by nonprofits and other organizations to promote the adoption of Proposition Fifty, an initiative on the 2002 ballot authorizing a new state fund for land purchases involving, among other sites, the CALFED ecosystem.

Venues

The California and Florida experiences suggest that foundations committed to ecosystem restoration as a conservation strategy should expect sustained policy engagement not simply at state and local jurisdictions, but especially with state, regional, and local administrative agencies responsible for resource and environmental management—fish and game, pollution control, forestry, water management, urban planning, and recreation bureaucracies among them. For example:

- In several Florida communities bordering the Everglades, the Surdna Foundation supported conferences between biodiversity experts and urban planners to promote greater attention on the impact of local city development on efforts to protect endangered Everglades animal species.

- In California, the Packard Foundation provided support enabling the Nature Conservancy to assist state and local officials in monitoring the decommissioning of dams on the Battle Creek River required for the regional implementation of several CALFED objectives.

Such examples amplify both the importance of policy implementation in ecosystem management and the imperative for foundations to create forms of engagement with administrative agencies in order to affect that process.

Such generalizations, however, seldom apply to foundations that consider themselves ideologically conservative or "libertarian." Charitable foundations on the right of the American political spectrum mostly eschew other venues of influence on conservation policymaking in favor of litigation. This preference is grounded on a widely shared conviction that resource conservation generally, and restrictions by public authority on land use in particular, are most significant to conservatives when they raise constitutional and philosophical issues about property rights and the appropriate limits of public authority over private property. Thus, conservative charities, such as the Scaife and the Coors Foundations, typically underwrite conservative public interest laws firms that initiate litigation, and conservative "think tanks" that encourage public dialogue, about property rights and related issues that may be implicated in conservation policymaking.

A discussion of venues would, in any case, be incomplete without recognition that one of the most important policy arenas for foundations engaged with resource conservation, and particularly those involved in the Florida and California ecosystem work, is the venue of public opinion. In the following discussion of tactical alternatives for policy engagement, the use of public opinion polls, the cultivation of media attention, the dissemination of public information, and efforts to influence the "grassroots" constituents of state and local public officials—all the apparatus of what Benjamin Starrett of the Funders' Network for Smart Growth calls "a deliberate and sophisticated effort to inform media and decisionmakers"—has been a recurrent theme in tactical discussions by so many informants that this "venue" almost seems preordained (Interview, August 20, 2002).

Tactical Choices: The Strategic Premises

Several fundamentals appear to guide foundation tactical choices for policy influence. First, engaged foundations act primarily through established environmental advocacy groups or other institutions legally distinguishable from the foundation itself. One major reason, of course, is that this permits foundations to support advocacy and many related activities by proxy, thereby avoiding the legal complications which might arise should this appear to be legally proscribed "lobbying."[9] Florida Audubon, as one example, was actively involved in advocacy in the Florida Legislature to propose a constitutional amendment in 1996 (Ballot Proposition Five) to increase state funding for public land purchases facilitating the Everglades ecosystem plan. The MacArthur and Surdna Foundations, among other grantmakers, provided general program support for Florida Audubon, anticipating that the money would, among other things, underwrite such advocacy. Implicit understandings between grantmakers and advocacy groups that grants will sometimes be targeted in fact, if not formally, for legislative advocacy is not uncommon. One Florida Audubon staff member observed that foundations often become deliberately ignorant about the political purposes to which their grants may be (intentionally) directed:

> Foundations often want to direct NGO activities but don't want to be perceived as manipulative. Foundations expect NGOs to create a foundation for political action . . . and they don't want to know that their money goes for political action. But foundations like groups such as Audubon because the foundation will get the collateral benefit of political influence.

Whether this customary strategy of political leverage through proxies is the most appropriate or efficacious means of exerting foundation influence upon public policy is now a matter of debate of significant proportions within the environmental grantmaking community. A *provocateur* in this debate has been the Pew Charitable Trusts. Pew's very assertive intervention in environmental policymaking at national and international levels, creation of affiliated institutions to promote and to propagate scientific research, and for others to aggressively advance a substantive policy agenda, and its

---

[9] The distinction between "lobbying" and other forms of advocacy is enormously important to philanthropies. Charities are subject to revocation of their tax-exempt status if a "substantial part" of their activities is "lobbying." Private foundations are even more strictly regulated by a prohibition for spending any funds on lobbying. However, "the federal rules define 'lobbying' very narrowly to exclude many activities that can affect legislative decisions [and] . . . the law contains robust safe harbors that permit foundations to make grants to public charities that lobby without having the grantee's lobbying attributed back to the foundation."

commitment to getting measurable [policy] results poses an alternative model of policy intervention which, if successful, may be very attractive to other environmental grantmakers.

Second, advocacy and other modes of political influence are often underwritten through grants ostensibly targeted for nonpolitical or nonpartisan purposes. The distinction between foundation funding of public information, roundtables, opinion studies, or related nonprofit activities and funding of legally proscribed advocacy is fragile and elusive in practice. Many foundation managers and their nonprofit grantees readily acknowledge that powerful political leverage can be exerted on local, state, and federal policymakers through ostensibly nonpartisan activities funded by grantmakers. Public opinion polls, for instance, may be commissioned by a foundation, or a foundation grantee, to provide nonpartisan information about public perceptions on an important issue such as the Everglades ecosystem restoration. If that poll suggests strong public approval for the project among the constituencies of state representatives anticipating a legislative vote on funding for the project, the judicious release of the polling data among legislators will become advocacy in fact if not in name. Grant-funded nonprofit activities are often described so vaguely as to permit generous latitude of interpretation. One informant, from Defenders of Wildlife, offered an example of this strategy: while foundations are very careful to state that they don't want their money used for lobbying, it can be used for educational outreach [which is often similar].

Tactical Choices: A Primer

While foundations involved in the California and Florida ecosystem projects have used a broad array of instruments for policy leverage, modalities are apparent:

A. **Funding Policy Analysis:** In both California and Florida, foundations frequently funded symposia, conferences, and other gatherings that brought together local officials, technical specialists, and stakeholders to identify and clarify significant policy issues *created as a result of a project's initiation*. Several large California foundations, for example, convened a meeting with CALFED officials to discuss how foundation investments could facilitate the program's implementation. As ecosystem restoration gains increasing scientific as well as political importance, some foundations are beginning to give much greater attention to funding scientific research intended to inform and support conservation efforts. Florida Audubon and Defenders of Wildlife, for instance, have both received modest grants in recent years to underwrite research on habitat conservation associated with Everglades restoration. The Moore Foundation is still among a few large foundations to identify scientific research as a major environmental priority.

B. **Funding Technical Support:** Scientific research associated with ecosystem planning, like other large conservation projects, is often underfunded. Foundation support for technical research is highly valued by a great many stakeholders because it enables them to create more competent advocacy in restoration planning. In Florida, the Dunn Foundation grantmaking to the Florida Sierra Club and the Surdna Foundation's support to the Florida Audubon Society underwrote influential technical studies related, respectively, to restoration of the Kissimmee River floodplain and Florida Bay pollution—in both instances, with significant policy impact.

C. **Supporting Advocacy:** Advocacy support assumes both familiar and innovative styles. Customary and frequent advocacy support is provided through creation and dissemination of information to the public and stakeholders on salient, current issues; operating support to nonprofits known to support specific policy positions; and cultivation of media interest in specific policy discourse. Opinion polling has been focused on specific publics (such as local policymakers, scientific or technical experts, opinion leaders), important demographic subgroups, or the general public.

  – A number of larger California foundations routinely commission public opinion polls related to currently important restoration issues. Especially when the results may yield advantage in policy leverage, the polls are often widely disseminated to the media and, particularly, to state legislators expected to vote on important restoration issues. For example, one California funder, anticipating the California Legislature's forthcoming vote on authorizing land purchases to implement the CALFED project, initiated opinion polling which revealed strong public support for the purchase; the polling results from each legislative district were then sent to appropriate representatives.

  – "Building capacity"—using foundation grants to underwrite the operating budget of nonprofits—often becomes advocacy by another name. Foundations supported Florida's Nature Conservancy in this manner to assist the Conservancy in persuading Congress and the Florida Legislature to purchase wetlands essential to the Kissimmee River Restoration phase of the Everglades project.

— Support for litigation illuminates how "capacity building" can readily transmute into policy advocacy. A great many of the environmental advocacy groups supported by foundation grants in both California and Florida have been, and continue to be, aggressive litigators; foundation grants also support organizations like the Resources Law Group, committed to litigation as a primary policy instrument. Litigation lies in a twilight zone between proscribed and permitted forms of foundation policy advocacy. Foundation and nonprofit staff recognize, however, that foundation grants are often intended, explicitly or not, to underwrite litigation meant to create or change legislative or executive policymaking.

— A more innovative approach to foundation advocacy is what Marcia Sharp has called "a diffusion strategy." This entails the creation or exploitation of communication networks (workshops, symposia, conferences, or existing associations) through which policy goals can be lodged on the funding agenda of other foundations—in effect, something akin to lobbying the lobbyists. This strategy is epitomized by the Funders' Network for Smart Growth. The Network "creates a more circuitous route to leverage of members' investments which involves a long-term and highly ambitious strategy to embed issues and knowledge into the program agendas of many different granting streams of many different foundations." (Sharp, 2002)

D. **Deploying Assets:** Foundations have historically promoted resource conservation across the United States by purchasing valuable land or conservation easements to protect property from development. In recent years, several foundations have effectively leveraged public funding of land purchases by collateral commitment of their own resources to the undertaking. "I'm amazed how much private dollars can move other projects" noted one consultant who acted as broker between several foundations and the state of California in a cooperative CALFED wetlands purchase. "Commitments of foundation money help to push projects to the top of the policy agenda. . . . Private foundations have this kind of influence that they seldom recognize." Such foundation capital may appear to be a traditional program-related investment (PRI), but when it is offered as leverage for public conservation spending, it appears to pack a political clout that resonates among policymakers. In particular, since 2004, many environmental grantmakers have felt growing pressure from their staff or board to invest foundation capital assets strategically as well, particularly in mitigating global climate change.

E. Oversight of Policy Implementation: Among some consultants, foundation staff, and nonprofit informants, there is an emerging perception that foundation decisionmakers are climbing a "learning curve" through experience with the California and Florida restoration programs. One increment on that curve is said to be an evolving awareness that funding the monitoring and oversight of program implementation creates an important pressure point in ecosystem policymaking. One reason is that ecosystem restoration projects are heavily dependent on "adaptive management" which means, in effect, that initial planning strategies may be altered over time when experience with previously untested policy designs demonstrates an imperative for change. Where and when these "adaptive" decisions occur may initially be problematic. However, awareness of the substance and occasion for these decisions through monitoring is likely to be a tripwire signaling important policy decisions of which stakeholders should be aware.

– This "follow-through" by foundation proponents of ecosystem developments also requires a new, more sophisticated conception of policymaking by many foundation staff. A few foundations, such as Hewlett, Packard, and Surdna, already appear cognizant about these implementation issues. Florida Audubon, for instance, sought foundation support to oversee implementation of sixty-seven separate Everglades projects managed by the Army Corps of Engineers.

– An innovative example of follow-through has been the Everglades Foundation initiative, begun in 2003 and continuing through 2008, to facilitate cooperation among the restoration stakeholders and to build technical expertise within their ranks to support the Everglades restoration. The Everglades Foundation did not dictate what recipients should do. The grants to private and public stakeholders were meant to promote efficiency and synergy within the common goals of the partner organizations and to encourage collaboration rather than competition on policy agendas. For example, the foundation established a weekly teleconference that provides an avenue through which the partner organizations regularly communicate and strategize. It also helped its partners form six regional advisory groups that focus on specific parts of the ecosystem, and then report back to the main group what is being accomplished and where additional resources are needed. "The foundation has fundamentally broken away from the traditional mold of grantmaker, and has become a working partner with its grant recipients, all with a common goal of saving, restoring, and protecting America's Everglades," observed Foundation CEO Mark Kraus (Interview, April 13, 2008).[10]

[10]According to Everglades Foundation CEO Mark Kraus, the Foundation also "hired a talented science staff to provide technical expertise and expert witnesses to support the efforts of the partner organizations."

Looking Ahead: The Implications

The evolution of foundation engagement in wetlands, habitat, and related conservation policymaking inevitably raises questions about the future—surely for the foundation staff, stakeholders, consultants, and others who are already pondering the implications. Some implications seem evident, some portentous, others unsettling in their contingency.

Are the Florida and California Experiences Typical?

Until the latter 1980s, it appears that foundations committed to resource conservation relied primarily on three strategies: program-related investments (mostly through the purchase of conservation lands or conservation easements on land); operating support to environmental advocacy organizations; and some indirect funding of policy advocacy and litigation. During the 1990s, it appears that growing engagement in large-scale ecosystem policy issues prompted many foundations to considerably diversify their grantmaking tactics and objectives. This diversification was especially evident in: 1) the increasing frequency with which foundations underwrote public opinion polling and targeted conferences, workshops, and specialized information flows specifically for legislative and administrative decisionmakers; 2) greater attention to using program investments individually, and collaboratively, to leverage governmental conservation investments; 3) greater receptivity and more initiative in discourse with environmental consultants over technical resources and new opportunities for environmental policy engagement; and 4) more focus on promoting and embedding policy-relevant conservation issues in agendas of other funders and affinity groups.

In these respects, the Florida and California narratives exemplify what seem to be innovative (or at least atypical) strategic and tactical decisions by the foundations engaged in efforts to influence conservation policy. This innovation may be a distinctive response to the emerging problems of policy engagement posed by the jurisdictional, economic, and ecological scale of ecosystem restoration. In particular, the intensive foundation engagement with state and local governmental entities, the growing attention to directly influencing the climate of community public opinion, and heightened sensitivity to improving the science base for policy advocacy may all be distilled from the quality of science and management issues implicit to extremely large-scale ecosystem policymaking. In any case, foundation attention to the politics of policy implementation has certainly become more acute and instrumental in foundation policy planning as a result of the generous timescale upon which ecosystem policymaking must necessarily transpire.

Additionally, the rising salience of large ecosystem issues in foundation policy discourse, both within and between foundations, bespeaks the growing influence of science consultative organizations, such as the Consultative Group on Biological Diversity, and a greater receptivity to their influence among the larger and wealthier environmental grantmakers. These consultative groups and their variants (for example, organizations offering both science and legal expertise to foundations) seem well on the way to claiming a secure position in the constellation of institutions collectively shaping the direction of ongoing foundation conservation policies, particularly among the foundations that are considered to be leaders in environmental grantmaking.

None of this amounts to a collective epiphany. Characteristically, a diffusion of innovation occurs when one or a few foundations appear to exploit an unfamiliar tactic successfully and spread the news, often through affinity groups. In many cases, the appearance of these tactics may also have much to do with the remarkable growth of foundation assets during the 1990s, enabling many funders to think more imaginatively (and expensively) about policy leverage. The profusion of newer policy engagement styles may also be an artifact of growing governmental involvement in very large ecosystem restorations and closely related projects which, in turn, increasingly compels foundations committed to conservation to come to terms with governmental policymaking in ways that might have been unnecessary a relatively few years ago.

What Is Success? What Is Successful?

Foundation officials themselves sometimes struggle at defining how to measure "success." (Responding to the question, one foundation environmental director explained bemusedly: "We are right now having a Berkeley professor do a study for us.") Generally, a measure of success is easiest when grants are dedicated to time- or event-bound projects. These objectives might include: 1) a specific policy action or decision, such as a legislative vote on a project authorization or a resource purchase, or the passage of legislation integral to a conservation program, or the initiation of litigation on conservation issues; 2) creating a defined knowledge resource, or underwriting conferences, symposia, or other conferences meant to disseminate or create information and ideas; 3) creating and disseminating information, such as public opinion polls, to media and the public; and 4) funding new organizational structures, or providing operating expenses for other organizations. Such projects are intended to produce results in a relatively short time; to have measurable consequences within a state, region, or community related to the foundation; and to create some tangible institutional product. Not surprisingly, these are the strategies which foundation officials and consultants most often cite as "successful."

Far more elusive of evaluation are foundation activities intended to have diffuse consequences temporally, geographically, or institutionally—support of activity to "educate" urban planners about the ecological implications of their work, for example, or funding to "build capacity" for greater activism among community-based environmental organizations. Indeed, foundation officials strongly committed to such activity express frustration that such programs often are prematurely neglected because satisfactory results are difficult to demonstrate. In any case, demonstrations of "success"—however measured—are the propellant for many long-term foundation programs. This may create a perverse situation when it comes to foundation engagement in the implementation of ecosystem restoration or other long-term conservation programs. Ecosystem restoration is typically implemented over many decades (the Everglades project is expected to require a minimum of thirty years). A rising sensitivity to the implementation aspect of environmental conservation may be evident among many foundations, as the California and Florida experiences suggest, but foundation involvement in such implementation may require engagement over many years, or decades, during which evidence of "success" may be tenuous long before it becomes evident (if it does). Whether foundations, however well-intentioned, have the robust institutional endurance that engagement with implementation policy may require is problematic.

What Is Risky?

The foundations involved with the California and Florida projects seem, with a few important exceptions, most averse to funding that betrays more than a dash of what can be called "The Pew Style."[11] The reference is to the Pew Charities' aggressive national and international promotion of many different environmental protection policies through virtually every traditional pathway for mediating influence on government. The Pew Charities typically create separate institutions to promote this advocacy, legally distant enough to avoid proscribed political "lobbying" yet subsidized largely through the Pew organization. Perhaps most importantly, the Pew organization intends to create and sustain high-visibility policy controversies and to plunge into existing ones without apology.

[11]On the Pew philosophy, see Douglas Johl, "Charity Is New Force in Environmental Fight," *New York Times*, June 28, 2001.

Still, some foundations concerned with the California and Florida endeavors have created subsidiary institutions committed to policy advocacy, if not quite so boldly as Pew. These organizations are kept at arm's length because they are either technically underwritten by NGOs who receive much of the necessary money through grants from the parent foundation; or they are independently incorporated consulting firms whose policy advocacy is largely supported by the foundation; or they are environmental advocacy groups. Thus, it appears to be the high intensity and visibility of controversy arising from engagement in policy advocacy that these foundations seek most to avoid.

Other kinds of risk to which foundations may quickly become averse, if they are not already, are engagement in policy implementation, in the sustained promotion of issues through "embedding" on other institutional policy agendas, and in other long-term funding commitments. The problem of distilling "success" from such continuing engagement has already been apparent. Additionally, the meltdown in foundation assets beginning in 2001–2003 amplified foundation concerns about the wisdom of long-term investments at a time of increasingly constrained resources. No other issue more pervasively weighs upon the discussion of future foundation grantmaking, environmentally or otherwise, than the implications of severely shrinking program assets—a matter of renewed concern with the economic recession following the "subprime meltdown" in the housing industry beginning in 2008.

How Firm the Foundations?

"People don't realize how much a cutback in foundation assets is going to influence future environmental grantmaking," observed a veteran consultant to California's largest environmental grantmakers. Virtually all the foundation informants offered variations on this theme. The most significant implication appears to concern how future environmental program resources will be reallocated. Long-term program commitments can be badly frayed by constricting assets and problematic results. Some informants have suggested that long-term investments, or large program investments to leverage public conservation spending, may be the most endangered budget items. The budgetary bloodletting, additionally, will compel difficult decisions not only about priorities within environmental categories but between environmental spending and other grantmaking domains. Through a budgetary ripple effect, a number of environmental advocacy groups active in the two state ecosystem projects have already anticipated a significant decline in foundation support and are rethinking their own environmental priorities.

It isn't apparent how amplifying budget constraints will affect foundation engagement in ecosystem policymaking for California or Florida. Nor can one predict how well the more creative strategic and tactical modalities, especially, will weather the oncoming winter of programmatic downsizing. However, nothing about the future of environmental grantmaking in either state is more problematic, or more consequential, than the answer.

REFERENCES

Billitteri, Thomas J. "Endowments Mark Fiscal Maturity for Environmental Groups." *Chronicle of Philanthropy*, December 3, 1998.

CALFED Bay-Delta Program (nd). "Facts About the Bay-Delta," available at http://calfed.ca.gov/pub_info_materials/about_bay_delta.html, last accessed 2003.

Chronicle of Philanthropy. "A Big Year for Big Giving." January 24, 2008.

Cortner, Hanna J., and Margaret A. Moote. 1999. *The Politics of Ecosystem Management*. Washington, DC: Island Press.

David and Lucile Packard Foundation. 2003. *Conservation Program Five-Year Framework 1999–2003*, 18.

David and Lucile Packard Foundation. "SF Bay Salt Pond Acquisition," September 9, 2002.

Dowie, Mark. 2001. *American Foundations: An Investigative History*. Cambridge, MA: MIT Press.

Dowie, Mark. "Support Grass-Roots Environmentalists." *Chronicle of Philanthropy*, April 20, 2006.

Eilperin, Juliet. "Environmental Groups Join Forces; Time Is Short, Challenges Are Enormous, Leaders Say." *Washington Post*, May 15, 2007, A13.

General Accountability Office (GAO). 1994. *Ecosystem Management: Additional Actions Needed to Adequately Test a Promising Approach*. Publication No. RCED-94-111.

Greene, Stephen G. "Preserving Open Space for the Ages." *Chronicle of Philanthropy*, July 29, 1999.

Jensen, Brennen. "Doris Duke Foundation Gives $100-Million to Help Slow Global Warming." *Chronicle of Philanthropy*, April 19, 2007.

Johl, Douglas. "Charity Is New Force in Environmental Fight." *New York Times*, June 28, 2001.

Malone, Charles R. 1997. "The Federal Ecosystem Management Initiative in the United States" (pre-print edition), appearing in Lemons, J., R. Goodland, and L. Westra (eds.), *Environmental Sustainability: Case Studies on the Prospects of Science and Ethics*. Dordreche, The Netherlands: Lluwer Academic Publishers.

Newman, Joe. "Project Aims to Protect Acres of Florida Wetlands." *South Florida Sun-Sentinel*, June 29, 2002.

Rogers, Paul. "Lawmakers *See*k Review of S.F. Bay Salt Pond Pact." *Contra Costa Times*, June 23, 2002.

Schwinn, Elizabeth. "Growing Number of Charities Bring the Environment into Their Appeals." *Chronicle of Philanthropy*, November 1, 2007.

Sharp, Marcia. 2002. "Foundation Collaborations: Incubators For Change." Paper prepared for the forum: *Leveraging Philanthropic Assets for Public Problem Solving*. The Center on Philanthropy and Public Policy, University of Southern California, May 13–14.

U.S. Environmental Protection Agency. 2002. Office of Water, Office of Wetlands, Oceans and Watersheds, *Threats to Wetlands*, Publication No. EPA 843-F-01-002d.

U.S. Environmental Protection Agency. 2006, May. Office of Water, *Economic Benefits of Wetlands*, Publication No. EPA 843-F-06-004.

Viederman, Stephen. "Don't Just Tweak the Corners." *Foundation News & Commentary*, January–February 2000.

Viederman, Stephen. "How Grant Makers Can Curb Global Warming." *Chronicle of Philanthropy*, February 7, 2008.

Williams, Roger M. "Sustaining Ideas on the Right." *Foundation*, January/February 2006.

Willman, David. "A Low-Cost Way to Help the Environment." *Journal of Philanthropy*, June 10, 2004.

Working Group of the South Florida Ecosystem Restoration Task Force. 1998, November. "Success in the Making: An Integrated Plan for South Florida Ecosystem Restoration and Sustainability."

Interviews

Bast, Joseph: CEO, The Heartland Institute

Brady, Richard: Staff Attorney, Pacific Legal Foundation

Brooks, Hooper: Director of Environmental Programs, Surdna Foundation

David, Britt: Director of Foundation Relations, Resources for the Future

Dietrich, Richard: Associate Director, Foundation and Corporate Relations, Sierra Club

Dowdle, Elizabeth: Staff Member, The Conservation Fund

Doyle, Mary: Director, Center for Environmental Study, University of Miami

Draper, Eric: Director, Florida Audubon

Farquahr, Ned: Foundation Relations, The David and Lucile Packard Foundation

Griffith, Stephen: Sierra Club, Washington, DC

Hamilton, Ralph: Director of Florida Philanthropy, John D. and Catherine T. MacArthur Foundation

Harvey, Hal: Environmental Program Director, The William and Flora Hewlett Foundation

Jackalone, Frank: South Florida Office, Sierra Club

Jenson, Robert: Director, Margaret Ordway Dunn Foundation

Kallick, Stephen: Assistant Director for Environmental Programs, The Pew Charitable Trusts

Kranzer, Bonnie: Former Director, Governor's Commission for a Sustainable South Florida

Katz, David: Vice-President for Development, Earthjustice

Kraus, Mark: Senior Vice President and CEO, the Everglades Foundation

Langston, Stuart: Consultant, South Florida Ecosystem Restoration Task Force

Lohr, Lynnn: Executive Director, Consultative Group for Biological Diversity

Mantell, Michael: Staff Attorney, Resources Law Group

Martin, Daniel: Foundations Relations, Moore Foundation

Rivet, Nicole: Foundation Relations, Defenders of Wildlife

Rogers, Jane: The San Francisco Foundation

Starrett, Benjamin: Director, Funders' Network for Smart Growth and Sustainable Communities

Schoonmaker, Susan: Staff Attorney, Resources Law Group

Taylor, Jeremy: Natural Resources Specialist, Heritage Foundation

Tejada, Claudia: Staff Member, Defenders of Wildlife

Ward, Katherine: Environmental Grantmakers Association

Williams, Diane: The James Irvine Foundation

Yabolnski, Christopher: Research Staff, Heritage Foundation

8

Foundations, Public Policy, and Child Care

Jack H. Knott and Diane McCarthy

Introduction

This chapter is concerned with the way foundations engage public policy in the area of child and youth development. The particular focus of the chapter is on child care, which is defined here to include pre-kindergarten care and learning, after-school care, and mentoring programs for children. Child care is a useful focus because it cuts across several policy issues. Employment policy includes child care as more women enter the workforce, causing parental work schedules to take away time for raising children. Alleviating poverty from one generation to the next is dependent on child care as poor families often have limited options for early learning activities and after-school programs for their children. Many families in poverty have only one parent. For these families, the success of welfare-to-work requirements depends on access to child care for the transition into the productive workforce.

Child care also plays a prominent role in future achievement and behavior patterns for adults. A growing body of knowledge shows the importance of early learning for adult outcomes and out-of-school programs for adolescents and teenagers in the development of behavior patterns that persist into adulthood. This knowledge has rekindled interest in universal child care,

Another version of this chapter was published by Sage Publications in *Administration & Society* 2007; 39; 319 under the title "Policy Venture Capital: Foundations, Government Partnerships, and Child Care programs." Material from that article is used here by permission of Sage Publications.

especially in a technological society that needs educated workers to compete in the global market.[1]

Not surprisingly, a number of foundations at the national and state level have adopted initiatives targeted at pre-kindergarten and after-school child care. These child care programs are often embedded in broader foundation initiatives that focus on community and neighborhood development or on children and families. This chapter analyzes child care programs in twelve national foundations that have made grants targeted for children and families. Within the children and family program area of these foundations, child care is the most frequently funded program emphasis (see Table 1).

The argument of the chapter is that foundations became involved in child care in general due to a number of factors, the most important of which were the increase in numbers of women in the workforce and improvements in knowledge of brain development in children. They became interested in systems and policy changes because they believed that these changes are necessary to achieve their programmatic goals for children and families.

In this way, foundations can be viewed as policy venture capitalists who invest in particular communities and programs expecting a return on their investment. They expect that their initial foundation investment will stimulate regulatory policy changes and financial investment by government and other nonprofits to produce a broader systems impact. Consequently, the foundations' specific goals and strategies for investment in child care have reflected their assessment of the risks of the political process and their perceived windows of opportunity to effect policy change. Tying investment to political risks and policy opportunities, however, despite a broad policy agenda for children and families, has meant that few foundations have innovated or led in child care policy. Most have played an important but targeted role of partnering with government, networking, leveraging funds, filling in gaps and inconsistencies, and evaluating and improving the implementation of government initiatives.

The chapter is divided into the following sections: 1) foundations and child care programs; 2) foundations and child care policy; 3) the specific goals and strategies that foundations use to engage child care policy; 4) the locations for policy engagement; and 5) conclusion.

---

[1]The data for the analysis was derived from the foundations' published reports and web sites. Written questionnaires were e-mailed or mailed to program officers involved in the child care area at each foundation and telephone interviews were conducted with senior officers at four of the foundations in 2002 and 2003. The telephone interviews were conducted to gain an understanding of the foundations' specific goals and strategies for engaging child care policy.

The Evolution of Foundations' Child Care Programs

Foundations are an important component of the child care sector, providing direct services, technical assistance, and funding for programs. They also fund research, carry out demonstration projects, and support advocacy groups. Scientific and social developments played important roles in bringing foundations into the child care program area (see Table 2). The Foundation for Child Development (FCD), for example, from the 1950s to the 1970s focused on genetic and birth defects in children. FCD's focus changed over time as the public became more aware of the underlying causes of child disease and disability (Foundation for Child Development, 2000). In particular, medical science gained more knowledge about the relationship between poverty and health, which led the foundation to develop an interest in the promotion of economic security for children, including child care for indigent families.

The Edna McConnell Clark Foundation was influenced in its program emphasis by the growing body of knowledge that showed that out-of-school time, including pre-kindergarten, formed habits of behavior and social relationships that lasted into adulthood. The foundation's earlier emphasis on in-school education policy for children shifted to an emphasis on out-of-school programs and care for children and youth. Similarly, a program officer at the Kellogg Foundation observed that, "Our early learning programs are mostly driven by research and by the whole area of brain science."

Some foundations were broadly involved in issues related to child well-being from the beginning and incorporated child care under this program umbrella. The child care emphasis of the W. K. Kellogg Foundation, for example, grew from the concern for child welfare of the foundation's founder and first president. Research on child welfare by the founder of the Annie E. Casey Foundation, as another example, showed that many troubled adults come from bad foster family experiences. Since 1966 the foundation has had a strong commitment to long-term foster care issues, and in 1983 the foundation expanded its focus to all disadvantaged and at-risk children. In 1999 the foundation initiated the *Making Connections* program that focused on channeling funding and policy priorities toward strengthening families in neighborhoods, including child care programs.

Sometimes a change in leadership or a related program emphasis can lead to an interest in child care. The Carnegie Corporation of New York, founded in 1911, shifted its program focus with the arrival of their new president in 1997 to an emphasis on knowledge as a way of improving the lives of citizens. To ensure the success of the United States in the twenty-first century, the Corporation sees basic educational skills as key to leadership development, hence their interest in early childhood education. A good example of how a program emphasis can spill over into child care concerns is the Upjohn Institute, whose primary focus is employment policy. The Institute became interested in work and family and through this concern developed an interest in child care; this interest was heightened further as more mothers entered the workforce.

Foundations and Child Care Policy

Providing grants for child care programs does not necessarily engage the foundation in child care policy. For example, at the time of this research, the Edna McConnell Clark Foundation explicitly rejected public policy as a focus, believing that the legal and political environment is too unchangeable for the foundation's programs to make a difference. The Gerber Foundation, too, did not take an active role in public policy but supported the policy efforts of other organizations through grants. The other ten foundations in this study had varying degrees of commitment to public policy, but those that had a policy emphasis have worked in policy for a long time. An exception is the W. K. Kellogg Foundation, which only adopted a policy focus in the 1990s when new leadership took over (see Table 3).

A BRIEF HISTORY OF CHILD CARE POLICY

The federal government has pursued several child care policies, beginning with the emergency nursery school program under the Franklin Roosevelt administration in 1933. During the Great Depression, child care policy rose to the surface of societal concern because of the harsh conditions that low family income imposed on children. By the 1940s, however, continued support for programs for all pre-school children had dissipated. During the Second World War the federal government passed the Lanham Act, which supported child care facilities in war-impacted areas of the country. Services were available to all mothers, regardless of family income, working in defense industries (Cohen, 1996).

In the postwar period, public policy shifted back to concerns about persistent poverty with the passage of the Head Start program. In the 1970s, a growing body of knowledge about the importance of early childhood development for success over one's lifetime brought a renewed emphasis on universal child care. Congressional legislation reflected this new emphasis on child development through the passage of the Comprehensive Child Development Act of 1971, which was vetoed by President Richard Nixon. In the late 1980s, however, a number of factors converged to recreate a societal interest and policy opportunity in universal child care. These factors included a growing welfare-to-work movement for welfare mothers, sparked by the perception of intergenerational welfare dependency; the growing number of women in the workforce; and the continued growth in knowledge about the importance of early child development. The government responded to these factors by passing the Family Support Act in 1988, the first universal entitlement for child care (Cohen, 1996; Klein, 1992). The passage of this act was followed in 1990 by two more legislative enactments in child care: the Child Care and Development Block Grant (CCDBG) and Title IV-A, At-Risk Child Care.

In 1996, the federal government passed the Personal Responsibility and Work Opportunity Reconciliation Act, commonly known as welfare reform, which replaced Aid to Families with Dependent Children (AFDC). This reform created the Temporary Assistance for Needy Families (TANF) block grants, consolidated several federal child care funding streams into a single Child Care and Development Fund (CCDF) block grant, and resulted in the decoupling of welfare from child care in many states. Since 1996, states have reallocated more TANF funds into child care than have been spent from the CCDF. One concern is whether the amount of public subsidy leads to quality child care. There is also concern about co-payment policies, which may force some of the poorest families into unlicensed care.

The federal government and the states also support child care through tax policy. The two major tax programs are the Dependent Care Tax Credit (DCTC) and the Dependent Care Assistance Program (DCAP). For 2007, the DCTC provided a tax credit of up to $1,050 for one eligible child in employment-related care and up to $2,100 for two or more qualifying children or dependents. In general, the higher the dependent care expenses and the lower a person's income, the larger the tax credit. The DCAP allows an employer to provide eligible employees up to $5,000 per year in tax-free child and dependent care benefits. Employees do not pay federal income tax, employers do not pay employment taxes, and neither employer nor employee pays Social Security and Medicare payroll taxes.

WHY FOUNDATIONS BECAME ENGAGED IN CHILD CARE POLICY

Many foundations believe that they cannot achieve or sustain their programmatic goals for children and families without significant systems change, including changes in public policy. Support for changes in child care policy fits within this broader rubric of concern for the well-being of children, as well as families and within some foundations' program emphasis on employment and community development.

Several foundations emphasize that the government's policymaking machinery in the United States is inadequate to meet the needs of children. The Annie E. Casey Foundation, for example, believes that the public systems that serve children and families are too narrowly focused, intervene only when a family or child is at a crisis point, and hold themselves accountable only by quantity of services rather than effectiveness. Casey thus supports decentralization of the government bureaucracy and better interagency cooperation at the neighborhood level, including better data and information sharing among agencies and parents.

Similarly, the Kellogg, Packard, Mott, and W. T. Grant Foundations focus on uncoordinated state, local, and national policies and the gaps and fragmentation in systems for children and families. These foundations are interested in creating a systems approach to public policy that includes a concern for how financing systems operate and how to improve quality standards. An official at the Packard Foundation sees the funding system for child care "as fragmented and under-funded, the quality of services is often mediocre, and the supply of personnel is inadequate." Packard supports more generous family leave benefits by employers, public financing of child care from birth to age three, and government support for enhancing after-school programs.

Kellogg emphasizes mobilizing, strengthening, and aligning the various systems of learning for children in vulnerable populations. These systems include schools, child care, families, and communities. As a program officer of the Kellogg Foundation remarked, "Our goal is to make child care a municipal issue rather than just an educational issue. The quality of life for the community depends on the quality and quantity of the child care systems." Kellogg is interested in the regulation of provider quality, certification for providers and teachers, and state-level subsidies for at-risk children.

These and other foundations support substantive policy prescriptions for children and families. The fully articulated vision of an alternative national policy for children and families in the U.S. is found in the FCD publication, *Our Basic Dream*, which argues that there is no excuse for a working family or its children to be "poor" or experience hardship (Shore, 2000). Working families meet their obligation to society and should be able to live "The American Dream." The foundation favors a comprehensive, coherent plan for families and children on the universalistic model of many European countries (see Kahn and Kamerman, 2002). Its policy goals include: welfare and employment policies that strengthen adult learning; universal access to early-learning programs; top-down program standards and quality incentives; improvement of the early education workforce; paid family leave; expansion of the Earned Income Tax Credit (EITC); and wage increases for early learning and adult learning workers.

Specific Goals and Strategies for Child Care Policy

Foundations espouse broad systems and policy change that they see as necessary to accomplish their programmatic vision for children and families. The challenge for foundation boards and officers is to spend the money entrusted to them wisely. They would not want to spend the money to simply duplicate government programs, for example. They would also not want to spend the money on activities that are already being provided by the private market. In both instances, foundation funding would add little or no net benefit for society. Consequently, foundations are often involved in efforts to create new public goods. This process of investing money in activities that produce new public goods is referred to here as "policy venture capital," a term borrowed from stock investing. But, rather than investment activities that fund innovation and the creation of new private goods, foundations can invest policy venture capital in the creation of new and innovative public goods.

The foundations' specific choices about policy goals and strategies in child care, therefore, depend on the kinds of risks they perceive in the political process, their recognition of windows of opportunity, and how they measure success. It also depends on the history of the foundation's grantmaking and the perceived level of knowledge about the problem. Many of the foundations use multiple approaches but emphasize one approach more than the others (see Table 4).

THE RISKS OF POLICY ENGAGEMENT

The decision to engage in public policy entails different kinds of risks for the foundation than do initiatives that focus on social programs. An obvious risk is the tax-exempt status of foundations, which prevents them from lobbying for specific legislative bills. While this tax-exempt status limits activity, most respondents did not feel it posed the greatest risk of policy engagement. The more important risk is the uncertainty of the political process to produce outcomes favorable to the foundation's goals. A foundation's program officers establish these goals in the development of program initiatives within the divisions of the foundation. The initiatives are then discussed and approved by the foundation's president and presented to the board of trustees. The foundation's program officers are held accountable for the achievement of these goals by the foundation's board, which measures the foundation's effectiveness and reputation as perceived by other foundations and the public.

One program officer stated, "The bigger risk is if you have a policy goal, too much of a successful outcome depends on the whims of politicians. The political winds can be quite devilish at times." Another program officer observed, "Politics by its nature is a risky business. It is much more risky than other programs. In politics despite trying hard and doing the right things, you may never reach your goal." The common concern among program officers is that, "You can put huge energy into something that is stillborn. The big risk is when everything is congealed, you could be wrong."

A foundation can also become too closely identified with one administration and find itself in trouble after an electoral change. A program officer commented that, "A major risk is the over-identification with the current administration in the partnership. Our partnership was tied to the Clinton-Gore administration. Bush is not so supportive. [We are] identified with a Clinton issue.... Partnering is always tricky, especially with the federal government, which is the ultimate gorilla. You can be pulled off the line."

Working through grantees also poses a risk. A program officer expressed the concern that, "There is a big risk in a grassroots strategy. We are a big funder of community organizing, which is risky because you empower people in poor communities. They have their own agenda and you don't know what it will be. It is filled with conflict." Another officer lamented, "What if we fund organizations that won't come through? What if we invest in organizations that are not wired into or hooked up politically? We expect local communities to change policy at the local level but some of these attempts fall flat on their face." Some foundations work with vulnerable communities and groups that do not normally have influence in the political process. A program officer explained, "In [two states] we worked with native peoples who don't normally have power or get involved in the policy process. We expected schoolteachers also to get involved in policy, something they had no experience with. That is a quantum leap."

Many program officers are substantive specialists rather than policy experts. These officers worry about failure to design or achieve policy goals and strategies that meet the expectations of the senior leadership, the board, or their peers. A program officer asked, "Does the program director have credibility and respect? How much policy information and understanding of political dynamics should directors be expected to know? We walk around with fear of not knowing enough."

The essence of risk for foundation officers is the probability of failure in achieving expected outcomes with the expenditure of foundation funds, as perceived by the foundation board, other foundations, and the public. To promote an initiative to the board requires building expectations of a successful program and a likely impact on policy and systems change. The foundation's senior officers establish their reputation by showing how activities that they have supported contribute to the foundation's mission. These accomplishments help the foundation justify its mission and expenditure of funds to the board and external constituencies.

STRATEGIES THAT INCREASE THE REWARDS AND REDUCE THE RISKS OF POLICY

There are several strategies that the foundations pursue to increase the rewards and reduce the risks of engaging in public policy. These strategies serve to increase the probability of achieving some measurable positive program results and some demonstration of impact on systems and policy change. While foundations advocate for broad systems and policy change, their actual activities are more narrowly focused and tied to the dynamics of the political and policy process. These strategies allow the foundations to demonstrate that they are making progress and achieving results in their quest for a better society.

Measuring Effort Rather Than Outcomes

Because connecting activities of the foundation or its grantees to policy impact is tenuous and difficult, foundations often measure success in terms of effort rather than actual policy impact. As one program officer stated, "We certainly like to see policy change as a direct result of our efforts, but this is not always possible." The officer then asked, "Have we had success in child care? Not really. Our investments in child care have been relatively modest compared to some other areas. In [our state] I think that we have had a measure of success. The state has increased its capacity and support for child care, but it is difficult to say that the changes we observe are due to the work of the grantees."

While political advocacy, networking, and public opinion activities are important for understanding policy effort, they do not constitute actual policy change. One foundation has set a goal of after-school programs for all children by 2010, but as the program officer observed, "Since this is unlikely to happen, how do we explain it to the board? What we do is say here's the progress we have made so far. We have had considerable success so far in developing the public will aspect of this.... We have been conducting semiannual polling and the proof will be in the pudding." This same officer stated that when child care funding was devolved to the states, "We set the goal of an after-school network in each state. If the networks are strong and thriving, that is a huge success. If the networks fizzle, we haven't succeeded with the initiative." In a similar vein, a program officer from another foundation defined success "in terms of leadership development in the communities. It is concerned with...who understands the politics of the communities, how to leverage funds and support in the community.... Every grant is political. Politics is concerned with who is benefiting and who is losing. Leadership and success have to do with more than expertise." He added that in some of the evaluations we look at "parents' involvement in politics, the role of the Chamber [of Commerce], and the Board of Education."

The long-term process of making a difference poses an additional problem for measuring success because it often extends beyond the length of the foundation initiative. A good example is the Joining Forces Initiative of the W. K. Kellogg Foundation, a program that was designed to improve child care quality and services, but is no longer operating at Kellogg. The evaluation of the program by Abt Associates focused on building local capacity for child care decisionmaking rather than examine the actual effect of the initiative on child well-being. A program officer at the foundation observed, "We get all fired up over it, but when the process is over, we end up going on to something else. It would be interesting to see what happens in 10–15 years, but we won't be there to know. [Our initiative] is simply too new to tell whether we are being successful." In considering this problem, a program officer from another foundation concluded that, "The best way to ensure policy success is to have grassroots support…. The need is to build a real grassroots constituency. If that isn't there, the program will not last." The point here is that the foundation can claim that even though no policy change has taken place, the foundation has succeeded in building a grassroots constituency that will advocate for change over time. Success is measured not by actual policy change but by the setting up of mechanisms that will increase the chances for change in the future.

Forming Partnerships and Collaborations

Many of the foundations in this study have formed partnerships with other organizations and the government to pursue child care policy (see Table 5). Partnerships with government in particular comprise both a risk and an opportunity. The risk is that the political administration will change and negatively affect the partnership. The opportunity is to leverage a greater impact on policy and programs than acting alone. Such an opportunity can reap important rewards for the foundation in terms of program success, accomplishment, national reputation as a major player, and influence in policy circles. The Kauffman Foundation, for example, entered into a partnership with five national foundations (Carnegie, Packard, Mailman, Ford, and the Institute for Civil Society) and six state-based child advocacy organizations, plus some state-based foundations such as the McCormick Foundation, to build greater public knowledge and awareness about the importance of early education, thereby building the public will to expand the supply and quality of early child care and educational resources.

The Annie E. Casey Foundation has also emphasized partnerships in its approach to engaging public policy. The *Making Connections* program is one component of a much larger campaign to help channel funding, policy initiatives, and public priorities toward strengthening families in neighborhoods. These efforts include numerous partnerships with national organizations such as the United Way of America, Points of Light Foundation, and Goodwill Industries, as well as national advocacy and policy groups such as the National Governors Association, Conference of Mayors, and National Conference of State Legislatures. These partnerships and other strategies are designed to expand the coalition of support, knowledge, and public will to recognize and strengthen families and neighborhoods.

Mott and Packard support a public-private partnership with the U.S. Department of Education (DOE), called the Twenty-First Century Community Learning Centers (CCLC), that provides quality after-school programming for low-income rural and urban children in thousands of schools across the country. The partnership, established in 1997, is designed to enable public schools to become community learning centers with expanded after-school learning opportunities, mentoring, and lifelong learning for adults. The program is administered and funded by DOE, while Mott and Packard have underwritten training and technical assistance for the centers.

Foundations that engage in partnerships with federal or state governments must deal with the risks of political change and administrative turnover. One foundation whose program was placed in jeopardy through political change decided to take a more strategic approach to government partnerships. They developed the following criteria for entering a partnership: 1) How close is the proposed partnership to the priorities of the foundation? 2) How many grant dollars need to go into the partnership and how many dollars will it leverage? 3) How does the foundation situate itself in the larger constellation of government activities? 4) Is there a population or intervention opportunity that is new and promising?

Foundations that pursue a grassroots approach also engage in partnerships. The W. K. Kellogg Foundation, for example, forms partnerships at the local level between educational institutions and community organizations, with the goal of promoting education and training for child care professionals. One of Kellogg's most interesting partnerships was the Joining Forces Initiative, which increased accessibility, affordability, and quality of child care for low-income families. This collaborative venture included partnerships with two local foundations—the Frey Foundation (Grand Rapids) and the Skillman Foundation (Detroit). In this project, Kellogg worked closely with the state government during the welfare reform of the 1990s, receiving $100,000 each year from the state legislature. This partnership was instrumental in the state legislature forming a children's caucus, an increase in child care subsidies from less than $100 million in 1994 to over $600 million in 2001, and the development of a referral system for the "Work First" welfare reform sites for parents entering the workforce.

In the evaluation of Joining Forces by Abt Associates, a critical impact was the increase in the capacity of the local community to engage in advocacy and decisionmaking on child care. Each community implemented a unique plan to involve broad resources and segments of the community. The expectation is that when foundation funding ends, these local coalitions will continue to live on and influence government decisions about child care. One important lesson of the initial phases of the evaluation was the crucial importance of including public sector partners in the coalition. These partners were able to influence the regulations and public subsidy of child care to remove barriers and provide needed financial support.

Assisting Local Grantees

The past success of the Joining Forces Initiative also shows the value of a related approach to reducing risk: assisting grantees in the communities in determining how to effectively engage the policy process. A program officer at Kellogg explained that the foundation "... provides the communities with experts on policy. We also set up evaluation mechanisms and networking meetings. We facilitate a sharing of ideas with each site and expect the grantees to set out clear policy objectives that are agreed on." Joining Forces has allowed communities to assess their needs and set their own priorities, thus achieving a level of local ownership and range of solutions tailored to the community. In addition, it demonstrates the value of reducing the risk of policy failure by maintaining a portfolio of projects that is flexible and diverse. A program officer from another foundation involved in a different initiative explains that flexibility and a diverse approach can also serve as a diversified portfolio for the program officer: "I have never had an out and out failure that is my Waterloo. I try to take a diversified approach with several things going on at the same time. It is better to build in flexibility and put evaluation into everything."

Vertically Integrating Programs and Policy Goals

In-house initiation of and control over projects and policy goals allows for closer attention to integration of priorities and measures of success. One program officer commented that, "We are very deliberate when we choose what problems and issues to work on and what goals to set. This approach allows us to employ the most strategic use of our resources. It also produces complementarities across programs, multiple effects, synergy, and an integrated portfolio. With the staff initiating programs and setting goals, we can better evaluate our activities." This approach entails greater deliberation. A program officer stated that, "We often hold meetings and consultation in the field for one and a half years with various practitioners and experts before we are prepared to launch an initiative." It also entails fewer and larger grants to target resources. Through these efforts the foundation seeks to develop a more concerted approach to grantmaking.

Some of the foundations in the child care area have created their own in-house capacity. Three prominent examples are the Upjohn Institute, Carnegie Corporation of New York, and the Edna McConnell Clark Foundation. In the case of Upjohn, research on child care is conducted in-house through the Family Labor Issues research hub as well as through grants to outside researchers. McConnell no longer designs initiatives and sends out requests for proposals to nonprofit organizations. Rather, the foundation researches potential organizations itself and is gaining capacity in organizational development, teaching these organizations how to conduct their own in-house programs and initiatives. Carnegie also produces in-house research reports from the Carnegie Task Forces on Meeting the Needs of Young Children (*Starting Points: Meeting the Needs of Our Young Children*) and the Carnegie Council on Adolescent Development (*A Matter of Time: Risk and Opportunity in the Non-School Hours; Consultation on After-School Programs*).

In her work on foundations and child advocacy, Sally Covington (2001) criticizes these top-down, in-house, and staff-initiated approaches as too removed from the advocacy community and the political process. She argues that they often do not reflect a broad vision of the causes of poverty and lead to relationships with other professional organizations, universities, and government agencies rather than with grassroots community groups. On the other hand, they allow program officers to develop a coherent approach to public policy and reduce the risk of failure in how the foundation measures success. They can lead to tangible and practical accomplishments that serve as an important reward for the foundation's efforts.

Building Reputation and Relationships

Reputation and relationships with policymakers are important for reducing political risk because they build trust and common expectations with policymakers. Each foundation plays to its strength in developing a reputation as a credible policy player. The W. K. Kellogg Foundation, for example, emphasizes the value of its projects in communities around the country as models for other communities. The Upjohn Institute emphasizes the quality of its scholarship and makes a concerted attempt to be at the forefront of econometric research on issues of public and private employment. Other foundations, such as the MacArthur Foundation, the Packard Foundation, and the W. T. Grant Foundation, emphasize the quality and credibility of the research that they fund. Packard for example emphasizes the "timely, objective information based on the best available research" (from the *Future of Children*, Packard Foundation). The Annie E. Casey Foundation builds its reputation through demonstration projects much like the Kellogg Foundation but also through partnerships, resource manuals, and publications that are used by policymakers and advocacy groups across the country.

Those foundations that rely on demonstration projects pursue a decentralized strategy as part of their effort to build relationships with policymakers. Relationships with policymakers in this context occur through local grantees, who often have connections with national and state policymakers. The formation of national partnerships also leads to relationships with policymakers through the connections that these organizations and their leaders have with appointed and elected government officials. Often foundations will hold workshops or conferences on family and child issues, including child care, and invite prominent legislators or other officials to participate, which allows these policymakers to meet first-hand with community people, researchers, and advocates on these issues.

The Kauffman Foundation placed an explicit emphasis on building a relationship with state legislators in Missouri through the creation (with the Danforth Foundation) of the Missouri Legislative Forum, a nonpartisan, information-sharing, and relationship-building program. The program was launched in 1999 as a three-year pilot program. Its purpose was to help the Missouri General Assembly make informed decisions about statewide issues that will improve the economic vitality and quality of life for Missouri citizens.

EXPLOITING WINDOWS OF OPPORTUNITY

One of the more prominent theories of how issues get on the public policy agenda is that windows of opportunity open and close depending on how ideas, advocacy, and political leadership converge or diverge from each other (Kingdon, 1997). Foundation program officers are aware of these windows of opportunity and consciously try to position the foundation to take advantage of them. One foundation officer commented, "There are moments when we perceive a window of opportunity and leap in with just-in-time activities, including papers, grants, and conferences. Foundations have a strong role in promoting policy discussion and taking advantage of the opportunity when it comes." Another program officer commented, "In the legislature, you have windows of opportunity that open and close with a change in politics. If you set ambitious goals [which I think we should do], you don't know how politics will develop to affect your success."

Foundations reacted to two policy developments in the 1990s that offered them new program opportunities and heightened concerns about children. These two developments were the passage in 1990 of the Child Care Block Grant Fund and Title IV for the states and the passage in 1996 of the welfare reform bill. Welfare reform in particular intersected with the programmatic emphases of the MacArthur Foundation and the Foundation for Child Development (FCD), bringing both foundations into child care policy. As an official from MacArthur observed, "We invested in child care because of the effects of welfare reform, the growth of women in the workforce, and the knowledge and experience from the field of brain development, which shows the critical importance of pre-kindergarten years for performance in school and future development." Similarly, the FCD believed that the shift from a national welfare policy to an emphasis on work and personal responsibility placed a much greater burden on low-income, working adults to care for the needs of their children. The FCD challenged the policy assumption that if parents are working, their children's essential needs will be met. The FCD's activities in child care, therefore, are largely a response to this shift in public policy.

A related policy strategy is to choose a political context for program initiatives that appears to be favorable to the policy outcomes the foundation desires. A program officer explained that, "We have been reading the tea leaves. We see what is happening in Florida. Forty states have pre-school funding by the state. We believe there is an opportunity here for extending policy change." He added that, "Before we started, we conducted a survey of the states, and we picked states where we thought something was going on, where there was a buzz." Another program officer observed, "There has been an increase in funding through the child care block grants to the states provided by the federal government. But through our studies we saw that the states really didn't know how to use that money very effectively to achieve access to quality care. For this reason we focused on state-level policymaking."

The existence of a policy champion or denizen seems especially important for taking advantage of windows of opportunity. One program officer described how a colleague of hers is a top policy expert who "saw an opportunity sitting on a platter and took it."

Some foundations have policy gurus but they may not be substantive experts in the various policy areas of the foundation. A program officer expressed concern that, "He is more an expert on the politics of the policy process than on policy per se. He knows what buttons to push but we still need to know the dynamics on the ground." It is especially helpful if the top leadership of the foundation has a policy interest and expertise. A program officer stated, "We have a wonderful president and vice president, both of whom are policy denizens. They are caring individuals who play an important intellectual role." She explained how the president had identified a policy opportunity that led to a major program for the foundation.

STAGES OF POLICY ENGAGEMENT

Part of the foundation strategy for engaging public policy depends on the history of the foundation's activities but also on the amount of information that is available on what works and what does not work. A program officer observed that, "The stage of the program is an important element of strategy. You may need to start with a demonstration project if there is little information about what does and does not work. In other areas, it would be better to do a meta-analysis, or in others to develop a communications plan because we already know what needs to be done. We need to keep circling through, though, to see what is needed."

The choice of which stage to fund is also a matter of risk and opportunity. Funding demonstration projects entails relatively little risk politically yet can show innovation and accomplishment for the foundation in several communities. The foundation can support the implementers of the demonstration projects in their advocacy for policy change, leaving the foundation one step removed from the political process. Demonstration projects are also expensive and often take years to implement. They do not work very well for timely intervention in the policy process. They do, however, build a repertoire of solutions for putting forward when the political environment becomes favorable to change.

Funding evaluations of existing government policies or analyses of alternative policy approaches, in contrast, can involve the foundation directly in policy and political change. Often these analyses are either developed in conjunction with or the results are provided to advocacy groups who use the new information to advocate for specific policy choices. These analyses can also sometimes be used to develop "public will," or in other words, to measure and influence popular public opinion on an issue.

Funding Demonstration Projects

Four of the twelve foundations in this study made funding for demonstration projects a primary strategy for engaging public policy on child care. Annie Casey and Kellogg have given substantial grants to several communities and cities across the country, while MacArthur and Kauffman have given demonstration grants in the state and city where the foundation is located. All four foundations have sought to empower, inform, and enhance the capacity of relevant players, including service organizations, businesses, communities, faith leaders, civic leaders, government agencies, and families. Kellogg's child care programs have tried to advance learning for infant, child, and youth development. Annie E. Casey has taken a broader approach that seeks to strengthen neighborhoods and families, including child care.

The four foundations expected demonstrations to produce several benefits. They foresaw the strengthening of the neighborhoods, communities, and families over time and beyond the funding period from the foundation. They also expected a growth of capacity in these communities to improve their situation through their own efforts, including the development of community leaders and advocacy coalitions for change. In addition, they promoted the adoption of these models in other communities through replication. The policy benefit comes indirectly through the use of these demonstration models for advocacy and communication to policymakers, including what kinds of public policies might need to be changed to make these new approaches succeed.

Since the political and policy context varies with each state, Kellogg has emphasized that the grantees must develop their own, indigenous policy goals to fit each state's needs and political context. Kellogg also funds relatively little policy research (with some important exceptions) but does have a high-quality evaluation research program that concentrates on evaluating the success or limitations of the foundation's demonstration projects. The results of the evaluations are used as part of the dissemination strategy to policymakers.

The Kellogg Foundation's primary child care program is the SPARK (Supporting Partnerships to Assure Ready Kids) initiative. This initiative is a pre-kindergarten program that encourages more seamless transitions to school. SPARK is in seven states and the District of Columbia. Each community is charged with developing a community blueprint for an infrastructure to support school readiness for vulnerable children. In the process of carrying out these projects, the eight sites are required to identify local, state, and national policy targets that may need to change for the program to sustain itself and spread to other communities. Besides SPARK, and its prior funding of Joining Forces, Kellogg funds two other programs that are related to child care: New Options for Youth, which supports partnerships between communities and colleges to create alternative learning environments for kids aged 14–20 in preparation for work or post-secondary education, and the Kellogg Youth Initiative Partnership, which promotes sustainable systems for youth in three counties in Michigan.

Annie Casey has a two-stage process at two different levels of generality. The first stage is a demonstration project, *Making Connections*, which began funding community centers and neighborhood groups in twenty-two cities through seed grants to help them with teachers, community challenges, and the development of promising approaches. The second phase narrowed the number of areas to ten cities that "most demonstrated the capacity, energy, and will needed to achieve concrete results for children and families" (Annie E. Casey Foundation web site, Frequently Asked Questions). The second phase is directed at providing training in family finance and savings, eliminating predatory lending practices, networking, improving communications, using data more effectively, and attracting investment. *Making Connections* is only one component of a larger campaign to support neighborhoods, which involves numerous partnerships with major national associations and nonprofit organizations.

These demonstration projects are very important for showing the foundations' innovative approaches to child care programs. They also serve as highly visible examples of how policy changes, if adopted more broadly across the country, might support these programs. In addition, through work in many communities, the foundations lay the groundwork for the building of community coalitions at the state and local level and sometimes at the national level for advocating for systems and policy change.

Supporting Research, Advocacy, and Communication

A second primary approach by some of the foundations is more direct and less costly but entails more risks because it seeks to work with national researchers and advocacy groups to change policy. The potential rewards are also greater in the short run if the foundation can get on the political agenda and gain the attention of policymakers. This approach centers on the goal of facilitating the generation of policy knowledge and ideas, working to bring think tanks and researchers together to create a policy discussion, funding efforts to influence public opinion on the idea, and then funding policy advocacy groups based on these ideas and discussions. Foundations that adopt this as an approach see the foundation as a direct facilitator connecting research, advocacy, and policy (Laracy, 2001). This approach builds on the important role of policy networks (Heclo, 1977) among academics, think tanks, professional associations, and professionals inside government agencies, which can form powerful coalitions and use information strategically in advocacy for policy change.

The four foundations that viewed themselves in this way give slightly differing explanations of this role. Carnegie said it believed that knowledge is the key to improving the lives of Americans, and policymakers need innovative ideas and knowledge to make more effective policy. MacArthur and Upjohn reported that they see the value of expertise and research for policy but believe that research must be translated and disseminated to policymakers before it will be used effectively. One official observed that, "We wanted to provide evidence-based practice on the natural experiments in child care for all the states and the federal government to consider as policy options."

Foundations also said they see themselves as a somewhat neutral place where partisan and contesting interests can come together to discuss policy issues. The Kauffman Foundation, for example, places the greatest emphasis on unbiased, objective information for policymaking that is not based on interest group or partisan attachments as a means to improve public policy. An official from the Annie E. Casey Foundation mentioned that, "The foundation allows for the questions to be posed in a safe place, where a discourse can occur on the issue." In a similar vein, through the Early Education Exchange, the Kauffman Foundation shares timely and important information in a neutral, nonpartisan setting in depth. Conferences at the Conference Center in Kansas City, Missouri, offer a venue for policymakers, funding agencies, and practitioners to share ideas on a system of high-quality early education for all children in America.

The two foundations that actively adopt this approach as a full-blown strategy are the Annie E. Casey and MacArthur Foundations. Both foundations have funded research and policy analysis of alternative options for the funding, practice, and cost of child care in the states following the introduction of the child care block grant. MacArthur partnered with the Institute for Women's Policy Research to support economic modeling of the cost of universal pre-kindergarten education. They also funded "research into what different states were doing and on how to fill the gaps in policy." MacArthur worked with the National Council of State Legislatures (NCSL), the Public Human Services Administration, the Leadership Forum of the National Governor's Association (NGA), and Zero to Three to share information, interconnect different policy networks, and generate a policy discussion. They then funded several advocacy and practice groups, especially in Illinois, based on these study results and discussion ideas, including the Day Care Action Council and an organization called An Ounce of Prevention, which administers Head Start funding. MacArthur feels that this combination of activities "was influential and used by the Governor's Task Force in Illinois in putting forward its pre-kindergarten program. The modeling also played a role in Massachusetts and in Washington, D.C."

The MacArthur Foundation also funds a "Special Initiative on Early Education and Care," which supports one of the core strategies in the Policy Research priority area. Grants are intended to enhance state and local capacity for improved policymaking on child care and to increase the supply of high-quality child care in low-income communities. The program supports evaluation research on local models in Chicago and on relevant multi-state projects around the country that add to the knowledge base of early education and care for policymakers and practitioners.

Annie E. Casey follows a similar strategic approach to policy engagement. They have funded, for example, the Teacher's College at Columbia University and the Department of Social Services in New York to develop a new simulation model of how to fund child care at the state level. They developed a system of projections that allowed them to alter the variables depending on state-level policy choices, which has led to new funding ideas for the early child care area. After conducting this analysis, the foundation sought to interact and create a dialogue with professional associations and policy think tanks which operate through the policy networks. It then funds advocacy groups in the policy community. As a program officer put it: "People in the policy community are decisionmakers themselves and a target for our efforts. The directors of large programs can have a zeal and network to role out the influence with policymakers. An example is the Head Start Association, which has a huge network of Head Start agencies. Another example is the network of private Family Resource Centers."

The Mott, Packard, and W. T. Grant Foundations are interesting in that they explicitly focus not just on advocacy and the development of awareness of issues, but also on evaluating the implementation of policies and measuring the effects of existing policies. The Mott Foundation in this respect focuses on evaluating the financing and budget impact of state policies on low-income communities and populations. This approach involves the administrative and policy implementation side as well as the agenda-setting side of policymaking. The W. T. Grant Foundation follows a similar approach. It works directly with policymakers in state governments in the legislative process to identify information and develop reports that inform legislation. It also conducts analyses of the impact of public policies and laws on youth development and the impact of education reforms on health, welfare, and juvenile justice. Similarly, the Packard Foundation works on the implementation of California's Children and Families First Act through technical assistance to the Children and Families Commissions.

In general, the foundations that said they focus primarily on research or on report writing engage the policy process in more stages than foundations that concentrate mostly on demonstration projects. The Upjohn Institute, for example, addresses policy issues at all stages of the policy process, from the identification of emerging problems to the evaluation of the implementation of existing statutes. Similarly, for foundations that have a substantial relationship with a single state or region, such as Packard in California or Kauffman in Missouri, the ties to the policy process tend to transcend the agenda-setting stage to encompass the legislative and implementation stages as well. As was indicated above, the Packard Foundation is working with the implementation of the Children and Families First Act.

The choice between community demonstration projects and national research and advocacy funding, however, is not only concerned with stages in the policy process. Demonstration projects constitute a bottom-up approach to policy, while national research funding represents a top-down approach. Funding the Urban Institute or Brookings Institution to produce a report on child care that is used by national advocacy groups does not involve community people in the strategy for changing policy. Demonstration projects, in contrast, engage community groups and organizations in devising an evaluation and advocacy strategy.

OTHER STRATEGIES

Besides these major policy strategies, foundations engage in other strategies that also provide rewards and opportunities for demonstrating practical success. For example, foundations fund the "development of public will" on a policy issue. This phrase means that the foundation will support media stories and the dissemination of information to influence popular public opinion on child care. Similarly, foundations spend considerable sums in communicating their ideas to civic groups, policymakers, and professional associations. Other related strategies include the development of databases or repositories for use by policymakers, or the provision of consultation and technical assistance. These activities provide tangible benefits in the policy process and allow the foundation to show successful efforts as inputs into policy change.

Dissemination and Communication

Regardless of approach, the foundations place a strong emphasis on dissemination strategies for communicating the results of demonstration projects and research to advocacy groups, civic leaders, and policymakers. Some of the foundations have separate public affairs departments or communications offices for actively pursuing this strategy. The foundations are very interested in media strategies for influencing the public will of citizens to support policy changes that raise the level of awareness of policymakers about policy solutions and social issues of importance to the foundations. They work with elite opinionmakers in the major civic and business groups and national associations to build support for change. They also use news media venues at all levels of government to send messages to policymakers.

Foundations that fund several demonstration projects, such as Kellogg and Casey, use media stories about these projects at the state and local levels. Casey also uses news media reports on its *Kids Count Data Book* for national news stories on the status of children in the country. A program officer emphasized that, "You need a social communications plan and evaluation. Through a policy advocacy effort, messages are communicated to all levels of government. The messages can be found on radio, TV, and in newspapers, the full range. We do this for specific policy areas at the state level."

More direct funding of communications strategies by advocacy groups is also supported. The Mott Foundation supports several programs aimed at pre-kindergarten and after-school child care. The "School Readiness" program funds policy advocacy and community organizing activities rather than demonstration projects to improve access to pre-school programs and to improve public policy. "Learning Beyond the Classroom" provides grants to generate and disseminate knowledge of promising practices and programs for expanded learning focused on improving outcomes for children.

This kind of approach also characterizes the Packard Foundation's efforts in child care, including *The Future of Children*, which promotes effective policies and programs for children by providing policymakers, service providers, and the media timely and objective information from the best available research of grantees, issues and idea guides, and press releases. Through the "Build Community and National Commitment to Children" program, Packard funds "projects that increase the effectiveness of advocacy efforts through sophisticated use of data, strategic communication, and outreach to nontraditional constituencies" (Packard web site).

Data Repository

Several of the foundations produce products that serve as resources for communities, advocates, and policymakers in improving child care and youth and families. The Kauffman Foundation, for example, seeks to increase the accountability of early education programs through the creation of a database that tracks readiness indicators among children entering kindergarten. These indicators are used to help build the public's will to more generously finance and sustain quality child care and early learning programs.

One of the best-known data repositories is the *Kids Count Data Book* published by the Annie E. Casey Foundation, which tracks the status of children nationally and in the states. The book documents the prevalence of well-being and problems and achievements of children through a variety of measures, including the continuing crisis of a lack of adequate and affordable child care for children of poor families. The Casey Foundation also publishes through the Technical Assistance/Resource Center (TARC) a series of guidebooks for families and neighborhoods, including "Child Care for Communities" and, in conjunction with the 1998 Data Book, "Child Care You Can Count On, A Comparative Resource Guide."

Technical Assistance, Training, Consultation

Another general strategy that foundations in the child care area pursue to engage policy is the provision of technical assistance to communities, youth organizations, and advocacy groups. Sometimes this technical assistance is in the form of grants for training of youth leaders or organizational staff and for parenting skills. Other grants focus more on community organizing and advocacy strategies and how to conduct evaluation research. The Kauffman Foundation's Youth Development Division, for example, supports the Early Education and School Readiness Program and the Out-of-School Program

Investments. The Early Education Program funds professional development of early education teachers and efforts to develop national accreditation standards.

Five of the twelve foundations in this study listed technical assistance as part of their general strategy for assisting communities, advocacy groups, and organizations to engage public policy. The Annie E. Casey Foundation established a Technical Assistance/Resource Center (TARC), as mentioned above. Mott provides technical assistance to grantees that are developing after-school programs.

ARE FOUNDATIONS INNOVATORS OR FOLLOWERS IN CHILD CARE POLICY?

Perhaps because of the need to adjust to the risks and opportunities of the political process, most of the program officers in the children and family area interviewed for this study did not see foundations in general as innovators in child care policy. One senior official, for example, stated, "In my experience, foundations have largely been followers … because they respond to proposals given to them by other institutions or individuals. They gear their programming to these other institutions which often develop the ideas." A senior officer at another foundation observed, "Foundations are mostly followers. Universities, think tanks, and other organizations conduct the research and originate the ideas." One program officer stated explicitly that, "In child care, we as a foundation didn't do anything innovative."

Answering the question of whether foundations are innovators or followers, however, is not quite this simple. Some of the same program officers who see foundations in general as followers emphasized that in their specific initiatives on child care their foundation acted innovatively. One reason for this discrepancy may be that foundations conduct little of their own research and rely on ideas, including policy ideas, from think tanks, universities, and advocacy groups. As one program officer stated, "We found people who are innovative and our contribution was to accelerate the pace of their ideas. In this sense, the foundation represents capital for good ideas."

Foundations are very good at developing creative ways to bring together and leverage existing resources. A good example is the Mott Foundation's partnership through the Twenty-First Century Community Learning Centers (CCLC) Program with the U.S. Department of Education (DOE). This program was initially authorized by Congress in 1994 with the goal of opening up schools to broader community activities. In 1998, the program was refocused for children in low-performing schools to provide child care after school and during other times when school is not in session, such as weekends or holidays. The school-based child care includes an academic program to enrich learning and improve performance and programs for children with special needs, such as counseling, recreation, and youth development activities. The program began as a federal program, but under the current administration's No Child Left behind (NCLB) Act of 2001, the DOE makes grants to the states, which in turn make competitive grants to providers.

This partnership with DOE allowed Mott to leverage a large amount of public funding, thereby reducing the risk of failure to influence public policy to produce a major program. It also gave the foundation a wonderful opportunity to produce significant rewards for achievement of a national child care program. The foundation program officer explained that, "Because this program is a partnership with the federal government, it looks like our child care activities follow rather than innovate in public policy. With a small amount of money, however, we were able to leverage a large amount of funding from the DOE."

The CCLC turned out to be a great window of opportunity for the foundation. The NCLB Act reflected the strong interest and support of the Bush Administration, which caused the program to grow from an appropriation of $40 million in 1998 to $1 billion in 2002. By 2002, the CCLC supported after-school programs in 7,500 rural and inner-city public schools in more than 1,400 communities nationwide. Such a growth of program represents a huge opportunity to any foundation or community organization that could become a partner.

The partnership also allowed Mott to provide innovative ideas for developing the program and its content and for gaining community support. The program officer stated that, "We wanted to demonstrate what works and how the policy can be tied to quality, access and equity. We also wanted to lead in building public will for after-school programs." In other words, the foundation innovated in designing and funding the program, developing best practices, and gaining public support.

On the other hand, the CCLC also demonstrates the tendency to measure success by the foundation in terms of dollars spent or program activities carried out rather than by actual impact on children. While the foundation lists the CCLC as one of its major success stories for engaging in public policy, an evaluation study carried out by Mathematica and funded by the DOE and the Mott Foundation showed relatively little impact on children's performance in school. There was limited academic impact, low levels of student participation, no improvements in safety and behavior for children, and negligible impact on developmental outcomes. These outcomes are much harder to achieve than simply spending money and engaging in activities.

The risk in this partnership approach is the dependency of the program on the presidential administration in power. CCLC was started by the Clinton Administration. The Bush Administration was not initially supportive until the passage of the NCLB Act, which served as a major stimulus to increased funding. The program is now tied closely to this Act and the Bush initiative. The current budget situation and the less than positive results of the evaluation caused the DOE to recommend a $400 million reduction in the program's budget in 2003 and a shift in funding from schools to community providers of child care.

As this example shows, understanding innovation in policy is not just a matter of whether the foundation or the government acted first in child care (Knott and Weissert, 1996). The question is more one of differing roles and contributions that foundations can bring to an issue versus what the government can accomplish. Some foundations identify gaps or inconsistencies in government policy and try to improve and coordinate systems. Others try to identify which policy approach of the government works best or is the most cost effective. These actions are taken partly in response to government programs, partly in response to researchers or policy analysts whom the foundations have funded, and only sometimes ahead of any government activity.

Jurisdictions: Locations of Child Care Programs

All of the foundations in this study operate at both the national and local levels in carrying out programs on child care (see Table 6). There may be an interesting inverse relationship, however, between a primary focus on research versus an emphasis on demonstration models and projects. The foundations that place the primary focus on research do so to influence state level or national policy in most cases. If these same foundations also support programs or projects, they tend to do so in the local area where the foundation is located. The MacArthur Foundation provides a good example of this mixture of research and programs. Its primary focus is research, which it funds on national and state studies of child care and other issues related to children and families. On the other hand, its individual demonstration projects are limited to the Chicago metropolitan area, and multisite projects must include Chicago. Grants for research and public policy may support work in Chicago, Illinois, or at multistate or national levels. Another example is the Kauffman Foundation, which funds policy research and analysis and advocacy activities nationally and at the state level but concentrates its program and demonstration project funds in the Kansas City area. The Packard Foundation also funds research and advocacy in child care nationally but concentrates its program funds for specific child care facilities in local areas in California.

In contrast, the W. K. Kellogg Foundation concentrates on national demonstration programs that have project sites in many different states. While the foundation conducts some national research as well, a substantial portion of its research budget is directed towards evaluation studies in these local areas where the demonstration projects are located. It tries to develop information on models of child care and youth development at the local level in specific communities that can be transferred to other communities in other parts of the country. It also uses evaluation data from these projects to develop models for state and national policymaking, although the evaluation focuses on the success of the program, not on the success in influencing policy. In addition, the foundation does support local demonstration projects and program funding in Battle Creek where the foundation is located and in Michigan.

Similar to Kellogg, the Annie E. Casey Foundation supports the *Making Connections* program, which is the centerpiece of the Neighborhood Transformation and Family Development Initiative. This program initially supported demonstration projects in twenty-two cities but now focuses on ten cities the foundation viewed as having the best chance of success following evaluation research. These specific measurable outcomes derived from *Making Connections* can be used for state and national policy advocacy. The foundation also, as has been discussed, supports national data collections and reports based on the *Kids Count Data Book*. Thus, Casey has succeeded in developing research and demonstration projects strategies at local, state, and national levels.

In sum, foundations in the child care area adopt strategies that cover a wide range of activities, including policy research, evaluation of pilot and demonstration projects, technical and training assistance, data repositories, development of public opinion, and communications support for advocacy groups. They also have formed intriguing collaborations with government agencies and legislatures, in addition to the more common partnerships among other foundations, associations, and nonprofit organizations. The child care foundations pursue both indirect grassroots strategies, relying on local foundations and other community organizations, and direct national strategies that rely on national news media, associations, nonprofit organizations, and federal government agencies. The grantmaking tends to be multiyear and multistage, with the first stage laying the groundwork for a more detailed and comprehensive plan in the second stage that includes policy goals and strategy. Grantmaking also occurs in the context of broad initiatives that support several more specific programs and projects, some of which concern child care while others focus on related areas of children, families, and neighborhoods.

Conclusion

Foundations became involved in child care due to a convergence of several factors, the most important of which was the research on early childhood development and after-school programs for adolescents and teenagers. This research demonstrated the value to society of universal child care and out-of-school education programs. Foundations eventually became engaged in child care policy because of an opportunity and a major perceived problem. The opportunity was the passage of the Federal Block Grant and Title IV, which gave the states funds to begin developing and thinking about universal child care. The major perceived policy problem was the passage of welfare reform, which required welfare recipients, including those with children, to move from welfare to work, even if they were single parents. This program greatly heightened the need for child care for the poor.

Foundations are both innovators and followers in child care policy. While they were not the primary impetus behind the federal and state governments adopting child care legislation, they have offered critically important help to the states in designing, funding, and carrying out appropriate and effective child care programs. They also hastened the expansion and adoption of universal child care in the states.

The particular policy strategies that the foundations have employed are related to the perceived risks and rewards the foundations confront when they engage public policy. The foundations' officers are judged on concrete accomplishment with the funds entrusted to them. The uncertainties of the political process may cause the foundations to lose or at least not fully realize their investment in child care. Consequently, the foundations have resisted moving too far out front in the policy debate and have looked for ways to exploit favorable political contexts, especially in the states, and to rely on grantees and other advocacy groups. They have focused on expansions, inconsistencies, gaps, and improvements in child care policy. They have also concentrated on activities that can be measured, such as the development of databases, demonstration projects, policy papers, the formation of coalitions and networks, and other inputs into the policy process. In addition, they have forged partnerships with government agencies, playing an innovative role in the context of a government initiative.

Some of the most promising approaches include partnerships with state legislatures and with federal agencies, the generation and sharing of information across policy networks, and the formation of broad advocacy coalitions. In government partnerships, the scope of impact is much larger because of government funding and the direct influence on policy. The government initiatives benefit from the foundations' research, technical assistance, and training. A coalition among several organizations fosters the sharing of research results, ideas, and information across policy networks. These partnerships and network coalitions include policy research, conferences, joint funding, program delivery, and evaluation research. In these ways, the foundations have become involved in child care policy from agenda-setting through implementation to evaluation.

If foundations are interested in policy change, paying attention to windows of opportunity and the building of policy networks in the political process are necessary strategies for success. Foundations are thus part of the much bigger conundrum of political and policy change in American democracy, which often goes in fits and starts and takes place incrementally over time. Given the multitude of competing interests in the democratic process, achieving success often requires being co-opted by the establishment to some extent and the building of partnerships with other powerful actors. It also requires working with many different political environments in the states and with diverse grassroots constituencies, which may not hold the same views as the foundation's board or senior officers. Such necessary actions for success in a multilayered democracy invariably entail compromises and practical choices that in some sense tarnish the foundation's grand vision for a better society. On the other hand, these strategies may more effectively bring about actual policy movement in a direction that reflects a broader consensus of democratic priorities.

Table 1. National Foundations Involved in the Children, Youth, and Family Area

	Youth law & justice	Education reform	Child care (pre-school, after-school)	Youth at risk (AIDS, reproductive)	Child welfare & child well-being	Domestic violence & child abuse	Healthy neighborhoods	Poverty & economic security
1. Annie E. Casey Foundation	x		x		x			
2. Carnegie Corporation of New York		x	x					
3. Foundation for Child Development			x		x		x	
4. Gerber Foundation			x		x			
5. William T. Grant Foundation	x	x	x	x				
6. Ewing Marion Kauffman Foundation		x	x				x	
7. W. K. Kellogg Foundation		x	x					
8. John D. and Catherine T. MacArthur Foundation	x	x	x					
9. Edna McConnell Clark Foundation	x		x			x		
10. Charles Stewart Mott Foundation	x	x	x					
11. David and Lucile Packard Foundation			x	x	x	x	x	x
12. W. E. Upjohn Institute for Employment Research*			x					x

*While Upjohn is a research institute rather than a foundation, they are included here because they make grants and have a unique type of involvement in child care.

Table 2. Reasons for Becoming Involved in Child Care

		Founded	Primary reason(s) why foundation became involved in child care
1.	Annie Casey	1948	Social interest of founder; Logical extension of existing child, family, and youth programs
2.	Carnegie	1911	Change in foundation leadership; Logical extension of existing child, family, and youth programs
3.	Foundation for Child Development	1900	Response to government policy actions; Developments in science of child development; Logical extension of existing child, family, and youth programs
4.	Gerber	1952	Social interest of founder
5.	WT Grant	1936	Change in foundation leadership; Logical extension of existing child, family, and youth programs
6.	Kauffman	mid-1960s	Developments in science of child development; Logical extension of existing child, family, and youth programs
7.	Kellogg	1930	Social interest of founder; Logical extension of existing child, family, and youth programs
8.	MacArthur	1978	Developments in science of child development; Workforce changes or other societal shifts
9.	McConnell Clark	1969	Social interest of founder; Developments in science of child development; Logical extension of existing child, family, and youth programs
10.	Mott	1926	Social interest of founder; Developments in science of child development
11.	Packard	1964	Social interest of founder
12.	Upjohn	1945	Workforce changes or other societal shifts; Logical extension of existing child, family, and youth programs

Table 3. Foundations and Child Care Policy

	Policy focus?	Level of policy	Major child care policy goals
1. Annie Casey	Yes	Local, state, national	Neighborhood control and mobilization; Coordination of a fractured system; Marketing and issue awareness; Improved quality and standards; Improved access and affordability
2. Carnegie	Yes	Local, state, national	Marketing and issue awareness; Improved quality and standards
3. Foundation for Child Development	Yes	State, national	Improved access and affordability; Improved quality and standards; Better child care workforce; Coordination of a fractured system
4. Gerber	No, but supports organizations that do	Regional, national	—
5. WT Grant	Yes	Local, state, national	Analysis of weaknesses or gaps in system
6. Kauffman	Yes	Local, state, national	Better child care workforce; Improved quality and standards; Marketing and issue awareness; Improved financing system
7. Kellogg	Yes	Local, state, national	Neighborhood control and mobilization; Coordination of a fractured system
8. MacArthur	Yes	Local, state, national	Marketing and issue awareness; Improved access and affordability; Improved quality and standards
9. McConnell Clark	No	—	—
10. Mott	Yes	Local, state, national	Improved access and affordability; Improved quality and standards; Coordination of a fractured system; Improved financing system
11. Packard	Yes	Local, state, national	Improved financing system; Improved access and affordability
12. Upjohn	Yes	State, national	Unknown

Table 4. Child Care Strategies Used by Foundations

		Major strategies used and/or funded
1.	Annie Casey	Partnerships and networking; Demonstration projects; Program and facility development; Marketing and issue awareness; Information for policy-makers; Technical assistance
2.	Carnegie	Research, evaluation, and policy analysis; Information for policy-makers; Marketing and issue awareness
3.	Foundation for Child Development	Research, evaluation, and policy analysis; Leadership development and training
4.	Gerber	Technical assistance; Marketing and issue awareness; Information for policy-makers; Program development and facilities
5.	WT Grant	Research, evaluation, and policy analysis; Marketing and issue awareness; Information for policy-makers
6.	Kauffman	Technical assistance; Demonstration projects; Program and facility development; Research, evaluation, and policy analysis; Partnerships and networking; Information for policy-makers
7.	Kellogg	Mobilization and capacity-building; Partnerships and networking; Demonstration projects; Program and facility development
8.	MacArthur	Research, evaluation, and policy analysis; Demonstration projects; Information for policy-makers
9.	McConnell Clark	Mobilization and capacity-building; Program and facility development
10.	Mott	Information for policy-makers; Mobilization and capacity-building; Research, evaluation, and policy analysis; Technical assistance; Leadership development and training
11.	Packard	Research, evaluation, and policy analysis; Information for policy-makers; Technical assistance; Program and facility development
12.	Upjohn	Research, evaluation, and policy analysis; Information for policy-makers

Table 5. Foundation Partnerships

		Partnerships
1.	Annie Casey	National foundations, advocacy and policy groups, schools and community groups.
2.	Carnegie	National foundations and local school-reform organizations. Partnered with several other foundations, including Kauffman and Packard, to start up the Early Care and Education Collaborative.
3.	Foundation for Child Development	Partnerships not significant.
4.	Gerber	Partnerships not significant.
5.	WT Grant	Partnerships not significant.
6.	Kauffman	National and state foundations, community groups, local governments, school districts. Partnered with Packard and Carnegie and other foundations for the Early Care and Education Collaborative.
7.	Kellogg	National and state foundations, state agencies, local governments, community groups, and schools. Also forges partnerships between schools and communities.
8.	MacArthur	Various public, private, and nonprofit organizations.
9.	McConnell Clark	Partnerships no longer significant, as McConnell Clark is focusing on organizational capacity building. Previously, forged partnerships between local governments, nonprofits, and residents.
10.	Mott	Various public, private, and nonprofit organizations, federal government agency.
11.	Packard	National foundations, state and local agencies, community groups, schools and universities. Partnered with several other foundations, including Kauffman and Packard, to start up the Early Care and Education Collaborative.
12.	Upjohn	Partnerships not significant.

Table 6. Grantees and Location of Child Care Programs

		Location of programs	Grantees
1.	Annie Casey	Baltimore and national	Nonprofits, universities, and policy research institutes across the country. Capital or direct research only in Baltimore. Seed grants to local community groups and civic leaders.
2.	Carnegie	New York City and national	Community groups and school districts, and individuals who are conducting research under the Carnegie Scholars program. No grants for capital projects.
3.	Foundation for Child Development	New York City and national	Nonprofit institutions for research, policy analysis, advocacy, leadership development, and a small number of program development projects in New York City. Does not fund direct service. Gives preference to projects that can affect formation of national policy on economic security for low-income families.
4.	Gerber	Western Michigan and national	Nonprofits in Michigan and nationally. Only supports capital projects or operations in Western Michigan.
5.	WT Grant	New York/New Jersey/Connecticut and national	Nonprofit organizations, primarily in NY, NJ, and CT. Does not fund capital projects or operations, and does not make grants to individuals.
6.	Kauffman	Kansas City, MO; Kansas and Missouri; national	A few regional or national organizations, but primarily Kansas City-area organizations.
7.	Kellogg	Kalamazoo and Detroit, MI; Michigan; national	Nonprofits in Michigan and nationally. Does not fund capital projects, conferences, or individuals.
8.	MacArthur	Chicago and national	National and Chicago-area nonprofits; in some program areas (such as Early Education and Care), funded demonstration projects must include a Chicago-area site. Besides grants, MacArthur supports low-cost loans and venture capital funds.
9.	McConnell Clark	Boston, New York City, and national	Under the Institution and Field Building model, restricts its Youth Development grants to direct-service nonprofit youth development organizations doing out-of-school programs in the Northeast Corridor (Boston to Washington, DC). Does not give grants to individuals or to international organizations.
10.	Mott	Flint, MI and national	Funds general-purpose support and specific projects. Gives preference to Flint area for capital and research, and does not fund projects outside of Flint unless they are part of a national demonstration or a Mott network of grants.
11.	Packard	Northern California; Pueblo, CO; national	Nonprofits, local governments, universities. Capital projects and direct services are only funded in Northern California.
12.	Upjohn	National	Grants are typically given to individual researchers with a PhD.

References

Annie E. Casey Foundation web site. "Frequently Asked Questions," available at http://www.aecf.org/Home/MajorInitiatives/ MakingConnections/FAQs.aspx, last accessed May 17, 2008.

Brooks-Gunn, Jeanne, Wen-Jui Han, and Jane Waldfogel. 2002. "Maternal Employment and Child Cognitive Outcomes in the First Three Years of Life: The NICHD Study of Early Childcare," *Child Development* 73(4) (July–August) pp. 1052–1072.

Cohen, Abby J. 1996. "A Brief History of Federal Financing for Child Care in the United States," *Financing Child Care 6*, 2, Center for the Future of Children, the Packard Foundation (Summer/Fall).

Covington, Sally. 2001. "In the Midst of Plenty: Foundation Funding of Child Advocacy Organizations in the 1990s," in *Who Speaks for America's Children: the Role of Child Advocates in Public Policy*, edited by Carol J. De Vita and Rachel Mosher-Williams (The Urban Institute Press) pp. 39–80.

Ewing Marion Kauffman Foundation. 2000. "When School is Out," Public Policy Report.

Foundation for Child Development. 2000. "One Hundred Years of Commitment to Children: Change and Continuity."

Heclo, Hugh. 1977. "A Government of Strangers: Executive Politics in Washington" (Brookings Institution: Washington, DC).

Kahn, Alfred J., and Sheila B. Kamerman. 2002. *Beyond Child Poverty: The Social Exclusion of Children* (The Institute for Child and Family Policy: Columbia University, NY).

Kingdon, John. 1997. *Agendas, Alternatives and Public Policy* (Addison-Wesley), 2nd Edition.

Klein, Abbie Gordon. 1992. *The Debate Over Child Care 1969–1990: A Sociohistorical Analysis* (State University of New York Press: Albany, NY).

Knott, Jack H., and Carol J. Weissert. 1996. "Foundations and Health Policy: Identifying Funding Strategies in Health Programming," *Policy Studies Review*, 14, 1 (Spring/Summer, 1996).

Laracy, Michael. 2001. "Recent Efforts to Better Help Low-Income Working Families Through Federal Tax Policy Generated Over $12 Billion Annually in New Support for Struggling Households," Working Paper, Annie E. Casey Foundation, August 21.

Long, Sharon, and Sandra J. Clark. 2002. "The New Child Care Block Grant: State Funding Choices and Their Implications," The Urban Institute (September).

Lowe Vandell, Deborah, and Barbara Wolfe. 2000. "Child Care Quality: Does it Matter and Does it Need to be Improved?" Report to the Office of the Assistant Secretary for Planning and Evaluation, U.S. Department of Health and Human Services, Washington, D.C. (May).

Mitchell, Anne et al. 2001. *Financing Child Care in the United States: An Expanded Catalogue of Current Strategies* (Kansas City: Ewing Marion Kauffman Foundation).

National Women's Law Center. 2003. "Credit Where Credit is Due: Using Tax Breaks to Help Pay for Child and Dependent Care" (Washington, DC: January).

The Packard Foundation. 1996. "Financing Child Care: Analysis and Recommendations," *Financing Child Care* 6, 2, The Center for the Future of Children, the Packard Foundation.

Phillips, Deborah et al. 2000. "Within and Beyond the Classroom Door: Assessing Quality in Child Care Centers," *Early Childhood Research Quarterly* 15(4) (Winter), pp. 475–496.

Scarr, Sandra, and Marlene Eisenberg. 1993. "Child Care Research: Issues, Perspectives, and Results," *Annual Review of Psychology* 44: 613–644.

Shore, Rima. 2000. *Our Basic Dream: Keeping Faith with America's Working Families and Their Children* (Foundation for Child Development).

Twombly, Eric C., Maria D. Montilla, and Carol J. De Vita. 2001. "State Initiatives to Increase Compensation for Child Care Workers," The Urban Institute (February).

9

Foundation Engagement in Education Policymaking: Assessing Philanthropic Support of School Choice Initiatives

Michael Mintrom and Sandra Vergari

Introduction

Since the mid-1980s, many states and localities in the United States have introduced public policies designed to give parents more choice over the schools their children attend. At the same time, a variety of private efforts have been made to secure more choice for families, especially those living in low-achieving public school districts. In this chapter we examine strategies philanthropic foundations have used to gain influence in school choice debates.[1] We focus on two elements of the school choice movement: the rapid emergence of charter schools and efforts to establish public voucher programs. While foundations have apparently fulfilled relatively limited roles in securing legislative support for the adoption of charter school laws, they have done much to support policy implementation and nurture the fledgling reform. With regard to efforts to secure publicly funded school vouchers, the foundation role has been critical. Here, we find foundations seeking to influence the policy agenda principally by using privately funded demonstration projects to generate evidence that voucher programs work.

[1]We thank the foundation and school choice policy experts with whom we talked for the helpful insights and facts they provided.

Some foundations have made significant efforts to influence the broader national conversation on public education and how schooling should be delivered. After discussing the national context briefly, we turn to the two focal points of the chapter. In order to gain insights on foundation efforts to support school choice, we document their activities in two states: California and New York. Our examination reveals how foundations have worked with and alongside other policy players to promote, secure, and support policy change. In our discussion, we identify some common strategies that foundations have used to make school choice a salient issue on the public agenda.

As foundations work to influence public policymaking, they face a series of strategic choices such as the jurisdictions in which to focus their efforts. Some foundations operate at the national level, others work in one or two states, while others concentrate on local settings. To some extent, choice of jurisdiction is driven by foundation capacity. Foundations seek to leverage their limited resources. Thus, they are likely to fund activities that they perceive as most likely to yield big payoffs in terms of their policy objectives. Smaller foundations may focus on geographically limited, local initiatives. In other instances, foundations may strategically target selected locales with the aim of drawing broad attention to their activities and motivating others—ultimately public policymakers—to replicate the initiatives elsewhere. Observing the unique position of philanthropic foundations in the policymaking community, Hersh (2000, p. 60) has observed: "Foundations possess the flexibility, efficiency, and trust no longer associated with government that can help initiate and sustain large-scale school reform."

What stages of the policymaking process might foundations seek to influence? Potentially, foundations can influence the definition of policy problems, help with agenda-setting efforts, support advocacy for policy adoption, assist in policy implementation, and engage in program evaluation. Foundations can also choose the policymaking venues in which to be active. Aside from seeking to influence the legislative process, many foundations seek to support policy change through court cases. In states where ballot initiatives are permitted, foundations may attempt to influence policy by helping to mobilize support for or against a given ballot measure.

Background on School Choice

The traditional public school system in the United States is characterized by a high degree of local control, with the assignment of students to schools based on residency. Students attend their local public schools and the cost of that schooling is covered by a combination of local property tax revenues, state aid, and targeted federal assistance. The assignment of students to schools based on geographic location has resulted in a one-to-one relationship between student and school. That is, in the traditional public school system, beyond choosing the school district in which they reside, families do not get to actively choose the schools their children attend. Meanwhile, public schools cannot choose who they will enroll. All children residing in a specified school district are eligible to receive free public education.

These arrangements have led a variety of detractors—including scholars, commentators, and activists—to observe that the traditional public school system in the United States represents a form of state-sanctioned monopoly. This monopoly, it is said, embodies many of the problems that arise when suppliers are immune from market signals. Most notably, public schools may not feel compelled to be responsive to families and to ensure excellence in the delivery of education for all students. Students whose parents cannot afford to reside in areas with high-quality schools and who cannot afford the tuition of high-quality private schools have no choice but to attend the local public school to which they are assigned. Since those schools hold an effective local educational monopoly, school leaders and board members may not think it imperative to carefully address concerns expressed by parents and students. According to critics, the institutional arrangements for governing public schools have led to declining standards and schools that have often failed low-income and minority children. Such concerns about the consequences of a public school monopoly are part of the "free-market" argument for school choice.

In the 1950s, the economist Milton Friedman proposed the idea of educational vouchers (Friedman, 1955, 1962). Under his plan, public dollars for schooling would be channeled through children. Schools would compete for students and, hence, for public funding. Schools that failed to attract a sufficient number of students would be forced to close. Schools attracting many students could be expanded or replicated. Friedman envisioned a system of privately managed schools funded by vouchers supplied to families by the government. Subsequent supporters of school choice have advanced other arguments for vouchers or variations on the idea. For example, Mario

Fantini (1973) argued that, for pedagogical reasons, families should have choices about the types of schools their children attend, since students respond differently to different educational environments. This could be called the "alternative schools" argument for school choice. During the 1970s and early 1980s, various local school choice experiments were developed, based on the alternative schools model. Many public school districts introduced "magnet schools" with specialized curricula to attract racially diverse groups of students. In some instances, such as in District 4 in East Harlem, New York, the local public schools were each designated as magnet schools, and parents were given considerable choice over the district schools that their children could attend (Meier, 1995). In 1987, Minnesota became the first state to allow "open enrollment," permitting students to attend public schools outside their districts, so long as spaces were available (Roberts and King, 1996). Following the Minnesota example, many states adopted variations on the open-enrollment idea in the late 1980s and early 1990s (Mintrom, 2000).

FOUNDATION STRATEGIES

What role have foundations played in shaping the discourse on public education and how schooling should be delivered? At the most general level, foundations have adopted a two-pronged strategy. On the one hand, several foundations have focused on the realm of ideas. For these foundations, the crucial task has been to support scholars and think-tank policy analysts to develop proposals for moving policy away from the status quo. On the other hand, many more foundations have engaged in specific actions targeted at the state or local level. These efforts have been designed to secure legislative attention, promote policy changes, or boost fledgling legislative initiatives.

As Convington (1997) has observed, since the early 1970s conservative foundations have used a variety of strategies to promote small government and greater reliance on markets for service delivery. With respect to educational reform, two conservative foundations have done a great deal to influence the climate of ideas. The Lynde and Harry Bradley Foundation, located in Milwaukee, Wisconsin, has served as a champion of school choice, through its support of pro-school-choice scholars and its active support of reform efforts, such as the introduction of a public voucher program in Milwaukee in the early 1990s (Witte, 2000). Similarly, the John M. Olin Foundation, until it officially disbanded in late 2005, was a consistent supporter of efforts to change the climate of ideas by funding the work of highly regarded scholars interested in market-based school reform.

In terms of advancing school choice as a policy idea, a significant degree of agenda-setting discussion followed the 1990 publication of John E. Chubb and Terry M. Moe's book, *Politics, Markets, and America's Schools*. Funding for the research in the book came from a number of sources, including the United States Department of Education. The Bradley and Olin foundations were also supporters. These two foundations again funded Moe's major, survey-based research effort that led to the 2000 publication of his book, *Schools, Vouchers, and the American Public*. Again, this book relied on research evidence as a strong basis for advocating greater use of vouchers in the delivery of public education. Likewise, Diane Ravitch and Joseph P. Viteritti's 1997 edited collection, *New Schools for a New Century*, resulted from a series of seminars and conferences supported by the Olin Foundation.

During the 1990s, the Olin Foundation consistently funded school choice seminars and projects coordinated by Paul E. Peterson, a Harvard scholar who has been a central figure in efforts to test the effects of small-scale voucher programs across the nation. In contrast, scholars who have taken a more skeptical view towards vouchers have typically not received foundation support. Jeffrey R. Henig, author of *Rethinking School Choice* (1994) and John F. Witte, author of *The Market Approach to Education* (2000) are two prominent researchers who have sometimes disagreed with school choice advocates. Aside from a grant Witte received from the Spencer Foundation— which funds a large amount of educational research on a broad range of topics—neither Henig nor Witte received foundation funding for the research agendas that culminated in these major publications.

Of course, the Bradley and Olin foundations have not been the only foundations that have supported academic efforts to examine school choice. Other foundations, such as the Annie E. Casey Foundation and the Walton Family Foundation, have supported scholarly research in this area. But the Bradley and Olin foundations had longer-term agendas to support efforts to influence public opinion and, ultimately, policymakers, regarding the best ways to deliver public education. These efforts have been significant, and they have helped to move discussion of the school choice idea to the point where it is now seen as an entirely legitimate policy option for discussion. However, for these efforts to gain real traction, evidence that school choice can actually work had to be developed. Hence, while some foundations have sought to move the national conversation, many others have worked in specific locations to transform ideas of school choice into functioning programs at the state and local level.

THE EMERGENCE OF CHARTER SCHOOLS

Open enrollment forms of school choice discussed earlier do not present opportunities for new types of schools to develop. In a key response to this concern, in 1991 Minnesota became the first state to adopt a charter school law. Charter schools are nonsectarian, publicly funded schools of choice that operate with freedom from some of the regulations that pertain to traditional public schools. Charter schools enjoy a high degree of flexibility over how they are governed and operated. In return for this flexibility, charter schools must be accountable to public officials and attract an ample number of students. If they do not meet appropriate standards of educational quality and financial management, charter schools may be compelled to close (Nathan, 1996). The creation of charter schools introduced important competitive dynamics to the public school system. Following Minnesota's lead, thirty-five states and the District of Columbia adopted charter school laws in the 1990s (Vergari, 2002).[2] In many ways, the introduction of charter schools, with public money following students, works to produce similar ends as a public voucher program.[3]

THE EMERGENCE OF VOUCHER PROGRAMS

School choice efforts have also been pursued through the introduction of public voucher programs. The most prominent voucher programs in the United States are in Milwaukee and Cleveland. In both cities, students can receive public funds to attend private schools. Importantly, those schools can be either religious or nonreligious. Beginning in 1999, Florida had a statewide public voucher program enacted by the state legislature, named the Opportunity Scholarship program. Students could obtain a voucher to attend a private school if the public school they had been attending had received a low performance grade from the state for two consecutive years. The Florida program was struck down by the Florida Supreme Court in 2006 because it was ruled to violate the state's constitution. Other state-level initiatives to establish voucher programs over recent years have run into similar difficulties. In 2003, Colorado lawmakers approved a state voucher program allowing state funds to support student tuition in private schools. However, the following year, the Colorado Supreme Court ruled 4–3 that the voucher program violated the state's constitution because it would have diverted local control over both expenditure of tax dollars and curriculum decisionmaking.

---

[2]There are forty-one charter school laws in the U.S. today, including one for the District of Columbia.
[3]As public schools, charter schools are subject to different regulations than private schools, such as maintaining nondiscriminatory admissions processes and adhering to state standards and testing regimes.

A program approved by the state legislature in Utah was outlawed before its implementation by a ballot initiative in November 2007.[4]

A significant form of private school choice that came into prominence during the 1990s has involved individual philanthropists and foundations providing vouchers to families so that they can afford to send their children to private schools. J. Patrick Rooney pioneered this model of philanthropy in Indianapolis in the early 1990s, following failed attempts by Indiana state legislators to adopt school choice legislation. Since that time, the idea has been copied by philanthropists in many other cities in the United States (Kahlenberg, 2003; Moe, 1995).

Research Questions and Study Design

Philanthropic foundations have been significant actors in promoting school choice both as a policy idea and a social practice. Foundations have provided substantial funding in support of the school choice movement. Additionally, they have coordinated advocacy efforts and engaged in information dissemination. In the pages to follow, we focus on the following research questions:

1. How and why have philanthropic foundations supported school choice, as manifest in the emergence of charter schools and foundation support of voucher programs in California and New York?

2. What choices have foundations made regarding selection of jurisdictions in which to work, stages of the policymaking process and policymaking venues (legislative, judicial, ballot initiative) to target, and types of instruments to deploy?

3. What have been the outcomes of foundation efforts to advance charters and vouchers in California and New York?

4. What lessons for theory and practice emerge from these findings?

Our findings are derived from case study work involving scrutiny of documents—policy reports, newspaper articles, academic journals, trade and foundation publications—and interviews of informants closely involved in foundation work and, more generally, in education policymaking. Rather than treat individual foundations as our units of analysis, our focus is on

[4]Maine and Vermont have long-standing, limited voucher programs that permit expenditure of state funds at private, nonreligious schools in cases where there is not a public high school near a student's residence.

policymaking communities and the roles that foundations fulfill—or seek to fulfill—within them. Our analysis sheds light on the school choice movement in California and New York, two different but dynamic sites of school choice advocacy. Both states have witnessed a variety of developments with respect to the adoption of charter school laws, the formation of active charter school networks, the proliferation of charter schools, and the introduction of privately funded voucher programs for poor families. We have chosen not to work through a laundry list of foundations and their contributions to school choice advocacy efforts. Instead, we examine the intentions and the actions of a select group of foundations. We focus on these foundations because we believe that, unlike others, they have played sustained and prominent roles in supporting school choice advocacy. While by no means exhaustive, this selective focus provides a parsimonious way of illuminating how foundations have attempted to influence education policymaking in California and in New York.

California

In the 2005–06 school year, 7.5 million students were enrolled in public and private K–12 schools in California. Of those students, 595,000 were enrolled in private schools, and 240,000 were enrolled in nearly 700 state-supported charter schools (California Department of Education, 2007). The students attending California public schools account for over 13 percent of all public school students in the United States (National Center for Education Statistics, 2007). California's public school system is far greater in size than that of any other state.

California's constitution permits citizen initiatives, whereby proposals for amendments to the state constitution and proposals for new state laws can be placed on the ballot for a vote.[5] The initiative process creates opportunities for individuals and groups to influence the public policy agenda in California. Use of this process has been a critical factor in setting the terms of debate and discussion of school choice in the state. The possibility that disgruntled citizens might use the initiative process to circumvent the policymaking authority of the state legislature has created important dynamics in the politics of school choice in California. The key role that money plays in allowing supporters and opponents of ballot initiatives to build public support for their positions provides opportunities for wealthy philanthropists and foundations to influence policymaking in California.

[5]This approach to lawmaking is used most often in California and a few other western states.

THE RISE OF SCHOOL CHOICE IN CALIFORNIA

Although ideas for school choice were discussed in California and elsewhere in the early to mid-1980s, at that time education policy experts were looking for ways to improve the public education system from within the current institutional arrangements. This was the high point of the "excellence movement."[6] That resulted in efforts to introduce stricter graduation requirements, greater reliance on standardized tests of student performance, and more rigorous standards for teacher certification.

The first successful effort to place a voucher measure on the California ballot emerged in 1992. Proposition 174 was included on the November 1993 ballot in California, but it was defeated at the polls by a margin of 7–3 (Olson, 1993). The political campaigning over this ballot initiative attracted national attention. The California Teachers Association spent $12.6 million to defeat the proposition. President Clinton and Secretary of Education Richard W. Riley campaigned vigorously against the California initiative to create a statewide voucher system (Flint, 1993; Lauter, 1993).

In 1992, lawmakers and other elected officials in California grew increasingly concerned by the possibility that a successful ballot initiative could circumvent the legislative process and create a public voucher system in the state. In response, Delaine Eastin, chair of the California Assembly Education Committee and Gary K. Hart, chair of the state Senate Education Committee promulgated separate bills allowing for the creation of charter schools in California. At that time, only one other state, Minnesota, had adopted such a law. Hart's bill was signed into law by Republican Governor Pete Wilson in September 1992 (Hart and Burr, 1996). This law opened the way for limited choice within the California public school system. Allowing the creation of charter schools served as an effective way to respond to the interests of parents and teachers wanting to pursue alternatives to the traditional public school system without the introduction of a much more radical, public voucher program.

During the mid- to late-1990s, the charter school movement grew in California. At the same time, there were ongoing calls for the creation of

---

[6]*Education Week* 24 April 1985 quotes Michael Kirst, speaking at the annual American Education Finance Association conference: "Mr. Kirst told the gathering that the excellence movement was now 'the only game in town,' and that they, as leaders of the education community, 'have a stake in keeping it going.'" He said that educators need to demonstrate that the excellence movement has been a success, otherwise a host of "major societal negative forces" could combine to curtail spending on public schools. Kirst was also quoted as saying public schools are now "on probation … to see if they can shape up." Kirst argued that choice will only become a major issue if the excellence movement is perceived to have failed.

public vouchers. Following developments in other states, in the late 1990s several private voucher programs were established in California. Of these programs, by far the biggest in the state have been associated with the national Children's Scholarship Fund, which has received large amounts of funding from the Walton Family Foundation. In Los Angeles, through the Southern California Children's Scholarship Fund program, in the 2007–08 school year, over 1,000 children from low-income families were supported to attend private schools as an alternative to attending local public schools. The Broad Foundation, located in Los Angeles, has been a long-term partner of the Children's Scholarship Fund and its efforts in Southern California. Likewise, in the Bay Area, a similar program established in the late 1990s and funded by the Children's Scholarship Fund has provided support to 4,000 children from low-income families to attend private schools in the 2007–08 school year.

Efforts to secure a public voucher program in California through ballot initiatives continued throughout the 1990s. However, it was not until 2000 that an initiative was once more placed on the ballot. This initiative, Proposition 38, was defeated at the polls by a margin of 7–3, just as in the case of the 1993 ballot measure.[7] By far the greatest proportion of funds in support of the initiative came primarily from a lone individual, Timothy C. Draper, head of the Redwood City-based venture capital firm Draper Fisher Jurvetson. Draper, who belongs to a family with close ties to the Republican Party both in the state and nationally, is said to have become involved in education after seeing the state of the public schools that his four children attended in the Silicon Valley town of Atherton, before he placed them in private schools (Palmeri and Himelstein, 2000). Draper is reported to have spent $25 million—half of it his own—on promoting Proposition 38. Draper gained support from foundations and other wealthy individuals. The "No on 38" campaign, financed primarily by the California Teachers Association, had a budget of $26 million (Sacramento Business Journal, 2000).

Since the early 1990s, school choice has achieved a strong degree of legitimacy as a topic for public policy discussion and debate in California. Charter schools have become part of the landscape of public education (Wohlstetter, Griffin, and Chau, 2002). Voucher initiatives have helped to promote public knowledge and discussion of alternatives to the traditional system of education delivery. Furthermore, private voucher programs have

---

[7]Catterall and Chapleau (2001) provide a detailed, sociopolitical analysis of voting patterns associated with support and opposition to Proposition 38.

become a potent means of demonstrating that there is an unmet demand for quality education among poor families in the state and that, when given an opportunity to leave their public schools, many parents will opt for private alternatives, even if it means footing at least some of the cost themselves.

During the 1990s, several new organizational entities emerged with the purpose of supporting charter schools in California, both through policy advocacy and by providing financial support and know-how to school organizers. Most prominent among these institutions, and continuing to go strong, has been the Charter Schools Development Center, part of the California State University Institute for Education reform located on the California State University Sacramento campus. The Center was established in 1993 by former state senator Gary K. Hart and his long-term associate Susan Burr. It is supported primarily by foundation grants. The California Charter Schools Association serves as a mentor for charter schools, channelling resources and ideas to members, and connecting them with other charter school educators. It also serves to coordinate charter school advocacy efforts, and its representatives have frequently made appearances in Sacramento to advance the interests of the state's charter schools. The Association, which began its life in 1993 as the California Network of Educational Charters, has been funded by membership fees and by significant amounts of support from foundations.

Discussion of school choice in California has also been promoted by various state-level think tanks. Among these, the most vocal school choice supporters have been the Independence Institute, the Reason Foundation, and the Pacific Research Institute for Public Policy. All have received substantial and ongoing infusions of financial support from foundations. Policy Analysis for California Education (PACE), a consortium operating out of the University of California at Berkeley, and Stanford University and RAND, located in Santa Monica, have also provided analysis and comment on voucher proposals and their likely fiscal and educational impacts. Typically, the analytical and evaluative work of these organizations has been funded through specific foundation grants. For example, RAND's extensive study, published as *Rhetoric Versus Reality: What We Know and What We Need to Know About Vouchers and Charter Schools* (2001), was funded by the Gund Foundation, the Spencer Foundation, the Annie E. Casey Foundation, and the Carnegie Corporation of New York.

FOUNDATION STRATEGIES IN CALIFORNIA

Foundations have provided considerable financial support to various organizations in California, with the goal of advancing general discussion and particular points of view regarding school choice. Wealthy individual philanthropists have also made major contributions to voucher campaigns, advocacy groups, and research and information dissemination efforts of state-level think tanks.

John T. Walton and the Walton Family Foundation. John T. Walton, who died in a tragic aircraft accident in 2005, was a major national actor in the school choice advocacy coalition. He made contributions both through his individual philanthropy and through the Walton Family Foundation. Walton explained his goals as follows:

> We have enthusiastically supported the charter movement—as well as vouchers and scholarships to private schools—because we believe empowering parents to choose among competing schools will catalyze improvements across the entire K-12 education system, benefiting all children regardless of the school they attend. The simple fact that charter schools are chosen by families, not forced upon them, will begin to change how Americans think about public education. (Quoted by Finn and Amis, 2001, pp. 98–99)

Walton supported all forms of school choice in California. As an individual philanthropist, Walton contributed $250,000 in support of Proposition 174 in 1993 (Zebrowski, 1998). He also joined forces with a variety of conservatives who backed Proposition 226, the Paycheck Protection initiative of 1998. This initiative was strategically designed to break the power of the California Teachers Association by making it necessary for the organization to receive written permission each year from every member before using portions of their union dues to support political campaigns. The initiative was defeated by a margin of 46–54.[8] Walton contributed $360,000 of his own money and another $50,000 from the American Education Reform Foundation he cochaired to this campaign (People for the American Way, 1999, p. 10). To support the development of charter schools in the state, the Walton Family Foundation has provided funds to individual charter schools, as well as to the Institute for Education Reform and to the California Charter Schools Association. Along with the Charter Schools Association, the Pacific Research Institute in California has benefited from Walton Family Foundation support for its analysis and advocacy of charter schools. The

---

[8]Reported (with no authorship attribution) in the October 7, 1998, issue of *Education Week*, p.11.

Walton Family Foundation has also provided substantial funding to private voucher programs in California.

The Broad Foundation. California-based philanthropist Eli Broad, founder of the SunAmerica insurance company, intends to find ways to improve the quality of education in the United States. To this end, he established the Broad Foundation in 1999. The Broad family's initial funding commitment to the foundation was $100 million and this was later increased to over $400 million. Eli Broad says that he is opposed to the large-scale use of publicly funded vouchers. In his view, competition can be an important impetus to improving school performance. Therefore, Broad supports charter schools and the use of private voucher programs to introduce a degree of "healthy competition" into the delivery of public schooling. In the end, however, Broad believes that would-be reformers must work with the present public school system (Broad, 2002). Hence, the Broad Foundation has developed a series of initiatives to support improvements in the public school system in a variety of locations across the United States. Broad is on the board of advisors of the national-level Children's Scholarship Fund and, in recent years, the Broad Foundation has provided significant amounts of support to the Southern California Children's Scholarship Fund.

Since 1999, the Broad Foundation has also funded the general operating budget of the California Charter Schools Association. In 2002, the Broad Foundation began supporting Excellence in Education Management (EXED), a not-for-profit charter school development and management organization that provides management systems and services to charter schools, including assistance with finding and building new facilities. The foundation has been supporting EXED's work to help address Los Angeles' vast school facilities needs, and to boost the presence of high-quality charter schools in the Los Angeles Unified School District.

The Morino Institute, located in Reston, Virginia, describes the Broad Foundation as one of a reasonably small number of "high-engagement grantmakers" in the United States. Perhaps the clearest example of the Broad Foundation's high engagement involves its work with the NewSchools Venture Fund.

The NewSchools Venture Fund. The NewSchools Venture Fund is a $100 million fund based in San Francisco. Three individuals with business experience cofounded this foundation: business partners John Doerr and Brook Byers, whose venture-capital firm provided seed money to many successful technology companies, and Kim Smith, an associate with experience in the education industry. According to Archer (2002), the NewSchools Venture Fund exhibits a form of philanthropy that differs from common gift-giving practice: "What makes them different is the degree to which they play an active role in guiding the efforts they support, and in the way in which they try to hold those projects accountable for results. How they operate reflects the mind-set of an investor more than that of a grantmaker." Among other investors, the Broad Foundation and the Bill and Melinda Gates Foundation have made significant contributions to the NewSchools Venture Fund. In recent years, over half of the Fund's resources have been devoted to establishing new premises for charter schools.

The revolving fund to build charter school facilities was the idea of Eli Broad (Bank, 2002). Under this plan, the NewSchools Venture Fund has purchased and renovated buildings and leased them for use as schoolhouses. Schools have been encouraged to purchase the buildings. When they do so, the money they pay is returned to the fund, which is able to acquire more buildings for renovation and sale. This innovative kind of activity helps to advance the charter school notion, and smooths the way for the creation of more charter schools in California. As such, it promotes school choice as both a practice and a policy idea.

In terms of philanthropic strategy, here we observe the skills that led philanthropists to success in the for-profit world being used to directly inform the practices of nonprofit organizations. Aside from grant money, Eli Broad has contributed time, expertise, and advice to the NewSchools Venture Fund. This has led some to label this kind of work "venture philanthropy" (Paulson, 2002, Venture Philanthropy Partners, 2002).

The Bill and Melinda Gates Foundation. Among its many activities, in recent years the Bill and Melinda Gates Foundation has pursued three philanthropic strategies to improve education. These involve removing the financial barriers that prohibit many minority students from pursuing higher education, developing strong education leaders through technology training, and the support of model schools. This last strategy involves the creation of small high schools that use technology and strong personal relationships among teachers, staff, and students to create personalized learning environments that help student achievement. In 2000, the Bill and Melinda Gates Foundation awarded $37 million in grants in California aimed at creating smaller, more personal learning environments. Of this amount, $16.4 million, or 44.3 percent, was directed towards three clusters of charter schools (Gewertz, 2001). The grants to charter schools were explicitly designed to support learning across school sites and the diffusion of innovations from charter schools to traditional public schools in California.

This support for charter schools has contributed to the growing momentum of school choice in California, and efforts to make charter schools a familiar part of the educational landscape in the state. By supporting charter schools, the Gates Foundation has also signalled to the broader foundation community that this is an education reform worthy of support and that it no longer presents a politically or educationally risky investment. Thus, we might think of it as philanthropy that supports the agenda of promoting public school choice. However, this is an instance where pursuit of that agenda appears to be secondary to the pursuit of a separate policy agenda— that is, having legislators provide more support to public education in ways that will allow small high schools to become a norm. The strategy of the Gates Foundation differs considerably from that of the Walton Family Foundation and the Broad Foundation. Nonetheless, there are points of intersection across the strategies of these foundations, and, taken as a whole, those strategies have been contributing in significant ways to the promotion of school choice.

SUMMARY

Efforts to introduce and establish charter schools and efforts to promote publicly funded vouchers would have occurred in California with or without foundation support. Foundations were not agenda-setters with respect to the charter school movement in this state. However, they have done much to support the implementation of charter schools. With respect to the voucher agenda, foundations have taken the lead in promoting private voucher efforts. These have been deliberately designed to promote policy discussion and change within the traditional public school system.

Foundations have predominantly relied upon funding efforts to support school choice in California. There have been some efforts to forge networks, but mainly this effort has been left to the nonprofit recipients of foundation support. Foundations in California have not typically worked together to support an overarching model of policy change. One observer told us that foundations in California are typically more interested in being "nicie nicie," and being seen to be supportive of low-risk policy efforts rather than thinking broadly and strategically about how best to secure long-term fundamental policy change. Interestingly, family foundations (Walton and Broad, for example) have tended to be more prepared to take risks in promoting school choice than other foundations.

With respect to school choice in California, foundations have tended to emphasize support for local entities, such as schools. Foundations have not overtly attempted to set the terms of the policy debate on school choice. However, efforts to establish private voucher programs have been deliberately pursued with the purpose of changing policy. A program officer at the Walton Family Foundation suggested that the private voucher programs represent "win, win" strategies. That is to say, they help poor children to immediately secure places in better schools. But the presence of the private voucher program serves to remind educational administrators and policymakers that the present public school system has not been responding appropriately to the needs of many poor children. Thus, the private voucher efforts have been intended to be agenda-setting with respect to public policymaking.

Most foundation support of school choice in California has involved provision of grants to key nonprofit entities for service delivery and, in some cases, development of policy advice. For the most part, the foundation efforts have not been especially innovative when compared with philanthropic efforts in other policy areas or, indeed, in other states where foundations have supported school choice efforts. That said, we did observe some efforts to develop new forms of funding, especially with respect to supporting the establishment of appropriate accommodation for charter schools.

Overall, philanthropic support of school choice in California has taken a variety of forms. This is hardly surprising since the foundations involved bring to the school choice issue different perspectives and preferences with respect to the policy outcomes they would like to precipitate. Because foundations often choose to fund the actions of others rather than take actions for themselves, it is possible to underestimate the role that foundations have played in shaping school choice policy in California. Yet the activities of John Walton and the funding strategies of the Walton Family Foundation showed a determination to change public attitudes towards school choice and, further, to influence policy debate on the topic.

In a different way, the efforts of Eli Broad and the Broad Foundation reveal an unusually high desire to use hands-on philanthropy—philanthropy that provides the funding for activities and then infuses innovative thinking that changes the very nature of those activities. Meanwhile, the NewSchools

Venture Fund has expected its grantees to produce specific results within particular time frames. Finally, the activities of the Bill and Melinda Gates Foundation in California have indicated a desire to influence policy through contributing to the success of publicly funded charter schools. From the outset, California's charter school law was intended to promote innovation in schools and to inform the practices of traditional schools. However, it is only through the support of philanthropic foundations, such as the Walton Family Foundation, that these schools have attained the financial and network-building capacity that has allowed them to make good on that promise.

New York State

New York State (NYS) is home to more than 4,000 public schools, 1,400 of which are in New York City (NYC). Across the state, there are 2.8 million students enrolled in public schools while 439,000 students attend non-public schools. The nation's largest school district is located in NYC, with one million students.[9] In contrast to California, citizen ballot initiatives are not permitted in NYS. Thus, philanthropists and foundations must seek other means by which to achieve their policy objectives.

THE RISE OF SCHOOL CHOICE IN NEW YORK STATE

School choice advocacy in New York State has been centered in New York City and in other urban areas plagued by poorly performing schools, including Albany and Buffalo. Wealthy individual philanthropists (many with experience on Wall Street), public charities, and private foundations have supported school choice in the state. They have operated or supported privately funded voucher demonstration programs as well as provided support to the charter school movement in the state. These philanthropists have supported the Manhattan Institute, a prominent think tank that facilitates networking, strategizing, and information dissemination among school choice interests. Several philanthropists who have provided generous financial support to school choice initiatives also hold seats on the Manhattan Institute's board of trustees. The Empire Foundation for Policy Research (a private, operating foundation established in 1991, and based in the Capital Region) has also been very active in promoting school choice initiatives in Albany and elsewhere in the state. The Empire Foundation was replaced by the Foundation for Education Reform and Accountability (FERA). This private, operating foundation was founded by Thomas W. Carroll in 2002.

[9]Data from New York State Education Department and National Center for Education Statistics.

Backed by philanthropists from Wall Street and the corporate world, FERA has tracked whether school districts in New York have upheld school choice provisions of the *No Child Left Behind Act of 2001*.

School choice advocates in the state face formidable opposition from the traditional educational establishment, including New York State United Teachers (affiliate of the American Federation of Teachers), the state's largest teachers union, and the state school boards association. Repeated attempts to secure a charter school law in New York were blocked by opposition from the politically powerful teachers unions and the Democratic majority in the state assembly.[10] In 1998, seven years after the nation's first charter school law was adopted, New York became the thirty-fourth state to permit charter schools. The Charter Schools Act was adopted during a special session of a lame-duck legislature. While the state has been a relative latecomer to the charter school scene, charter school advocates have worked rapidly and deliberately to capitalize upon the enabling legislation.[11]

School choice proponents, based in the Manhattan Institute and the Foundation for Education Reform and Accountability, are linked to other school choice proponents in a network that includes the Charter Schools Institute of the State University of New York (SUNY), the New York Charter Schools Association, and the BISON Fund in Buffalo, a public charity. SUNY is one of the public entities authorized to approve charter schools in New York State. The Charter Schools Institute is SUNY's entity for approving new charter schools and overseeing the schools, the resource center provides technical assistance, and the association is engaged in various forms of technical support and policy advocacy.

Charter school opponents have sought to roll back the reform via the legislature and the courts. The charter schools association tracks all legislative bills pertaining to charter schools and mobilizes opposition to any bill that is viewed as a threat to the viability of the charter school movement in New York State.

FOUNDATION STRATEGIES IN NEW YORK STATE

While the strategies of foundations supporting school choice in New York State are multifaceted, three key trends stand out. First, in both the voucher

---

[10]Charter school bills pertaining only to New York City were introduced in the NYS Assembly during the 1991–92 and 1993–94 legislative sessions. These bills died in committee. In subsequent sessions, a couple of statewide charter school bills also died at the committee stage.

[11]For additional information on charter school dynamics in NYS, see Vergari (2002).

and charter school arenas, foundations have supported focused initiatives intended to showcase the potential of school choice policy. Second, foundations have supported public information campaigns involving both research and strategic use of the media to attract favorable attention to school choice initiatives. Third, foundations have provided funds to charter school support entities such as the New York Charter School Resource Center and the New York Charter Schools Association. For example, the Charles Hayden Foundation, a private foundation based in New York City, has awarded grants to both entities. The first major policy victory of the New York Charter Schools Association was a successful effort to have charter schools designated by the state education commissioner as local education agencies (LEAs), thereby rendering charter schools eligible for state and federal funds available only to LEAs. The association mobilized the state's diverse collection of charter schools to push for the designation. As a result of the victory, charter schools can apply for government grants available to LEAs without having to ask school district officials—many of whom are opposed to the charter school idea—to endorse their proposals.

The charter school law opened up many new options for philanthropic support of school choice and advancement of the school choice idea. Charter schools enjoy public funding, and foundation dollars permit charter schools (such as the Brighter Choice Charter Schools discussed below) to fulfill objectives that would not be possible with public funds alone. In turn, receipt of public funds permits the achievement of objectives that might not be possible if philanthropy were the sole source of available funds.

The Student/Sponsor Partnership, New York City. In 1986, Peter Flanigan founded New York City's first private voucher program, the Student/Sponsor Partnership, now called Student Sponsor Partners. This publicly supported charity combines tuition support with mentoring. It has enabled students from the worst high schools in NYC to enroll in parochial schools. The program has served about 3,000 at-risk inner-city students.

Peter Flanigan is an advisor of UBS Warburg LLC, an international investment banking firm based in New York City. Flanigan also sits on the board of trustees of the Manhattan Institute, and is a member of the board of advisors for the major national voucher foundation, the Children's Scholarship Fund. Flanigan has also served as Chairman of the Board of Children First America (an assumed name for the public foundation incorporated as Children's Educational Opportunity Foundation America), a prominent national public foundation that operates its own programs and also provides funding for school voucher initiatives.

The Children's Scholarship Fund. The Children's Scholarship Fund (CSF) is a publicly supported charity based in New York City. It was founded in 1998. The late John T. Walton and Theodore J. Forstmann (cofounder and senior partner of Forstmann Little & Co.) were founding cochairmen of the board of advisors for CSF. They provided an initiation grant of $100 million to the fund in order to provide opportunities for low-income families to send their children to private schools. The Children's Scholarship Fund has partnerships with programs in various locales and almost 29,000 children are in CSF programs nationwide. The average scholarship is $1,399 with families paying an average of $2,084 toward tuition (Children's Scholarship Fund, 2008).

In 2001, the Walton Family Foundation provided $21.7 million to the Children's Scholarship Fund. The Children's Scholarship Fund can be viewed as an ally of Children First America as John Walton formerly sat on the Children First America board. Children First America reportedly cooperated with the Children's Scholarship Fund to turn over 34 of 46 Children First America programs and shared leads on prospective programs, several of which partnered with the Children's Scholarship Fund (Children's Scholarship Fund, 2002).

Philanthropist Virginia Manheimer and the Brighter Choice Foundation. In 1996, Virginia Manheimer (formerly Virginia Gilder) committed to provide $1.5 million to fund the A Better Choice (ABC) scholarship program in Albany, New York. The program was established in June 1996 as a project of the Empire Foundation, directed by Thomas W. Carroll. Carroll is a prominent, active school choice entrepreneur in the state who previously held research, fiscal, and administrative posts with Governor Pataki, State Senator Joseph Bruno, the State Assembly Republican Conference, and the New York State Division of the Budget.

The ABC program was later renamed "A Brighter Choice Scholarships" (ABCS) and was managed by the Brighter Choice Foundation, a private operating foundation founded by Carroll. The program offered fifty private school scholarships for low-income students in grades 1–6 who were attending poorly performing inner-city public schools in the Capital Region. Students were selected via lottery. The scholarships were capped at 50 percent of tuition, up to $1,000, and guaranteed for three years. Subsequently, the lottery-based ABCS program offered another 50 scholarships to Capital Region students at all poorly performing public schools, excluding Giffen Memorial Elementary.

In December 1996, the Empire Foundation announced the ABCS-Giffen scholarship program. This precedent-setting initiative offered every student attending Giffen Memorial Elementary School in Albany a scholarship to attend any private school. According to state test scores, Giffen was the worst-performing school in the Capital Region and was among the worst-performing schools in the entire state. Other indicators such as attendance rates, incidence of violence, and suspension rates also provided evidence of Giffen's troubled status. The voucher paid up to 90 percent of tuition, up to $2,000, and was guaranteed for three years or through sixth grade, whichever was greater (the initial ABCS-Giffen offer was for 50 percent of tuition capped at $1,000, identical to the lottery-based ABCS program). In contrast to the initial lottery-based program, every K–5 student currently attending Giffen was eligible for the scholarship. The program's focus on a single troubled public school was a deliberate strategy, and it was the first such program in the nation.

The Empire Foundation actively sought and received local and national media attention for the ABCS-Giffen voucher program. In addition to being covered by the *New York Times*, and the *Washington Post*, the program was featured on the cover of *Forbes* magazine in 1997.

What have been the outcomes of the ABCS voucher program? The Empire Foundation reported that it conducted baseline testing of participants in the Giffen voucher program in 1997, but the foundation did not release data on the academic performance of the voucher students—a fact emphasized by critics of Empire and its school choice advocacy. Instead, the Empire Foundation focused on publicizing several significant changes at Giffen that many say were provoked by existence of the private voucher program. These included leadership and staff changes and replacement of Giffen's language arts program with the *Success for All* program.

The ABCS case was precedent-setting in that the Empire Foundation and its philanthropist/backer targeted a single failing public school. The program led to the exodus of about 100 students (the Empire Foundation and Albany City School District disagreed on the precise number) and the outcome was significant change in the organization and curriculum of Giffen Memorial Elementary School.

The BISON Fund. The Buffalo Inner-city Scholarship Opportunity Network (BISON) Fund is a nonprofit charitable organization founded in 1995. It is a privately funded voucher program that provides scholarships to low-income families in Buffalo, the state's second-largest city. In 1999, BISON was chosen to administer a $1 million matching grant from the Children's Scholarship Fund. This partnership enabled BISON to provide scholarships to more than 1,250 children during the 1999–2000 academic year.

Buffalo has been chosen by CSF as one of its partner cities. This partnership provided the BISON Fund with a $1 million matching grant. BISON was required to raise $250,000 per year over four years and achieved this during mid-2001. In 2001, Buffalo was among 17 of 38 original partner cities to receive a second matching grant from CSF. The Children's Scholarship Fund extended its commitments to the BISON Fund with an agreement to match BISON's fundraising intake at 50 percent on the dollar. In addition to CSF, BISON Fund supporters include philanthropists and corporate and family foundations.

CHARTER SCHOOLS

Personnel from the Empire Foundation participated in drafting the Charter Schools Act in December 1998, and school choice advocates were determined to have several charter schools up and running by the start of the 1999 school year in September. The SUNY Charter Schools Institute announced a fast-track application process, and by September 1999, three new charter schools were operating in the state: one in Albany and two in New York City.[12] By the 2007–08 school year, there were 99 charter schools in the state with 25,000 students enrolled (Center for Education Reform, 2007).

Brighter Choice Foundation, Albany. The Brighter Choice Foundation, a private operating foundation based in Albany, was founded in 2001. Among other school choice activities, it provides start-up grants, school facilities, a revolving loan fund, and technical assistance to eight schools in Albany, including the Brighter Choice Charter School for Girls and the Brighter Choice Charter School for Boys. M. Christian Bender is the executive director of the Brighter Choice Foundation. He was previously employed by Austin & Co., an insurance brokerage, where he established insurance programs for independent schools and charter schools in New York State. Bender serves on the board of the Bender Family Foundation, which has

---

[12] In addition, two conversion charter schools opened in New York City.

provided major philanthropic support to educational, cultural, and civic institutions in the Albany region.

The Brighter Choice Charter Schools (BCCS) in Albany were founded by Thomas W. Carroll, who had been president of the Empire Foundation (the same organization that founded the nationally known private voucher program in Albany). Carroll successfully raised millions of dollars in loans and donations to renovate and enlarge an historic public school building in Albany that had faced demolition and replacement by a drug store. His accomplishments have been praised by both school choice supporters and historic preservationists.

The founders of BCCS aim to make the companion single-sex schools exemplary schools of choice. The schools comprise the nation's first public single-sex elementary charter school in which boys and girls are educated in the same building but in separate classes. In contrast to most elementary schools, where students spend most of the day with one teacher who provides instruction in a range of subjects, students at Brighter Choice are educated by several teachers, each of whom instructs students in a specific subject such as reading, math, or history.

The Brighter Choice Charter Schools have received significant attention in the local and national media, including the *Wall Street Journal*. As in the case of the Empire Foundation and the ABCS private voucher initiative, the Brighter Choice Foundation has made use of the mass media a key part of its strategy for advancing school choice. A ribbon-cutting opening ceremony for the schools in 2002 was attended by the Albany mayor, several state lawmakers, and business and community leaders. Carroll has also offered tours of the new school to lawmakers who have expressed opposition to the charter school reform as a means by which to show them, first-hand, what the idea looks like in practice and, ultimately, to try to lessen their opposition.

U.S. Education Under Secretary Eugene W. Hickok visited the Brighter Choice Charter Schools in 2002 and one reason for the visit was to "get people to pay attention to it, because I think it has the potential to be a national model" (Brighter Choice Charter Schools, 2002). This visit by a high-profile federal education official and Hickok's favorable remarks lent considerable political legitimacy to Brighter Choice.

A significant foundation-supported component of the Brighter Choice Charter Schools is the "Learning Guarantee," offered to students who attend the schools for three full school years and complete the state's fourth grade tests. In addition, parents must sign and return report cards, attend all requested meetings by school personnel, perform volunteer work, and ensure that the student participates in any recommended school-sponsored tutoring programs. If the student fails any of the fourth-grade state tests and the parents or guardians attribute this to the education provided by the school, the Brighter Choice Foundation will provide a privately funded scholarship of $2,000 or full tuition, whichever is less, for attendance at another school in the Capital Region.

Virginia Manheimer, who funded the private voucher program in Albany, also supported the Brighter Choice Charter Schools. For example, in 2000, she agreed to back a loan guarantee of up to $350,000 for a loan covering building-related costs of the Brighter Choice Charter Schools. Manheimer also sat on the board of Children First America.

Several other philanthropists, many with connections to the Manhattan Institute, have supported the Brighter Choice Charter Schools. Richard Gilder, Manheimer's ex-husband, is a senior partner at Gilder Gagnon Howe & Company, a private money-management firm and a chairman emeritus of the board of the Manhattan Institute. In 2000, he agreed to back a loan guarantee of up to $375,000 for a loan covering building-related costs of the Brighter Choice Charter Schools. Bruce Kovner is chairman of Caxton Associates, one of the largest investment management firms in the U.S. He is also a member of the Manhattan Institute board of trustees. In 2000, Kovner agreed to back a loan guarantee of $375,000 for the Brighter Choice Charter Schools. Roger Hertog is President and COO of Sanford C. Bernstein and Company, a global investment research and management company, managing more than $80 billion in assets worldwide. He is chairman emeritus of the board of the Manhattan Institute. In 2000, Hertog pledged to donate $150,000 to the Brighter Choice Charter Schools. Robert W. Wilson is a private investor. In 2000, he agreed to back a loan guarantee of up to $350,000 for a loan covering building-related costs of the Brighter Choice Charter Schools.[13] At the time, he was also a member of the Manhattan Institute board of trustees.

In 2002, Thomas W. Carroll was joined by the BISON Fund in Buffalo and other school choice supporters in Albany to apply for a $5 million federal grant to advance public school choice in Albany and Buffalo. The lead applicants, the Brighter Choice Charter Schools (for which Carroll serves

[13]Financial figures from the Brighter Choice Charter Schools charter application, 2000.

as chairman), were eligible for the federal grant due to their legal status as a local education agency (LEA). In October 2002, the U.S. Department of Education announced that Brighter Choice Charter Schools would receive one of thirteen major grants awarded under the federal Voluntary School Choice Program, authorized by the *No Child Left Behind Act of 2001*. The other awardees were state departments of education or school districts. Carroll and his allies have aimed to dramatically expand the number of students in Albany and Buffalo who choose alternatives (e.g., charter schools, magnet schools, public schools in other districts) to traditional public schools in those cities, thereby compelling the two troubled school districts to reform. Indeed, the Brighter Choice Foundation is responsible for founding seven of the eight charter schools operating in Albany in 2008, and yet another Brighter Choice school is set to open in Fall 2008.

Beginning with Children Foundation, New York City. The Beginning with Children Foundation is a New York City-based operating foundation founded by Carol and Joseph Reich to increase educational opportunities for children. Prior to 1989, Carol Reich was employed as a developmental psychologist and Joseph Reich was a Wall Street investment banker. Mr. Reich also serves on the board of the Manhattan Institute.

The Beginning with Children Foundation developed an alternative school in Brooklyn that was named the most improved elementary school in New York City in 1997. The school is viewed as a model for elementary school reform and it was converted to a charter school in 2001. The Beginning with Children Foundation enjoys a noteworthy partnership with the Pfizer Foundation (of the Pfizer pharmaceutical company). The Pfizer Foundation, Inc. was established by Pfizer, Inc. in 1953. Its mission is "to promote access to quality health care and education, to nurture innovation and to support the community involvement of Pfizer people." In 1991, the Pfizer Foundation donated its former administration building in Brooklyn to the Beginning with Children school. This was accompanied by a $500,000 grant. The Pfizer Foundation recently donated a second building and $750,000 to expand the Beginning with Children charter school to the eighth grade. The Beginning with Children Foundation has also received support (e.g., $206,000 in 2001–02) from the Charles Hayden Foundation. In 2000, the Beginning with Children Foundation opened a second charter school, the Community Partnership Charter School, also located in Brooklyn.

Walton Family Foundation. As in California, the Walton Family Foundation has provided significant support to the charter school movement in New York State. For example, in 2001, the Walton Family Foundation made grants to at least seven operating, approved, or proposed charter schools in New York State. While the Walton Family Foundation funds a variety of initiatives in its home state of Arkansas, its national philanthropy is focused largely on school choice initiatives.

SUMMARY

Private foundations at the local, state, and national levels and public charities are actively engaged in supporting school choice in New York. The "educational establishment" that supports the traditional public education system—and defends it from threats to the status quo such as charter schools and vouchers—enjoys significant political resources and power in New York. Yet, to the surprise of some observers, New York now has a relatively robust charter school law, 99 charter schools in operation, and an active charter school movement. National and local private foundation support and charitable organizations have also been key in facilitating the development of private voucher programs in Albany, Buffalo, and New York City.

Grantmaking private foundations such as the Walton Family Foundation have provided valuable financial support to charter schools and to the entities that nurture and support charters. At least one New York-based private foundation has required that a charter school operate for at least two years before it will consider making a grant to the school. This stance diminishes its own risk but also precludes charter school access to foundation funds when they are most needed—during the start-up phases of founding and initial operation. In contrast, the Walton Family Foundation provides support to charter schools during the riskier, early stages of planning and operation.

School choice entrepreneur Thomas W. Carroll enjoys credibility in local, state, and national school choice policy networks. He has been skillful in attracting foundation support for various school choice initiatives and at establishing operating foundations for the advancement of the school choice idea in New York. His operating foundations have emphasized use of the mass media as a means by which to communicate the "good news" about school choice and to boost the legitimacy of the school choice idea in the minds of the public and policymakers. The ABCS voucher program and the Brighter Choice Charter Schools in Albany have each been the subject of favorable attention from national media outlets.

Advocates of school vouchers and their foundation supporters aim to place vouchers and the general notion of competition in public education on the public policy agenda in New York. As emphasized by one foundation official, the goal of the voucher movement "is not just to save kids but to also have the secondary effect of improving the public schools" via policy change.

School choice activists in New York and their local and national foundation allies discuss policy challenges, opportunities, and strategies with one another via phone conversations and organized gatherings. Most foundation support of school choice in New York has involved provision of grants for particular schools, programs, or charter school support services. An emphasis on careful evaluation appears to be underutilized as a potential instrument of foundation activity in New York.

Overall, New York State is home to a network of school choice supporters including wealthy philanthropists who have established private foundations for grantmaking purposes; Thomas W. Carroll's private operating foundations; the Manhattan Institute; the SUNY Board of Trustees; the New York Charter Schools Association; and local affiliates of the national Children's Scholarship Fund, a publicly supported charity. Philanthropic support for initiatives such as the A Brighter Choice Scholarships and BISON Fund programs permitted school choice entrepreneurs such as Carroll to build expertise, demonstrate that they are credible policy players, and build networks. The Manhattan Institute commissions and disseminates research and policy reports on school choice programs.

General Observations

Here we discuss several key observations based on the findings from our two case studies. First, foundations and individual philanthropists in both California and New York have provided significant sums of *financial support* to voucher and charter initiatives. Moreover, the Children's Scholarship Fund and Children First America facilitated local efforts to establish private voucher programs and permit students to escape failing public schools. On the charter school front, the Walton Family Foundation has promoted the development and sustenance of numerous new educational entities. Additionally, wealthy philanthropists at the local level have supported noteworthy school choice initiatives. In total and over time, these initiatives—some supported primarily by national foundations, some by local foundations, and others by joint efforts—have prompted substantial discussion about education reform among scholars and policymakers, and in the popular press, just as the foundations and the school choice policy entrepreneurs whom they support had intended.

Second, foundations have supported *research and information dissemination* on school choice initiatives and their implications. Earlier, we noted the number of foundations that funded the 2001 RAND Study on vouchers and charter schools. In another case, research on the Children's Scholarship Fund by Peterson and Campbell (2001) was funded by the Lynde and Harry Bradley Foundation, the Milton and Rose D. Friedman Foundation, the Gordon and Laura Gund Foundation, and the John M. Olin Foundation.[14] In attempts to "get the word out," the web sites of several foundations contain links to research and other school choice organizations. The Brighter Choice Foundation in New York State has been skillful in attracting favorable media attention for its school choice initiatives. The Milton and Rose D. Friedman Foundation has touted its own "world-class public information campaign, including television, radio and print advertising ... which highlights the benefits of school choice for children, families and society as a whole ... [and] ... is helping to shape the debate all over the country" (Milton and Rose D. Friedman Foundation, 2002). The Friedman Foundation has also supported efforts to protect school choice reforms from court challenges.

Third, foundations have forged valuable local, state, and national *networks* dedicated to the school choice concept. School choice activists and their foundation allies discuss policy challenges, opportunities, and strategies with one another via phone conversations and organized gatherings. In 2002, the New Schools Venture Fund hosted a "summit" during which more than 250 philanthropists, education entrepreneurs, educators, business leaders, policymakers, and scholars gathered to discuss education reform issues "and the progress of education entrepreneurship in improving our public schools" (New Schools Venture Fund, 2002). Matching fund programs such as those of the Children's Scholarship Fund have also promoted networking among local and national school choice entrepreneurs.

Fourth, foundations such as Children First America have been *recognized by governors and other policymakers* for their contributions to school choice efforts. Leaders such as Thomas W. Carroll and M. Christian Bender at the Brighter Choice Foundation have cultivated valuable relationships with

---

[14]The Olin and Bradley Foundations have provided funds in support of their strategy to encourage the intellectual community and opinion leaders to embrace school choice concepts.

local, state, and federal officials. These foundations and others, such as the Beginning With Children Foundation, have operated model school reform demonstration programs.

Finally, foundations such as the Walton Family Foundation and the Brighter Choice Foundation have *gained respect and credibility* for their approaches and activities. The Walton Family Foundation does not accept applications for its charter school funding program; it engages in its own targeted selection process. The Brighter Choice Foundation has benefited directly from Carroll's previous network of philanthropic supporters at the Empire Foundation. Through his achievements on the school choice front, he has shown himself to be a credible policy player. In addition, Brighter Choice Foundation executive director Bender helps operate a widely regarded family foundation in New York's Capital Region. Thus, he brings not only expertise to the Brighter Choice effort but also social capital.

A second set of findings pertains to similarities in the political strategies of foundations in both California and New York. For example, rather than use the term "students" to refer to the primary beneficiaries of school choice, foundation documents consistently use the more emotionally evocative term "children." Similarly, instead of using the term "vouchers" to describe the funding programs to support students' attendance at private schools, foundations use the more politically appealing term "scholarships."

A third discovery is that the "movers and shakers" in the school choice foundation world have impressive backgrounds in the corporate and investment sectors. Many of the major philanthropic supporters of school choice in New York State have experience on Wall Street. Similarly, philanthropists like Eli Broad and John T. Walton brought significant corporate experience to their foundation work. This cache of business and investment acumen enhances the ability of foundations to make strategically wise decisions when choosing where and how to focus their support of school choice advocacy. Moreover, foundation leaders of this kind are helping to bring private sector concepts to discussions about public education. It is easy to understand the appeal of market-based school choice programs to successful business leaders with a natural affinity for entrepreneurship and marketplace principles as well as experience in a competitive marketplace.

Fourth, foundations support each other. The Broad Foundation has contributed to the Southern California Children's Scholarship Fund, an affiliate of the Children's Scholarship Fund cofounded by John Walton.

Walton, in turn, has contributed to the Broad Foundation. In 2001, the Walton Family Foundation gave $100,000 to the Friedman Foundation. In March 2001, the William E. Simon Foundation began to award two philanthropy prizes: The William E. Simon Prize in Philanthropic Leadership and the William E. Simon Prize in Social Entrepreneurship. The prizes "identify and recognize outstanding individuals who made a difference in their communities either through philanthropic and charitable investments, or by creating successful social service projects to assist those in need." The Prize in Philanthropic Leadership includes a $250,000 cash gift which the winner donates to the charity or charities of his or her choice. The prize in Social Entrepreneurship includes a $250,000 gift to the awardee for his or her unrestricted use. In 2001 the first Prizes were awarded to John T. Walton and Peter M. Flanigan (William E. Simon Foundation, 2002). As we have noted, both were active in providing school choice scholarship money to low-income, inner-city students.

Sometimes reformers do not want programs to be formally evaluated for fear that the results will not be politically favorable. They may argue that a given reform initiative is too young for a valid evaluation of its impact. While foundations are funding various voucher and charter initiatives in California and New York State, there is not a concerted effort to track the success rate of the participants in each of the programs. Questions have been raised about the credibility of studies on school choice that are funded by foundations that are on record as being in favor of school choice programs. Inevitably, these studies produce conclusions that place school choice initiatives in a favorable light. Similarly, studies funded by members of the opposing advocacy coalition (e.g., American Federation of Teachers, 2002) inevitably suggest that school choice programs are faulty. The school choice policy community would benefit if: a) foundations engaged in systematic, objective evaluations of the school choice initiatives they support, and b) foundations that have not indicated a strong preference for or against the school choice idea supported research on school choice programs.

The June 2002 U.S. Supreme Court decision in *Zelman v. Simmons-Harris* indicating that public school voucher programs—when structured properly—are constitutional, opened the way for renewed efforts to secure public voucher programs via the citizen initiative and the legislative process. However, voters have turned down nationally publicized public voucher ballot measures in California, Michigan, and Utah. Foundations may decide that the public has not been sufficiently "softened up" (Kingdon, 1995) in favor of such a dramatic change in public education and instead continue to try to win hearts and minds over time via demonstration programs and promotion of charter school policies.

Conclusion

Among the general public as well as policymakers, foundations are typically associated with charity work, not with the explicit promotion of particular public policy positions. Further, many foundation personnel see themselves as distinct from and somewhat above the messy world of politics and policymaking. Foundations like to be viewed in positive ways, and this makes them averse to actions that might be construed as overtly political. The foundations discussed in this chapter have apparently been most comfortable—and, in many ways most successful—when they have pursued public policy goals in ways that go hand-in-hand with charity work. The development of private voucher programs represents a significant innovation in foundation strategy. For those who are not fully attuned to the motivations behind this development, private voucher efforts might appear as nothing more than charity. But it has been charity explicitly designed to send important messages to policymakers about problems in the traditional public school system and how those problems might be appropriately addressed. In New York, this charity work was crucial for helping specific foundations gain legitimacy as players worthy of a close hearing in public policymaking circles.

While foundations do not have authority to propose a bill, sign a bill into law, or hand down a court ruling, they wield significant power in the education policymaking arena. According to our findings, foundations that support school choice, by engaging in it directly or by funding the efforts of others, are active in the policymaking process, especially at the problem definition, agenda-setting, and policy implementation stages. In addition to promoting a public climate supportive of school choice, foundations have played a crucial role in protecting school choice policy successes. Thus, their efforts to support the charter school movement have helped make charter schools an institutionalized feature of public education. At all times, foundations and their allies supporting school choice have pursued their policy goals in the face of fierce opposition from the more established, embedded advocacy coalition representing the traditional public education system.

References

American Federation of Teachers. 2002. "Do Charter Schools Measure Up? The Charter School Experiment After 10 Years." Policy Report. American Federation of Teachers.

Archer, Jeff. "Venture Fund *Seeds* School Innovations." *Education Week*. April 24, 2002.

Bank, David. "California Venture Group *Seeks* to Fund Charter School 'Brands.'" *The Wall Street Journal*. April 10, 2002.

Bison Fund. 2002. "The BISON Scholarship Fund," available at http://www. bisonfund.com/aboutbison.html#whosupports.

Brighter Choice Charter Schools. Press Release. September 19, 2002, available at http://www.brighterchoice.org.

Broad, Eli. 2002. "Transforming Public Education," available at http://www. broadfoundation.org/eli/index-int.shtml.

California Department of Education. 2007. " Fact Book 2007: Handbook of Education Information." Sacramento: Department of Education.

Catterall, James S. and Richard Chapleau. 2001. "Voting on Vouchers: A Socio-Political Analysis of California Proposition 38, Fall 2000." Occasional Paper No. 42. National Center for the Study of Privatization in Education. New York: Teachers College, Columbia University.

Center for Education Reform, Charter Numbers, September 2007.

Charter Schools Institute. 2002. "Charter Schools in New York: A New Choice in Public Education." Policy Report. Albany: State University of New York.

Children First America. 2002. "Backgrounder/Overview," available at http:// www.childrenfirstamerica.org/about/backgrounder.htm.

Children's Scholarship Fund. 2002. "Children's Scholarship Fund Opens NASDAQ Trading." July 11, 2002, available at www.scholarshipfund.org/ press/releases.asp.

Children's Scholarship Fund. 2008. Web site, available at http://www. scholarshipfund.org.

Chubb, John E., and Terry M. Moe. 1990. *Politics, Markets, and America's Schools.* Washington, DC: The Brookings Institution.

Covington, Sally. 1997. *Moving a Public Policy Agenda: The Strategic Philanthropy of Conservative Foundations.* Washington, DC: National Committee for Responsive Philanthropy.

Empire Foundation for Policy Research. n.d. "A Brighter Choice Scholarships." Clifton Park, NY: Empire Foundation, available at http:// www.efpr.org/abcs.htm.

Fantini, Mario D. 1973. *Public Schools of Choice.* New York: Simon and Schuster.

Finn, Chester E., and Kelly Amis. 2001. *Making it Count: A Guide to High-Impact Education Philanthropy.* Washington, DC: The Fordham Foundation.

Flint, Anthony. "US Education Chief Blasts Voucher Plans as 'Surrender.'" *The Boston Globe.* October 22, 1993: 37.

Friedman, Milton. 1955. "The Role of Government in Education." In *Economics and the Public Interest,* ed. Robert A. Solo. New Brunswick, NJ: Rutgers University Press.

Friedman, Milton. 1962. *Capitalism and Freedom.* Chicago: University of Chicago Press.

Gewertz, Catherine. "Philanthropy." *Education Week.* November 22, 2000.

Henig, Jeffrey R. 1994. *Rethinking School Choice: Limits of the Market Metaphor.* Princeton, NJ: Princeton University Press.

Hart, Gary K., and Su Burr. 1996. "The Story of California's Charter School Legislation." Phi Delta Kappan 78: 37–41.

Heritage Foundation. 2001. "School Choice 2001: What's Happening in the States." Washington, DC: Heritage Foundation.

Hersh, Richard H. "Foundations for Change." *Education Week*. February 9, 2000: pp. 60, 40.

Hirsch, Eric D., Jr. 1996. *The Schools We Need And Why We Don't Have Them*. New York: Doubleday.

Kahlenberg, Richard D. Ed. 2003. *Public School Choice Vs. Private School Vouchers*. New York: Century Foundation Press.

Kingdon, John. 1995. *Agendas, Alternatives, and Public Policies*. Second Edition. New York: HarperCollins.

Ladner, Matthew. 2001. *Just Doing It*. 5th Edition. Bentonville, AR: Children First America, available at http://www.childrenfirstamerica.org/.

Lauter, David. "Clinton Urges 'No' Vote on School Voucher Initiative." *Los Angeles Times*. October 5, 1993: A3.

Meier, Deborah. 1995. *The Power of Their Ideas: Lessons for America From A Small School in Harlem*. Boston, MA: Beacon Press.

Milton and Rose D. Friedman Foundation. 2002. "Mission," available at http://www.friedmanfoundation.org/aboutmission.html.

Mintrom, Michael. 1997. "Policy Entrepreneurs and the Diffusion of Innovation." *American Journal of Political Science* 41: 738–770.

Mintrom, Michael. 2000. *Policy Entrepreneurs and School Choice*. Washington, DC: Georgetown University Press.

Mintrom, Michael, and Sandra Vergari. 1996. "Advocacy Coalitions, Policy Entrepreneurs, and Policy Change." *Policy Studies Journal* 24: 420–435.

Moe, Terry M. Ed. 1995. *Private Vouchers*. Stanford, CA: Hoover Institution Press.

Moe, Terry M. 2000. *Schools, Vouchers, and the American Public*. Washington, DC: The Brookings Institution.

Nathan, Joe. 1996. *Charter Schools: Creating Hope and Opportunity for American Education*. San Francisco: Jossey-Bass.

National Center for Education Statistics, Digest of Education Statistics, 2007, Table 33. Year of Data: 2005.

New York State Education Department. 2001. "New York: The State Of Learning." Albany: NYSED.

Olson, Lynn. "Novel Voucher Plan Suffers Resounding Defeat in California." *Education Week*. November 3, 1993.

Paulson, Amanda. "Venture Philanthropists Extend Reach." *The Christian Science Monitor*. February 4, 2002.

People for the American Way. 1999. "Privatization of Public Education: A Joint Venture of Charity and Power." April 20, 1999. Washington, DC: PFAW, available at http://www.pfaw.org/issues/education/reports/CSF-report-text.html#bedfellows.

Peterson, Paul E. and David E. Campbell. 2001. "An Evaluation of the Children's Scholarship Fund." Cambridge, MA: Program on Education Policy and Governance, Harvard University.

Ravitch, Diane, and Joseph P. Viteritti. Eds. 1997. *New Schools for a New Century: The Redesign of Urban Education*. New Haven: Yale University Press.

Roberts, Nancy C., and Paula J. King. 1996. *Transforming Public Policy: Dynamics of Policy Entrepreneurship and Innovation*. San Francisco: Jossey-Bass.

Sabatier, Paul A. 1988. "An Advocacy Coalition Framework of Policy Change and the Role of Policy-Oriented Learning Therein." *Policy Sciences* 21: 129–168.

Sacramento Business Journal. "Cranked Up and Running Hard." November 3, 2000. p. 11.

Steiger, Fritz S. 2002. "Children First America President and CEO Fritz Steiger's Farewell." Bentonville, AR: Children First America, available at http://www.childrenfirstamerica.org/avfc/082902.

Stevens, Mitchell L. 2001. *Kingdom of Children: Culture and Controversy in the Homeschooling Movement*. Princeton, NJ: Princeton University Press.

Student Sponsor Partnership. 2002. "SSP History," available at http://www.sspshp.org/ssphistory.htm.

Venture Philanthropy Partners. 2002. "About Venture Philanthropy Partners," available at http://www.venturephilanthropypartners.org.

Vergari, Sandra. Ed. 2002. *The Charter School Landscape*. Pittsburgh: University of Pittsburgh Press.

Vergari, Sandra. 2002. "New York: Over 100 Applications in Year One," in Sandra Vergari, (ed.) *The Charter School Landscape*, pp. 230–252. Pittsburgh: University of Pittsburgh Press.

Walton Family Foundation. 2001. "Grant Awards 2001," available at wffhome.com/2001_awards.html.

White, Eileen. "California Voucher Effort Stopped By Its Backers." *Education Week*. November 16, 1981.

William E. Simon Foundation. 2002. "William E. Simon Prize Program," available at http://www.wesimonfoundation.org/found.nsf/prizepurpose.htm?OpenPage&charset=iso-8859-1.

Witte, John F. 2000. *The Voucher Approach to Education: An Analysis of America's First Voucher Program*. Princeton, NJ: Princeton University Press.

Wohlstetter, Priscilla, Noelle C. Griffin, and Derrick Chau. 2002. "Charter Schools in California: A Bruising Campaign for Public School Choice." In *The Charter School Landscape*, ed. Sandra Vergari. Pittsburgh, PA: University of Pittsburgh Pres.

Zebrowski, John. "Five Fat Cats and a Flip-Flop." *Mother Jones*. September 29, 1998.

10

Conclusion

James M. Ferris

The history of foundation engagement in public policymaking underscores the point that the differences in approach "most often reside in the external environment, the specifics of the policy domain, the opportunities presented by differing political circumstances, and the changing expectations Americans have of the public sector" (Smith, Chapter 3). With that in mind, this volume has developed a framework that identifies factors that influence the decision to engage and the strategies and tactics that foundations have for leveraging their philanthropic assets—money, knowledge, and networks—for policy change. This framework is then examined in considerable detail in the context of four varied policy issue areas in which foundations have participated—school choice, wetlands preservation, child care, and health care access.

These four areas provide a range of policy issues, settings, and foundation activities that demonstrate the spectrum of foundation involvement in public policymaking. The policy issues are tightly focused, involve action at the various levels of government, demonstrate varying degrees of public acceptance of the role that government should play, and exhibit very different foundation ecology from issue to issue. This variation provides a reasonable and realistic illustration of the framework developed in the framing chapters and a "test" of the propositions and conjectures suggested in them, in particular the conceptual model developed by Ferris and Mintrom in Chapter 2.

The analysis of these cases has important lessons for those who are engaged or are contemplating becoming engaged in public policy work.[1] It helps to reveal what it takes, including the possible risks and rewards of such engagement, the patterns of how foundations that have engaged in public policy do their work, and identifies different profiles that emerge. Finally, the volume suggests the implications for foundation practice.

The Decision to Engage: What It Takes

The benefits of public policy work are substantial. Foundations have the potential to increase their impact by leveraging their assets—dollars, knowledge, and networks—to solve public problems. However, foundations do not take a single path to such work, nor do they always fully comprehend the complexity of engaging public policy that, together, place a premium on a clarity of values and an enduring commitment to engaging the policy process.

PATHS TO POLICY ENGAGEMENT

The path to public policy engagement is not linear or singular. Foundations come to public policy work in various ways and with various attitudes and perspectives. Some foundations begin with a mission to create change by affecting public policy. This is likely to result from dissatisfaction with existing policies or concern with addressing emerging or persistent problems. Other foundations come to engage public policy after recognizing that grant dollars can only go so far in creating important social change.

Foundations seem to take two prevailing attitudes in engaging policy. Some foundations partake in the process in a relatively aggressive manner, trying to force a particular solution, while others work more deliberately, seeking the best solutions to the problem. The first approach is more ideological; the foundation understands the problem and has determined the desired solution.[2] The second approach emphasizes the importance of understanding the problem and analyzing a range of potential solutions that lead to better outcomes, as defined by the foundation's objectives.

---

[1]These cases begin with foundations that are engaged in the policy process, so it is oriented to explaining the strategies and tactics that foundations adopt in their policy work. Nevertheless, these four cases also underscore some important lessons for those foundations that are considering whether to engage the policy process.
[2]There is wide recognition of the recent success of "conservative" foundations that are driven by a set of ideological principles in contrast with the perceived lack of success of more "progressive" foundations that are engaged in public policy but focused on a more policy analytic approach to public policy. *See* Kuttner (2002).

As these cases demonstrate, foundations may take a number of paths to address policy issues, and may bring a variety of attitudes along with them. Some foundations begin with a focus on an issue, such as an interest in improving public schools. Others begin with a focus on a solution or type of solutions such as vouchers or market-based school policies. Others come to an issue in a more circuitous route, such as foundations that care about welfare reform because of its impact on children, which is their primary focus, or those foundations that join in efforts to preserve wetlands as a vehicle for pursuing social justice and sustainable development.

THE COMPLEXITY OF THE POLICY PROCESS

The four case studies also underscore the importance of recognizing and accepting that public policy work is complex—it is messy, unpredictable, and open-ended—which inevitably brings risk. Foundations must weigh this risk—both in terms of political risks and unrealized outcomes—against the potential payoff of creating desired social change via public policy.

Public policy is contestable. Many players participate, both inside and outside the formal decisionmaking structures, representing different constituencies with their own set of values and interests. Foundations must understand that policy work is not neutral; they must adopt a point of view. For example, foundations undertaking efforts to create school vouchers believe that more competition will increase the quality of education and work to advance such policies; at the same time, others in the policy arena, often teacher unions, work to oppose those efforts due to the perceived negative consequences of voucher programs on their constituencies. In addition, foundations working to preserve environmental resources encounter opposition from those that have property rights to the use of those resources as well as those with economic interests in development.

Foundations that seek to influence policy decisions do so in the context of a policy process that is unpredictable and uncertain, and clearly beyond the control of any individual or organization. As a consequence, foundations need to be poised and ready to act as opportunities occur. This suggests that foundations need to create an infrastructure for foundation engagement both by developing their own capacity as well as relationships with partners—other funders, researchers and think tanks, and advocacy groups. If a foundation decides to weigh in on a particular issue after it is already under active consideration by policymakers, it is often too late to act.

The policymaking process is open-ended. It is dynamic and ongoing and it does not end with policy adoption. There is a strong perception that policy adoption is the heart of policy work, perhaps as a result of its discrete nature, an aspect that may make it easier to observe success. But, the ultimate outcomes of public policy work rest with effective implementation. This is clear in efforts to preserve wetlands, where adopting the policy is only one step towards acquiring land and preserving it; likewise, chartering new schools is only one step towards constructing, organizing, and running an independent school.

WHAT IT TAKES

The in-depth analysis of these four cases underscores the fact that foundations should be sanguine about the commitments that public policy engagement requires. Public policy work has a large potential payoff, but it comes with considerable risks. The risks are of two kinds: political risks that arise from contentious issues, and accountability risks that arise from failure to achieve policy change. A foundation is likely to be best equipped to engage public policy if it is comfortable, firm, and clear in its values, and if it is willing to commit to public policy work for the long term. It must also be flexible and responsive to the opportunities that emerge, willing to deal with ambiguity in terms of outcomes, and tolerate the risks involved.

Policy Engagement: Where and How

Foundations have a wide range of points at which they can work to impact the policy process and an array of strategies and tactics from which they can choose. The four cases examined reveal that foundations vary considerably in their choices of stages in the process and are not limited to the legislative process or a single level of government. What emerges is a range of patterns that lead to different foundation profiles—from investor to entrepreneur—in the policy process.

STAGES IN THE POLICY PROCESS

Foundations play important roles throughout the policy process—from agenda-setting to policy adoption to implementation. Some foundations focus on particular stages, typically the agenda-setting stage or the implementation stage. Others use a more encompassing approach, working to have an impact across the various stages of the policy process. In the context of the four cases examined here, fewer foundations appear to operate at the early stages of the policy process when compared to those that engage at the implementation stage.

Foundations engaged in the early stages of the policy process have a clear sense of what they would like to accomplish in terms of issues and solutions. They underwrite research and analysis, frame problems, and craft policy alternatives. These foundations tend to adopt a proactive posture and attempt to drive policy agendas by injecting ideas into public policy conversations. For example, foundations promoting school vouchers have invested heavily in research and analysis, demonstrations and experiments, and the dissemination of lessons from one community to another and from state to state, to place the issue on the public agenda. Similar efforts are found in health care, where foundation efforts have focused on raising public awareness of the problem of the uninsured by providing reliable and credible information about the scope of the problem, and stimulating conversations about possible policy solutions and courses of action to increase coverage. Likewise, foundations that have an interest in children's issues have worked to develop indicators on the status of children to underscore critical issues and to determine whether or not conditions are improving.

For a public policy to have the desired impact, it must be implemented effectively. Foundations can play an important role at the implementation stage in increasing the likelihood that the policy will achieve the desired results. Foundations are well-positioned to provide necessary resources and scrutiny. Their long-term involvement can help ensure that policies are implemented according to design. Foundations can work to help individuals take advantage of new government programs created through public policy, evaluate the effectiveness of new public programs, and, in some instances, even assist government in the delivery of programs.

Numerous examples of foundation efforts at the implementation stage exist in these four cases, including securing the requisite capital and structures to construct and operate charter schools, amassing the resources and creating the networks to acquire and preserve wetlands in the Cal-Fed Project and the Florida Everglades, working to ensure that those eligible take advantage of health access programs provided by the state of California, and helping states in the Midwest implement the child care provisions of welfare reform. In all of these instances, foundations have forged constructive relations with government agencies, either directly or through their nonprofit partners.

Although foundations have considerable leeway to operate directly in both the early stages and later stages, they can also participate at the policy adoption stage, i.e., the passage of specific legislation, through general support of nonprofit advocacy groups. While foundation/nonprofit partnerships are important throughout the entire policy process, they are at a premium at the policy adoption stage. This is particularly true for those foundations that wish to increase the odds that efforts at agenda-setting are translated into policy decisions. By providing operating grants, foundations can enable advocacy organizations to be effective players at this stage in the process, not only for a single issue but also in an ongoing capacity for grassroots involvement in the open-ended policy process.

BEYOND THE LEGISLATIVE PROCESS

The legislative process is not the only venue for policy engagement. The courts and administrative agencies are also important leverage points for particular policy issues. The courts and administrative agencies often make critical decisions, such as whether a policy is constitutional or whether public agencies have implemented legislation as intended. It is, therefore, important to view venues as complementary points of engagement rather than "either-or" choices. This is particularly true when policies that are being pursued in the legislative arena raise legal questions or involve regulatory or administrative decisions.

Foundations can be more actively involved in these venues since the prohibitions on lobbying do not apply. To the extent that such actions impact the successful realization of policies adopted in the legislative arenas, foundations need to stay involved. Again, foundations are likely to be involved through their nonprofit partners, though in these venues, foundations are not bound by the same funding restrictions that apply to the legislative process. For example, the constitutionality of vouchers has been raised by those opposed to this particular avenue of school reform. Thus, in addition to securing passage of school vouchers, proponents have been active in arguing the constitutionality of vouchers before the courts. Likewise, many of the critical decisions that impact wetlands preservation are made by administrative agencies at the state and local levels.

WORKING AT DIFFERENT LEVELS

The federal system poses interesting choices for foundations that are engaged in the policy process. While there are some issues that play out at a single level of government, many develop at multiple levels.[3] As a consequence, foundations are challenged to formulate strategies for working on policy issues that are often not neatly in sync with their scale or scope.

Foundations that are interested in influencing issues nationally may find investment in basic research and development to be an essential component of their strategy. Policy research and development, like other forms of research and development, need not be duplicated across state and local jurisdictions. For example, those advancing notions of school choice have developed demonstration projects to provide evidence of the impact of school organization and governance on learning outcomes. Similarly, foundations interested in child care have contributed to research on the impact of child care in the early years, and those promoting wetlands preservation have contributed to an understanding of ecological science.

On the other hand, foundations with a state or local perspective are more likely to focus on applications. These foundations can focus their efforts on how policy ideas can be applied to the local context and, where relevant, create the public will to place the issues on the state or local policy agenda. It is possible that demonstration projects can occur in a localized way that creates the evidence for replication as well as the capacity of grassroots action for continual engagement in the policy process, such as in the case of the Kellogg Foundation's approach to child development.

PROFILES OF POLICY ENGAGEMENT

The analysis of the four policy issues reveals that there is considerable variation among foundations in terms of the breadth and degree of foundation involvement and the willingness to assume risk.

Some foundations develop a broad-based approach working across multiple leverage points, while others focus on a particular niche. Foundations that adopt a broad-based approach often work to move an issue from agenda-setting to adoption, and ultimately policy implementation. In other instances, they use a multipronged approach by working multiple venues or jurisdictions. Other foundations focus on a particular niche in the policy process. There are a few that tend to work at the front end in terms of problem definition, agenda-setting, and creating a public will for action. But those foundations that target a single point most frequently seem to focus on

---

[3]As previously mentioned, in order to illuminate some of the issues that arise in policymaking in a federal system, we made a conscious decision to examine policy issues that have an important state or local dimension.

the implementation stage. This is not surprising; the implementation stage of the process plays to the strength of foundations and involvement in this stage is likely to be more comfortable for them. The work is clearly legally permissible; the primary focus is to provide financial resources; outcomes are likely to be more tangible and show foundation impact; and, the environment is likely to be less politically contentious.

The breadth of engagement appears to be guided by a foundation's perception of the greatest opportunity for contribution, which is determined by a mix of its organizational imperative, the policy environment, and the efforts of other foundations. For example, among those working in health, foundations with greater resources working at the state and local levels tend to use the full array of strategies and attempt to impact the process through the range of stages, rather than carving out a distinct area of engagement.

Another important characteristic of a foundation's profile is the willingness to assume risk. It is clear from the discussion thus far that foundations that choose to engage public policy understand that there are inherent risks. But even among the foundations doing policy work, there is a range of risk-taking that is reflected in their strategic decisions about where and how to engage the policy process. Foundation involvement ranges from that of an investor to that of a policy entrepreneur. Foundations that engage the process as an investor provide the funding that enables others to shape policy agendas, advocate for policies, and to work to see that they are effectively implemented. There are, however, some foundations that play an entrepreneurial role. These foundations are willing to incur risk by aggressively pursuing policy changes, not only by investing their dollars, but also by taking a proactive role in terms of pushing ideas, policy options, and in some cases, even solutions. They seek out partners that will develop policy ideas and build networks. In some instances, they will help to identify, create, and nurture them. In addition, they are willing to build and leverage their own connections—their own political capital—with policymakers to realize policy change. The foundations that assume the role of a policy entrepreneur understand the importance of knowledge and connections, in addition to their dollars, in leveraging change.

Implications for Foundation Practice

Engagement in public policymaking has important implications for foundation practice. Thus, foundations that choose to do policy work should consider what it takes to be effective in terms of governance, staffing, grantmaking, and networks.

A foundation engaged in policymaking must be clear about its values, understand the political risks, and recognize the degree of ambiguity in impact and outcome that characterizes policy work. This implies that policy work be conducted with the full support of the foundation's board. The board needs to understand the potential that such work can have on furthering the foundation's goals, and the conditions required for conducting such work, including resources, staffing, and grantmaking programs. Moreover, the board should have realistic expectations about the likelihood of success and the political risk, as well as the length of the commitment required. This is particularly important in an era of strategic philanthropy where a premium is placed on results.[4]

Foundations that are committed to engaging public policy require certain capacities beyond programmatic expertise. Two important skill sets for foundations engaged in public policy work are an understanding of the policy process—the actors and institutions in and around government in the relevant policy domains—and strategic communications—the ability to frame issues and generate support among the public and policymakers. It is increasingly common for foundations to appoint key staff with these abilities. Some policy areas require expertise of a specialized nature that may be difficult or inefficient to obtain through staffing such as environmental science, and may rely on consultants to provide the expertise.

Another critical dimension is staff stability. As noted in the four cases, staff expertise is necessary but not sufficient. In order for foundations to be effective in public policy, they need to develop and nurture connections with those in the policy community, in particular with those in government. Stability among foundation executives and program staff that are engaged in these relationships is essential, as trust and respect take time to establish and such relationships tend to be personal in nature rather than institutional.

There are also implications for the grantmaking practices of foundations. Of course, the strategies that foundations adopt for their public policy work will have an important impact on grantmaking practices. The analysis of the law and policymaking processes provides some important insights about grantmaking. Obviously, grants for core operating support provide foundations with a means to support nonprofit advocacy groups that are engaged in lobbying. Moreover, operating grants can be instrumental in building and sustaining the capacity of policy networks and their members.

[4]In recent years, there has been a focus on developing evaluation approaches for public policy grants that allows for benchmarks for performance cognizant of the uncertainties associated with policy work. *See* Guthrie, et al. (2005 and 2006) and Reisman, et al. (2007).

This all suggests that grantmaking be viewed as a tool for building the infrastructure for policymaking rather than as a means for supporting discrete projects. In addition, multiyear funding commitments are pivotal given that policy work is open-ended.

Clearly, there are advantages if foundations can develop the capacity to work together. The nature of this work can range from simply sharing information and coordination to co-funding to collaboration. Such cooperation can take many forms, from ad hoc to more structured and formal arrangements such as affinity groups, collaboratives, and regional associations. Whatever the form, there is a need to ensure that such arrangements match the policy work to be done. This may require realigning current foundation associations or developing new structures. In an era of decentralized policymaking mechanisms that enable action locally and are then shared to create impacts elsewhere, working together can be a distinct advantage to the philanthropic community.

The Road Ahead

As foundations engage public policy, it is critical that they bring the full range of their assets to bear. Foundation grants are instrumental in funding research and development, advocacy, and implementation and evaluation. Yet, foundations can make an even greater difference than simply being an investor in public policy. Foundations are uniquely positioned to create the infrastructure for public policy—linking the knowledge, experts, and policymakers—that enables the conversations about public problems, policy alternatives, preferred solutions, and policy outcomes. They can choose to assume the role of policy entrepreneur. Foundations that assume such a role should understand that public policy work is not undertaken without risks, and without challenging well-established foundation practices. Each foundation needs to develop its own philosophy, strategies, and tactics for advancing public policy, including whether to engage it in the first place, and if so, whether to simply invest in policy work or to adopt a more entrepreneurial role.

Foundations must also be ready to confront the tension that occurs between their role as social institutions with a long-term perspective and the increasing pressures to produce demonstrable results. Indeed, the paradox of policy engagement in an era of more strategic philanthropy is that the greater the potential for impact, the less reliable the evidence of effectiveness given the messiness of the policy process. As we have seen in all four of the policy areas studied, while foundations are interested in advocating for broad changes in public policy, their work tends to be more narrowly focused and linked intentionally to the realities of the policy process. Indeed, the tendency to focus on implementation is, in part, the result of the limited risks at that stage. As foundations from various viewpoints accept the challenge, the policymaking process will benefit, and philanthropy's contribution to society via policy will be enhanced.

References

Guthrie, Kendall, Justin Louie, and Catherine Crystal Foster (2005, October). *The Challenge of Assessing Policy and Advocacy Activities: Strategies for a Prospective Evaluation Approach (Part I)*, prepared for the California Endowment by Blueprint Research and Design, Inc.

Guthrie, Kendall, Justin Louie, and Catherine Crystal Foster (2006, October). *The Challenge of Assessing Policy and Advocacy Activities: Moving from Theory to Practice (Part II)*, prepared for the California Endowment by Blueprint Research and Design, Inc.

Kuttner, Robert. "Philanthropy and Movements." *The American Prospect.* July 15, 2002.

Reisman, Jane, Anne Gienapp, and Sarah Stachowiak (2007). *A Guide to Measuring Advocacy and Policy 2007*, prepared for the Annie E. Casey Foundation by Organizational Research Services.

About the Authors

James M. Ferris is the founding Director of The Center on Philanthropy and Public Policy at the University of Southern California. He is a Professor in the School of Policy, Planning, and Development and holds the Emery Evans Olson Chair in Nonprofit Entrepreneurship and Public Policy. He specializes in the economics of the public and nonprofit sectors, public finance, and public policy. His current work focuses on the changing landscape of philanthropy, foundation strategy for public policymaking, and the efficiency of philanthropic markets.

Contributor Affiliations

Lucy Bernholz is the Founder and President of Blueprint Research & Design, Inc., a strategy consulting firm specializing in program research and design for philanthropic foundations.

Jason Gerson is a Public Policy Consultant and Contractor in Washington, D.C.

Jack H. Knott is Dean of the University of Southern California School of Policy, Planning, and Development and holder of the C. Erwin and Ione L. Piper Dean's Chair.

Diane McCarthy is affiliated with the Department of Biological Sciences at the University of Illinois-Chicago.

Michael Mintrom is Associate Professor and Deputy Head of the Department of Political Studies at the University of Auckland.

Thomas R. Oliver is Associate Professor of Population Health Sciences at the University of Wisconsin School of Medicine and Public Health. He also serves as director of the Health Policy Program at the University of Wisconsin Population Health Institute.

Walter A. Rosenbaum is Acting Director at the Bob Graham Center for Public Service and Professor Emeritus of political science at the University of Florida.

James Allen Smith is Vice President, Rockefeller Archive Center, and Director of Research and Education.

Thomas A. Troyer is an attorney in the Washington, D.C. office of the law firm Caplin & Drysdale. He is also a trustee of the Natural Resources Defense Council, and a director of the Democracy 21 Education Fund and the Children's Defense Fund.

Douglas Varley specializes in advising private foundations at Caplin & Drysdale and is Adjunct Professor of Law at Georgetown University.

Sandra Vergari is Associate Professor in the Department of Educational Administration and Policy Studies, and a faculty affiliate with the Department of Public Administration and Policy at the University at Albany, State University of New York.

Index